*Planning the development of universities**
A series of reports based on an IIEP research project

Vol. I. IIEP seminar on planning the development of universities, Paris, 7-11 July 1969
(Basic discussion paper/ Summary report of the seminar/ Case study on
Leningrad State University/ Case study on the University of Sussex)

Vol. II. Analysis of the questionnaire of the project 'Planning the development of
universities'
(Summary of the findings from the questionnaire/ Introduction and the structure
of the sample/ The state of replies/ University growth/ University autonomy and
the involvement of different bodies in the internal decision-making process/
Trends of change in university structure (1958-68)/ Structure of the student body/
Teaching staff/ Innovation in the teaching work/ Evaluation of teaching
programmes/ Research in the universities/ Source of university finance/ Use
of indices for university planning/Past and future factors of change in
the university/ University functions and their priorities/ The tables/
Appendix I. Method of analysis of the questionnaire/ Appendix II. The
questionnaire/ Appendix III. Glossary of terms)

* Further volumes to appear.

Planning the development of universities—II

Analysis of the questionnaire

Victor G. Onushkin
assisted by B.C. Sanyal and G. Bartagnon

Paris   1973
Unesco: International Institute for Educational Planning

The IIEP research project on 'Planning the development of universities' is being carried out with financial assistance from the Swedish International Development Authority (SIDA), the Canadian International Development Agency (CIDA) and the Ford Foundation.

Published in 1973 by the United Nations
Educational, Scientific and Cultural Organization,
Place de Fontenoy, 75700 Paris
Printed by L. Vanmelle, S.A., Mariakerke/Ghent

ISBN 92-803-1058-5

Preface

This volume is the second in the series of IIEP publications on "Planning the Development of Universities", the first being the report of the inaugural seminar of the research project. This seminar suggested that one of the aims of the project should be to draw up a manual for heads of universities containing the most interesting and useful conclusions from existing experience in planning university development in different countries of the world. This the project team has done by means of a questionnaire and case studies. The case studies investigated particular areas of university planning in depth and will be the subject of a subsequent publication, but the present volume sets out the findings of the questionnaires which were circulated to universities in fifty countries of the world.

I think it is true to say that it has fulfilled the request of the seminar—a vast amount of information was collected (readers will find over 200 tables in the second half of the publication) which provides a factual basis for an analysis of the state of higher educational development and university planning and management. Both general and in many cases detailed conclusions have been drawn and I would stress that the diagnosis is founded in fact—all too often generalizations and conclusions are drawn by persons responsible for educational development which are based on individual observations and impressions. Firstly, I would say that the analysis demonstrates the great need for introducing new managerial methods into university administration. This work, in many universities, is still at a very early stage and more importantly, most of these universities are ill-equipped to use planning as a tool for balanced development. It is obvious that the weakest point in university management is the lack of proper information systems and therefore this should be considered as one of the most urgent areas of work when modern management techniques are to be introduced.

The above point interests me greatly, but there are other more far-reaching conclusions of the analysis which, though they do not contradict the impressions gained by other researchers in this field and simply because they are based on facts, sound highly alarming. I will mention just a few of those which struck me particularly—for instance, the widening gap between university performance and the socio-economic needs of countries and the growing difference between the level of university performance in the developing and developed countries. These should attract the concern of governmental policy-makers and of the university community at large. Perhaps we may draw some hope from the fact that at the same time another important conclusion is that though in the past decade quantitative aspects of university development were the major concern of university heads, in the present decade universities indicated that they intend to concentrate their attention on the quality of work, including closer links with real socio-economic needs and consequent reform of curricula, more innovation, improvements to the quality of teaching and research personnel and the development of recurrent education at the higher level.

I am also gratified that the research project, besides providing a clear picture of the situation of university development, has had some useful practical consequences. For instance, when the universities were asked to complete the questionnaire, some of them became aware of certain gaps and faults in their administration and accordingly began to revise information and managerial systems. In this way the questionnaire has already served a useful purpose. Then the actual analysis of the questionnaire itself broke new ground in that for the first time a computer programme had to be devised to cope with analysis of this type of information on an international basis. This experience will be used by other research projects. In addition, the questionnaire and the methodology of its analysis have been and will be used by some countries at the national level to study the present state of their own university planning and management in detail.

As to other practical benefits to be derived from the information obtained and conclusions, these will serve as a factual basis for further research into problems of higher educational development since they highlight the areas of most pressing need. As for myself, I am particularly happy, as head of an international training centre for educational planners, to have this document for use as material in our own training programmes. I am sure that all working in this field will find it a useful and informative guide on the present state of university planning and development.

Finally, I would like to express my thanks to all those universities who participated in the project by completing a questionnaire—this was a concrete indication of the interest and importance of the research.

RAYMOND POIGNANT
Director, IIEP

Contents

Analysis of the questionnaire

I. Summary of the findings from the questionnaire

The research project undertaken at the International Institute for Educational Planning (IIEP) on 'Planning the development of universities' was instituted in 1969 in order to look into the problems of higher educational development, planning and management. These problems are attracting more and more attention in the different countries of the world and the following analysis of data obtained from a questionnaire allows us to draw some conclusions which are of great importance in the diagnosis and evaluation of the existing situation with regard to the development of universities in many countries. It also enables us to obtain an impression of the perspectives and to work out some recommendations for improving university planning and management.

This is important since at the present time development planning in the universities can be particularly useful (and in some cases is already proving to be so) in the search for solutions to some of the problems which universities are facing. However, it must be understood that planning can be really effective only when it becomes a specific form of modern university management. We do not believe it to be the panacea for all university ills and, indeed, its effective use depends to a great extent on whether the socio-economic conditions in the country are such as to encourage its use.

The questionnaire was drawn up, revised and tested with the help of experts from all the different continents of the world and it covered most aspects of university activity. It asked for basic information on the university, data on university operations, functions and objectives, academic problems and teaching materials, governance and management of the university, decision-making and planning mechanisms, and assessments of past and future changes. In addition, it sought to establish the availability of information and other elements which might improve university planning and management and the ability to meet the requirements of modern society.[1]

. The questionnaire is presented in Appendix II.

To obtain any worthwhile diagnosis it was necessary to seek the collaboration of a representative sample of universities and, at the international seminar at the IIEP in July 1969, it was suggested that a sample of about 100 universities would be sufficient to represent the whole. Selection was made in close co-operation with the Secretariat of the International Association of Universities and the following criteria were considered to be particularly important from the point of view of assuring that the sample was representative :

1. Existence of planning systems in higher education : this was felt to be important since it reflects differences in the socio-economic and political structures of countries ;
2. Level of economic development : in accordance with the recommendation of the Governing Board of the IIEP, more than two-thirds of our sample are universities in the developing countries and less than a third are from the developed ;
3. Geographical location ;
4. Size of the university ;
5. Emphasis on field of study ;
6. Type of control—either public or private ;
7. Admission system.

Finally, 169 universities (a number which we hoped would be sufficiently large to allow for refusals and yet still give a reasonably balanced sample), which met the above criteria, were requested to co-operate. Agreement was received from 107, of whom eighty from fifty different countries eventually sent in completed questionnaires in time for the computer analysis.

An immediate positive result of this stage of our work was that the universities, merely by being asked for information, were made aware of the defects in their management and information systems ; some of them informed us that they had been stimulated to start planning and statistics offices or groups and committees in order to improve their planning and management.

The data which we received in the questionnaires were processed, with the help of the Unesco computer, according to a special programme formulated for this particular type of research. We understand that this is one of the first if not the first, experiment with this type of analysis on an international basis.

Because of the pioneer character of the work, obviously some difficulties were encountered, particularly with collecting the information from the universities, but, nevertheless, the questionnaire and its analysis were important aids to a diagnosis of the present situation. Those interested will find more detailed descriptions of the analysis in Appendix I.

Some of the most important general conclusions which can be drawn from our analysis of the available data are given in the following sections.

1. The pace of university development

The decade under review (1958-68) has been one of very rapid growth in higher education in all parts of the world and this is likely to continue in the next decade. Important changes and innovations took place in the higher education systems of some countries, but this process has, in general, been too slow, which in itself has aggravated the situation and has given rise to new problems.

A detailed analysis of the growth rates of different university components and their relative consistency or imbalance was made. This covered student enrolment, academic staff, instructional space, operating expenditure, research funds and library items. These should demonstrate to a great extent the conditions under which universities carry out their basic functions of teaching and research and reveal the major difficulties or discrepancies in their development. Some of the findings are :

(a) Growth rates vary considerably from one group of universities to another, demonstrating that not only general problems common to the development of all universities should be analysed in depth, but also certain specific features of groups and even peculiarities of individual universities.

(b) Universities with an *open system of admission experienced much more serious imbalances and discrepancies* than universities with a selective or mixed system.

(c) A very obvious social tendency in the composition of the student body is a higher annual growth rate for female enrolment, especially at the undergraduate level. However, *this tendency did not bring them to parity with the male students,* although their proportion of the student body is now much higher than a decade ago. Much remains to be done in this direction in many countries.

(d) With the exception of North America, *the most striking imbalance may be observed everywhere in the development of the university library,* which is one of the most important bases of the teaching-learning process. Growth rates were so often found to be much lower than other sectors that, obviously, this matter deserves very serious attention and investigation.

(e) It was noticed that *in those classifications for developed countries and public universities, space has proved to be a factor which could not be increased at the same rate as enrolments.* Evidently, planning methods and innovation are urgently needed in this area.

2. Quantitative and qualitative aspects of university activities

In the past decade the universities were pre-occupied with dealing with problems of quantitative growth, but there is a general feeling and belief among the heads of universities that *in the future decade the focus of their activities will be on the development of qualitative aspects.* This does not mean they consider quantitative growth will be less important, but it cannot take place without bringing serious qualitative changes.

Analysis of fifteen factors of change which might create difficulties in the universities shows that the most serious problems which universities faced during the past ten years were, in order of importance : increase in enrolments ; the need to increase the volume and sources of finance ; the need to expand facilities ; the increase in applications ; and the need to expand teaching and research staff. In sixth place was the need to adjust the curriculum to fit changing social and economic needs, which was followed by the need to improve the quality of staff. As one can see, *the importance of qualitative changes followed closely after quantitative developments, but emphasis was given to the quantitative aspects.* In the universities' view, these were coped with well except for the two most serious problems of finance and facilities. However, there were less serious problems which had not been considered and were dealt with very poorly ; for example, the increase in applications relative to the number of places available and those aspects of university activity which were influenced by socio-economic needs. The latter, consisting of the differences between the distribution of graduates by speciality and the manpower needs, and the availability of refresher courses and continuing education, was ranked very low for university reaction.

As for the future, the qualitative aspect of university life is considered as the more serious problem for the next ten years ; this includes the need to alter the curriculum and university structure to meet changing needs and to expand and improve the quality of teaching and research staff. As can be seen from the analysis, the universities consider that they will be able to deal with these problems and this is in accordance with our analyses of changes in structure and courses and the growth of staff. For example, according to our data, teaching staff expansion has resulted in the proportion of junior-level staff rising in comparison with the situation which existed in 1958, but, reassuringly, this has not meant any decline of academic qualifications and in some cases our figures would indicate that junior-level staff were more highly qualified in 1968 than they were in 1958. However, what is necessary is more attention to their pedagogical qualifications and to the provision of special training, which, to some extent, would be a substitute for lack of teaching experience.

3. The widening gap between the developing and developed countries in university performance

Despite the very rapid growth of higher education in the developing countries, the gap between their performance and that of the universities in developed countries is not diminishing but widening, particularly in such areas as the availability of qualified teaching staff, relevant material resources and, subsequently, the quality of teaching and training of students and the amount and quality of research work.

Our analysis shows that :

(a) During the decade under review a very rapid growth took place in the number of students, which was in general higher in the developing than in the industrialized countries but was, nevertheless, very uneven from country to country. But a very important phenomenon which should be noted is the higher growth of graduate students in comparison with undergraduates. This tendency *was much stronger in the developed than in the developing countries.*

(b) Although the teaching staff has tended to grow rapidly in the decade under review, and seems, in general, to have met the expansion in student enrolments in most parts of the world, *the question of teaching staff appears to have posed a particularly difficult problem for some developing countries, particularly in Africa and Latin America.*

(c) *Research activity developed much faster in the universities of industrialized countries in Europe and North America than in other countries.* This may seriously influence the relative quality of the training of undergraduate and, especially, graduate students in the developing countries and should be borne in mind when planning the future development of universities, particularly in view of the necessity to increase the university contribution to national economic and social development.

(d) *The trends in innovation were similar in both developing and developed countries, although the gap between them was rather wide.* It is realized that the difficulties to be overcome in using new teaching and learning techniques are greater in the developing countries—finance, expertise and equipment are not so readily available—but in view of the problems posed by expansion, it might prove worth while making a greater effort in this area.

4. The university and socio-economic needs

In the majority of universities (with the exception of universities under both central government and institutional-level planning, e.g. universities in the socialist countries), *there is a serious and, in many respects, increasing gap between their activities and the actual social and economic needs of their countries.* Universities do not possess adequate information on these needs and, very often, their autonomy is used not to establish closer links between the university and the progressive development of society, but to isolate themselves.

This is shown throughout our analysis but can be seen particularly in Chapters V, VI and VII, as follows :

(a) The universities as a whole do not make systematic use of information on the socio-economic needs of their countries; for example, only 16 per cent of the universities had adequate information on the number of graduates in relation to the demand for them.

(b) With regard to the evaluation of teaching programmes, our sample reveals that efforts were undertaken by the majority to up-date and develop their curricula according to changes in knowledge and to the social and economic demands. As can be seen, the situation is very diverse throughout the world, but it would appear that more serious efforts are being made by the universities coming under central and institutional planning to carry out evaluation and to adjust their teaching programmes to the actual demand. However, *as a rule, the non-involvement of representatives from industry or manpower planners would mean that, overall, evaluation procedures are far from satisfactory* and energetic efforts should be made by universities to work out a permanent and reliable mechanism to link their basic activities to the rapidly changing national social and economic needs.

(c) Similarly, those universities which are already planned at both the national and institutional level are more innovatory in both teaching and administrative structures. This is, no doubt, due to their familiarity with the overall socio-economic needs of their countries.

(d) Generally universities do not use some important types of information on their students, as can be seen from the poor response to questions on drop-out rates and the reasons for them (there had been no serious attempts by the universities to investigate these matters) and from the paucity of data available on the socio-economic background of students. The latter shows an alarming situation where, for the majority of respondent universities, the basic tendency is growth in the number and proportion of students from the upper- and middle-level income groups. The number of students from the lower income group is increasing in absolute terms but their proportion remains low. It should be noted that most of the information received came from the developing countries and shows that they, at least, paid some attention to this matter. This very important social problem has, or will have, a great influence on planning the development of universities.

(e) We asked a question about the role of the university in the political and social life of the country and, although opinion questions were usually answered by all the universities, in this case 14 per cent of our sample were not able to reply—in fact, some of them stated that opinions were divided within the university on this subject. The figures for the overall sample show that 48 per cent of the universities felt they had a limited or indirect role, which was mainly educating students and carrying out research, and 5 per cent did not think they had any influence at all. Only 38 per cen considered themselves as an important factor. In all cases, they had a social more than a political or economic role—proving again their weak links with the economic needs of the country.

(f) Analysis of the obstacles facing the universities shows many of them to be aware of external influences, but *a rather common situation is that, while it is felt that socio-economic needs should be met and the university should change and develop accordingly, tradition and resistance encountered from both staff and students have delayed reforms.*

(g) The universities in our sample, according to the opinions of their principals, enjoy a rather high degree of autonomy in all the most important areas of their activity. The lowest degree was in finance, but even here the score indicates 'partial' autonomy. Classified by planning systems, one sees that universities working under both national and institutional plans enjoy a more *balanced* autonomy, i.e. their degree of autonomy is similar in all areas of activity. Their highest degree of autonomy was in finance, but there was not a great difference between this and other areas. However, other sub-groups had a rather wider range, between high degrees of autonomy in the basic areas of their activity (curricular planning, staff recruitment, setting of academic objectives, etc.) and a lower financial autonomy. One would presume that a university can really enjoy a high degree of autonomy in a particular field or area only if it is supported by a similar degree of autonomy else- where, especially in finance. Balanced degrees of autonomy provide the basis for the balanced development of the university.

Apparently, the most important differences in the degree of autonomy are due to the socio-economic structure of the country. Autonomy is generally considered to be important for university development ; this might well be so, but, *at present, practically all universities enjoy a high degree of autonomy and, therefore, their most important problem is how to use it in the most effective way, in accordance with the progressive social and economic trends of their respective countries.*

(h) Analysis of the involvement of different bodies in internal decision-making shows a variety of situations in the various types of universities. Generally, however, it does follow a more or less traditional pattern where students and teaching and research staff, especially at the junior level, are either playing no role at all or a less important role than they should if universities really want to democratize their decision-making processes.

5. *The importance of higher educational planning for university development*

In most countries of the world there is no proper higher educational planning at the governmental or institutional level. In those cases where some efforts in this direction have taken place, planning was either indicative in character or was minor at the university level. In general the managements of higher education systems and of individual universities have a traditional character and universities, as a rule, do not use modern techniques and methods of planning and management.

At the same time, *the opinion is shared by the heads of all the universities in our sample, that modern planning and management can and should be used as an instrument for solving the difficult problems they are facing.* For example, analysis has shown that serious efforts were made during the decade under review towards the broadening of interdisciplinary study and towards better co-operation among the different units within the universities. Nevertheless, the majority of universities feel a great need for further innovation in their management and planning and for the establishment of planning and institutional research units.

Also, there has been a considerable amount of structural change in the universities, but, from the percentages of units dropped (36.3 percent), added (92.5 per cent) or re-organized (58.8 per cent of the universities), it seems that *they are more inclined to add than to re-organize.* Addition does not necessarily bring any improvement in the structure and may bring new problems. Improved overall management and planning can be brought about only by a systematic and balanced approach to the whole university.

6. A necessity to develop the university information system

Our basic assumption in this study is that modern university planning and management should be based on an adequate information system, and therefore the essential factor in the planning of higher education is the amount and quality of information readily available in a form which can be used by planners and managers. The major conclusion one can draw from our analysis is that *the majority of universities, although facing very serious problems in their development, have neither reliable information nor mechanisms to analyse it.* This does not mean they are not concerned about their problems and are not doing anything to solve them, but rather they are not taking advantage of modern planning and management techniques and are neglecting to make efficient use of methods which are available.

Analysis of the state of replies shows *many universities have a serious lack of information for planning and decision-making purposes.* This includes, in particular : the amount and type of research ; the number of applications accepted ; background information on students ; use of staff time. None of these can be ignored in the planning and management of universities. *Thus major developments and innovations are needed in the information systems of most universities*. The fact that it took rather a long time for the universities to complete the questionnaire (a mean of four months) supports this conclusion. Apparently, the information which *is* available, is in a form which prevents the university administration from making good use of it in their everyday activities.

With regard to the indices used by universities for planning purposes, our questionnaire listed fourteen, covering both qualitative and quantitative characteristics of university functions, which would be useful. They included: ratio of acceptances to applications ; number of graduates in relation to demand ; student/teaching staff ratio ; rate of drop-out ; proportion of graduate students in the student body ; proportion of new courses in the curriculum ; etc. The utilization of indices, such as these, runs through each level of university planning and management. They can, for instance, be used to identify areas where resources are under-utilized and, subsequently, assist the allocation and utilization of resources in forward planning and thus lead to better informed decision-making.

The results of the analysis of information on the utilization of basic resources were very surprising. One of these was teaching and research staff. Obviously, proper utilization of their time can make a major contribution to the amount and quality of university activity, but only 27 per cent of the universities had adequate information available on the distribution of staff time between teaching, research and other activities, and 58 per cent of the universities did not have any information at all. The situation is likewise not very good for other basic resources. For example, only 39 per cent of universities had adequate information about the number of hours per week instructional space was used ; only 34 per cent had information about the availability of teaching and research equipment ; and 40 per cent knew the ratio of books available per student. Forty-four per cent of universities said that they knew the unit cost per graduating student.

As for other indices, only half the universities had adequate information concerning the ratio of applications to acceptances ; 44 per cent knew the rate of student drop-out ; and 42 per cent the proportion of new courses in the curricula per year. Only 23 per cent of the universities in the overall sample had adequate information on the proportion of research of a high professional calibre.

We are far from thinking that the availability of data on different activities in the university and an actual information system are one and the same thing. Not all data are informative. That is why it is extremely important to have methods and criteria for selecting data, the analysis of which will be significant and on which a university information system can be built. In other words, information gives the basis for decisions and planning, but not the decisions themselves. It is very important to have adequate methods of analysis, adequate criteria for evaluation and, also, an adequate mechanism for decision making on the basis of that information.

7. Personnel for planning in the universities

In the majority of countries, there is no special training for university planners and administrators. Some universities have taken the first steps and have made a study of the situation with regard to institutional planning. However, lack of properly trained management personnel has meant that many universities work on an improvised basis.

8. University experience in planning and management

It is, therefore, important that the experience of those universities which have obtained practical results in planning their development and modernizing their systems of management in tune with the changing social and economic needs of their countries, should be generalized and made available to others. This may provide a spur to the majority of universities in their efforts to modernize their management and planning systems.

II. Introduction and the structure of the sample

This paper presents an analysis of data obtained from a questionnaire circulated in connexion with the IIEP research project 'Planning the development of universities'; the results given in the following pages represent an important part of the research undertaken at the IIEP on this project, which was instituted in 1969 in order to look into the problems of higher educational development, planning and management—problems which are attracting more and more attention in different countries of the world.

Recent decades have been characterized by marked socio-economic and political changes in the world and by important events in many countries. One of the most significant contemporary trends is the development of the scientific and technological revolution, which is seriously influencing all aspects of social life. It is obvious that there exists a close interdependence and interrelationship between scientific and technological progress, economic and social changes in society and the development of higher education (the training of highly-qualified specialists). These same decades are therefore characterized by a very rapid growth of higher educational systems in practically all the countries of the world. The situations in which different higher educational systems, as well as individual institutions, perform their functions have become more complicated and many universities are now facing many serious problems, imbalances and difficulties.

In the present situation, development planning in the universities can be used (and in some cases is already being used) to find adequate solutions to the problems which universities are facing. Certainly, planning can only be really effective in our opinion when it becomes a specific form of modern university management. It should also be made clear that we do not believe planning at the university level is the panacea for all ills. Indeed, planning can be an effective tool of university management only if the socio-economic conditions in the respective countries are such as to encourage its use.

The planning of the development of both higher education as a whole, and of its various parts, can succeed only if, besides the existing socio-economic prerequisites for planning in any country, the peculiarity of this field of human adtivities is taken into account. Its peculiarity is that the system of higher education produces and distributes knowledge and the subject and object of this process is a human being.

When planning the development of a part or the whole of a higher education system, one must try to consider, together with the economic aspects, the aims, responsibilities and functions of higher education. It has an important social and political role to play in every country and the organization of the teaching process and what is actually taught will contribute to the fulfilment of this role. All these elements together, not any individual element, are the subject of higher educational planning.

In the light of the above, the aims of the project were formulated as follows :

1. To analyse the most important and interesting tendencies in the development of universities (past, present and future) ; to generalize the most valuable experiencies in university planning and management, and to identify difficulties and shortcomings.

2. To work out a system of tools and methods for university planning and management which might be used by the heads of universities to reveal hidden or under-utilized reserves, to make the most efficient allocation of existing limited resources and, generally, to result in an improved decision-making process which will better adapt the university to the socio-economic needs of the country.

3. To formulate recommendations for the use of modern methods of university planning and management in different situations and circumstances which might be useful to the heads of universities in their day-to-day activities.

The questionnaire was formulated at the IIEP with the assistance of experts from several countries and it covers a large number of questions concerning different aspects of university activity. The basic aim of the questionnaire was to collect some important information for a diagnosis of the present situation of university planning and management in different parts of the world. Thus, we asked the heads of universities about the most important past, current and future tendencies of university development, about the availability of information and other elements which might improve university planning and management and its ability to meet the requirements of modern society. Our questions, therefore, covered basic information on the university, data on university operations, functions and objectives, academic problems and teaching materials, governance and management of the university, decision-making and planning mechanisms, and assessment of past and future changes.

Obviously, to obtain any worthwhile diagnosis we should have to seek the collaboration of a representative sample of universities, since we could not hope to cover all of them. At the International Seminar at the IIEP in July 1969, it was suggested that a sample of about 100 universities would be sufficient to represent the whole. Our selection was made in close co-operation with the Secretariat of the International Association of Universities. Several criteria which were considered to be important from the point of view of assuring that the sample was representative, were used in this selection, as follows :

1. The existence of planning systems in higher education : this was felt to be important since it reflects differences in socio-economic and political structures of the countries, e.g. those universities with both central government and university planning are in the socialist countries ;
2. The level of economic development of the country : in accordance with the recommendation of the IIEP Governing Board, our study was oriented towards the needs of the developing countries. Therefore, about two-thirds of the universities in our sample were from developing and one-third from industrialized countries. For a more precise analysis of the situation, we used not only the general distribution into developing/developed countries but also considered the level of economic development in terms of GNP *per capita ;*
3. Geographical location : here the standard Unesco regional classification was used : Africa ; Asia ; Australia and Oceania ; Europe ; North America ; and Latin and Central America ;
4. Size of the university : for the purposes of our sample, we tried not to include either very small or extremely large universities ;
5. Emphasis on the field of study : not all higher educational institutions, including universities, teach all the different fields of study and, therefore, some balance had to be sought between pure science, the humanities, social sciences and professional training. This criterion was combined with a classification on different functions, such as emphasis on undergraduate teaching, graduate teaching, research and teacher training ;
6. Types of control : the differences between government-controlled and private universities were taken into account ;
7. The method of selecting students entering the university : this criterion is very interesting as it should show up both particular and common problems of universities with admission policies which are either open, selective or some mixture of the two.

We therefore selected 169 universities which met the above-listed criteria ; a number which we hoped would be sufficiently large to allow for refusals and yet still give us a reasonably balanced sample. In the event, 107 universities agreed to co-operate, of whom eighty from fifty different countries eventually sent in completed questionnaires in time for the computer analysis. We have since received eight more questionnaires. The main reasons given for inability to co-operate in the project were lack of proper information, lack of staff to take charge of the work, and thirdly, in only a few cases, that the university was already too busy in completing questionnaires from the government or other sources.[1] Eight universities, after having agreed to co-operate, dropped out because of difficulties in obtaining the necessary information and in the remaining eleven cases, illness and transfer of staff or university reform were given as reasons for delay.

One of the immediate positive results at this stage of our work was that some universities who had difficulties in completing the questionnaire owing to lack of information, informed us that they had thus been stimulated to start planning offices, offices of statistics or other groups or committees to improve planning and management.

Although not all the universities whom we invited responded to the question-naire, nevertheless, we have rather a satisfactory sample of universities. Percentage distributions within the above listed criteria among the eighty universities are shown on the opposite page.

As one can see from these figures, we have 72.5 per cent of universities from developing and 27.5 per cent from developed countries, which corresponds to the requirements laid down previously. It is also worth noting that the majority (about three-quarters of the responses), were from universities which possessed at least some elements of planning and whose experience should be particularly valuable for our research.

Also, if we compare our sample with the existing global situation, in one criterion (the number of students), we see that our percentages almost coincide with those calculated from world-wide data. In our sample, universities with 0-5,000 students represent 45 per cent of the total and the global percentage is 48 per cent; universities with 5,000-10,000 students are 25 and 23 per cent respectively; and for universities with 10,000 students and over the figures are 30 and 29 per cent respectively. Certainly, this one criterion is not sufficient to judge how representative our sample is of the global situation, but our analysis of the data received from the questionnaires, compared with generally available information on the situation in different regions of the world, leads us to the conclusion that our sample is sufficiently representative to make a general diagnosis of the situation of university planning and management, especially in relation to developing countries. For example, we have in our sample fourteen universities out of a total of about fifty qualified institutions of higher education existing in Africa; in Latin America seventeen universities from eleven different countries responded, which means about half of the Latin American countries are represented.

1. Even though they could not participate in the study, most of the universities stated that they considered the improvement of their planning and management as important.

1. *Existence of a*
   planning system   *Percentage*
   Central government and
   university planning   6.2
   Central government
   planning only   3.7
   University planning only   21.3
   Some planning mechanisms   42.5
   No planning mechanisms   26.3

2. *Level of economic*
   development
   Developing countries   72.5
   Developed countries   27.5

3. *GNP per capita*
   (in US $)
   0-100   16.3
   100-200   16.3
   200-300   21.2
   300-400   7.5
   400-500   —
   500-1,000   11.3
   1,000-2,000   11.3
   2,000 and over   16.3

4. *Geographical location*
   Africa   17.5
   Asia   28.7
   Australia and Oceania   3.7
   Europe   22.5
   North America   6.3
   Latin and Central America   21.3

5. *University size by*
   number of students   *Percentage*

	IIEP sample	World distribution[1]
0-5,000	45.0	48.0
5,000-10,000	25.0	23.0
10,000 +	30.0	29.0

6. *Emphasis on field of study*
   Pure science   11.3
   The humanities   8.7
   Social sciences   5.0
   Professional training   28.7
   No special emphasis   46.3

7. *Emphasis on university*
   function
   Undergraduate teaching   71.3
   Graduate teaching   22.5
   Research   2.5
   Teacher training   3.7

8. *Type of control*
   Private   20.0
   Public   80.0

9. *Type of admission system*
   Open   11.3
   Selective   72.5
   Mixed   16.3

In our opinion, where the distribution of universities in our sample might seem disproportionate in comparison with the global distribution, this does not affect its relevance, for even the small sub-classifications of a few universities

1. *Sources: Digest of Educational statistics, 1969,* Washington, Office of Education, U.S. Department of Health, Education and Welfare, 1969 (USA universities only are taken into account).
   International handbook of universities, 1968, Paris, International Association of Universities, 1968.
   Commonwealth universities yearbook, 1970, London, Association of Commonwealth Universities, 1970.

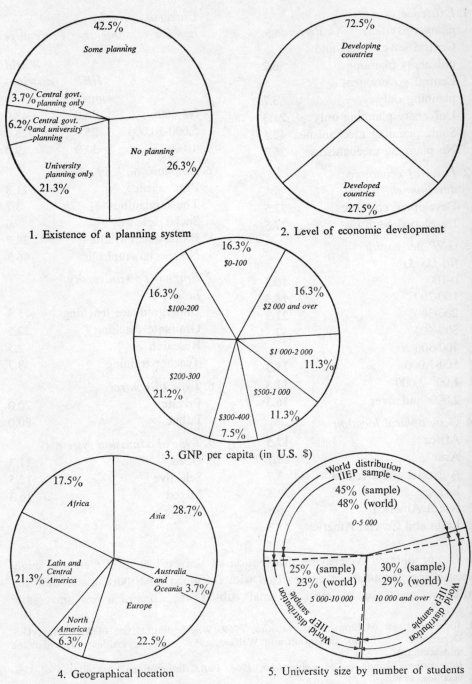

FIGURE 1. *Percentage distribution of sample by classifications*

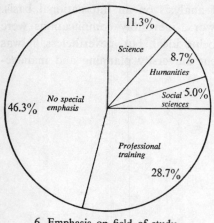

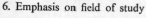

6. Emphasis on field of study

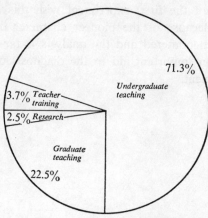

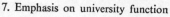

7. Emphasis on university function

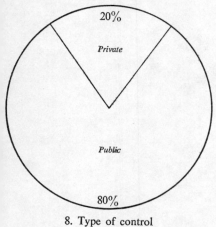

8. Type of control

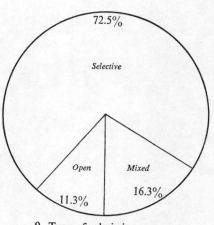

9. Type of admission system

FIGURE 1 *(continued)*

represent more or less homogeneous groups of higher educational institutions. For example, this is true of universities or university-level institutions located in industrialized countries. Here, of course, we took into account the very significant socio-economic and political differences in these groups and a great variety of situations is represented.

The data which we received in the questionnaires were processed with the help of the Unesco computer according to a special programme formulated for this particular type of research. We understand that this is one of the first, if not the first, experiment with this type of analysis on an international basis. Because of the pioneer character of the work, inevitably complications were encountered and the analysis is far from being ideal, but, nevertheless, it was an important aid to the diagnosis of present university planning and management.

III. The state of replies

One of our basic assumptions for this study was that modern university planning and management should be based on an adequate information system, and, therefore, the essential factor in the planning of higher education is the amount and quality of information readily available in a form which can be used by planners and managers. The questionnaire was thus intended to concentrate on finding out what the university knows about itself, for example : data on its past operations ; its basic functions and objectives ; its research and academic programmes ; teaching materials ; its administrative and decision-making processes. Certain questions were designed to obtain as much statistical and factual information as possible so as to permit an analysis of each university in its own context, to gain an idea of its character, structure and tendencies and, as far as possible, to amass comparable data. Besides these purely factual questions, there were others which asked for opinions on different university problems and whose aim was to obtain estimations from the people who run the universities of, for instance : the degree of university autonomy ; the need for reorganization ; the use of new media ; problems encountered during the past decade ; their reaction to them and the difficulty that this same problem will present in the future ; and so on. Despite the fact that these opinions are to some extent subjective, it is possible with a large enough number of opinions to draw some conclusions which will reflect objective trends more or less precisely.

Although it is difficult to analyse responses to open questions, some of them were included in the questionnaire to provide for more specific information from particular universities.

A broad examination of the degree of response shows that questions relating to opinions and judgements received a higher response from most universities than questions requiring factual data. For some questions the degree of non-response was quite high, but we considered that lack of information is also informative in that identification of areas where information does not always exist is one of the objectives of the current study. This absence of information, however, may be either because the data are really not available in the university, or because the form in which they are available is not suited to our question. In other cases there were responses which we could not analyse because of problems of the interpretation of terms. (This persisted in spite of the attachment of a glossary to the questionnaire. See Appendix III.) This applies particularly to data relating to operating and capital expenditure, for we found that when the totals were broken down into the various items of expenditure, the figures were no longer comparable. There were also occasions when questions were not applicable to particular universities : for example, questions demanding information on some fields of study were not applicable to universities where they were not taught. This reduced the rate of response and, when considering these questions, this fact should be borne in mind.

It should be noted that many statistical questions demanded figures for three separate years from a decade (1958/59, 1963/64, 1968/69) and that the percentage of non-response would, in these cases, represent for the most part lack of figures for the early years. We should also point out that, for these questions, 13 per cent of the total possible response could not in any case have been given because some universities were established after either 1958 or 1963.

We have considered the state of replies according to the different sections of the questionnaire, which were as follows: background information; basic data on university operations; university functions and objectives; academic programmes and teaching materials; governance and management; decision-making and planning mechanism; assessment of past and future changes.

1. Background information

Response to questions relating to the background of the university was almost complete. This was obviously due to the general nature of the questions asked, namely, year of foundation, type of institution, current total number of students, disciplines taught and an opinion of the degree of university autonomy in specified areas of decision-making. The average percentage response to the two latter questions was 99 per cent.

2. Basic data on university operations

This is the section of the questionnaire where the rate of response varied most significantly, ranging from almost complete response to some questions (such as the number of working weeks per year and such general information as, for instance, the total number of students by type), to a very low rate of response (17 per cent) to the question on the socio-economic origins of the students

Only 14 per cent of the universities were able to state the numbers of students by parental occupation, but 34 per cent reported the geographical location of their homes and 23 per cent gave the number by source of financial support. This type of information on students is essential for planning, but it appears that most of the universities do not possess it.

Statistics on the number of applications to the university were also scanty. The ratio of applications to acceptances is a very useful tool as an index of individual demand for education in specific disciplines. However, we should take into account the fact that universities do not always receive applications for admission directly, nor do they always make decisions concerning admission. But it is clear that, without such basic data, rational and reliable planning cannot be implemented.

Statistics relating to the percentage of student drop-out were available from a slightly larger number of universities, 26 per cent. The number of degrees granted was given by just over half of the universities, but the differences in the structure of degrees and diplomas and the problem of terminology created some difficulties in making a comparison of the data. The numbers of academic staff were available also from about half of the universities and about the same percentage (55 per cent) reported the proportion of staff coming from abroad.

With regard to financial questions, 56 per cent gave their total operating and 52 per cent their total capital expenditures, but due to difficulties of terminology, as mentioned above, the itemised expenditure could not be compared. However, this was not a problem when considering the total expenditures. The percentage of the university budget allocated to the library was reported by 68 per cent of the universities.

Statistics relating to the volume of research work were available from less than half of the universities—43 per cent reported the amount of money received for different types of research work, but only 22 per cent were able to state the actual number of research projects. The number of universities completing the section on numbers of graduate students engaged in research was almost nil.

Half of the universities reported on changes in available instructional space during the last decade; 63 per cent were able to state the total number of library items, but most of the other figures relating to the library were approximate and could not be used for analytical purposes.

Ninety-five per cent of universities reported the number of weeks they were fully functional per year.

3. University functions and objectives

This section was concerned mostly with the judgements and opinions of the heads of universities. It also contained some very general types of factual

31

questions, such as whether a particular function was performed or not. As mentioned before, such information was furnished by most of the universities. About 90 per cent of the universities gave their ranking for present types of functions and also for areas they would most like to see developed.

4. Academic programmes and teaching materials

This section consisted of questions asking for statistics or for factual information on courses, academic structure and teaching materials—here, particularly, the response to statistical questions was much lower than elsewhere. About 60 per cent of the universities reported the total number of courses offered and 63 per cent their degree of change during the last decade. Only 31 per cent were able to give the composition of course requirements in different fields of study, and an even lower percentage (22) the course requirements in fields other than the major subject. The question as to whether there was any kind of continuous evaluation of the existing courses received a complete response, as did that on the involvement of different persons in this evaluation.

Information on the past, present and future use of new media in the teaching process was provided by 73 per cent.

5. Governance and management

In this section of the questionnaire we were interested in innovations in university management and, because most of the questions were of the simple yes/no type, the response rate was almost 100 per cent.

6. Decision-making and planning mechanism

The degree of involvement of different agents (government, industry, university administration, staff, students) in the various areas of decision-making was reported by 86 per cent of the universities. A very important question in this section was the availability of different types of information for planning purposes. We did not ask for the actual data but simply whether they were available or not, adequate or not, and if not available, whether they were desirable. Because of the nature of the question, the rate of response was almost 100 per cent.

7. Assessment of past and future changes

This section required the opinions and judgements of university principals. The response rate was high—90 per cent reported on the past and future change in different aspects of university activity, their reactions to those changes during the past decade, and their expected reactions during the next decade. Although all the universities reported whether a particular factor of change will continue to occur in the future, a lesser number (94 per cent) estimated the degree of desirability.

When analyzing the replies of the different groups of universities according to our sub-classifications, we noticed that information on major aspects of activity was, in general, substantially better where planning exists at both the central and university levels or at the central level only, than at universities without planning or with only some elements of planning. When classified according to the level of economic development the response rate from universities in developed countries was better, but the difference is not very striking for some kinds of information are more readily available in developing countries. This includes, for example, information concerning teaching loads, the number of publications by the staff and operating expenditures.

Obviously, the exact percentages of the replies do not mean a great deal since we are dealing with only a sample of universities but, nevertheless, an analysis should characterize the overall situation more or less precisely. Figure 2 illustrates the information given in this chapter.

The major conclusion from a general analysis of the state of replies is that at many universities there is a serious lack of information for planning and decision-making purposes. Even taking into consideration problems of terminology, the unsuitable format of our questions for some universities, etc., it is evident that the poor state of replies to some of our questions can be interpreted as a lack of attention to several important aspects of university life. These include, in particular, the socio-economic background of students, the reasons for drop-out, the amount and type of research work, the number of publications by the staff, etc., none of which can be ignored in the planning and management of universities.

Therefore, major developments and innovations should be made by most universities to their information systems. Because it took many universities rather a long time to complete the questionnaire (rarely two months, sometimes a year, the mean being four months) this conclusion is borne out. Seemingly, the information available is in a form which prevents the university administration from making good use of it in their everyday activities.

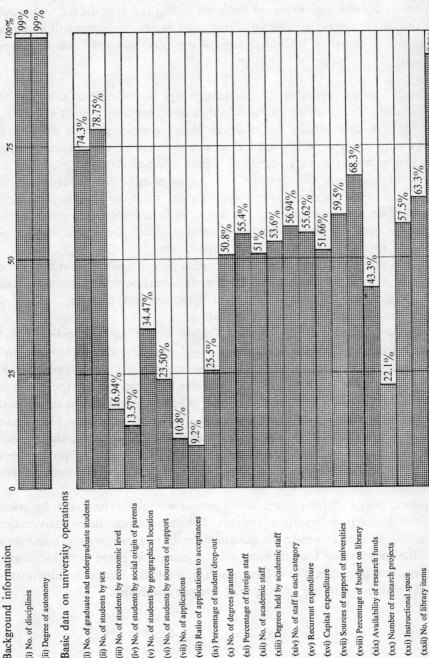

1. Background information

   (i) No. of disciplines
   (ii) Degree of autonomy

2. Basic data on university operations

   (i) No. of graduate and undergraduate students
   (ii) No. of students by sex
   (iii) No. of students by economic level
   (iv) No. of students by social origin of parents
   (v) No. of students by geographical location
   (vi) No. of students by sources of support
   (vii) No. of applications
   (viii) Ratio of applications to acceptances
   (ix) Percentage of student drop-out
   (x) No. of degrees granted
   (xi) Percentage of foreign staff
   (xii) No. of academic staff
   (xiii) Degrees held by academic staff
   (xiv) No. of staff in each category
   (xv) Recurrent expenditure
   (xvi) Capital expenditure
   (xvii) Sources of support of universities
   (xviii) Percentage of budget on library
   (xix) Availability of research funds
   (xx) Number of research projects
   (xxi) Instructional space
   (xxii) No. of library items
   (xxiii) No. of weeks the university works

FIGURE 2. *Detailed response rate for questionnaire, in percentages of the total sample*

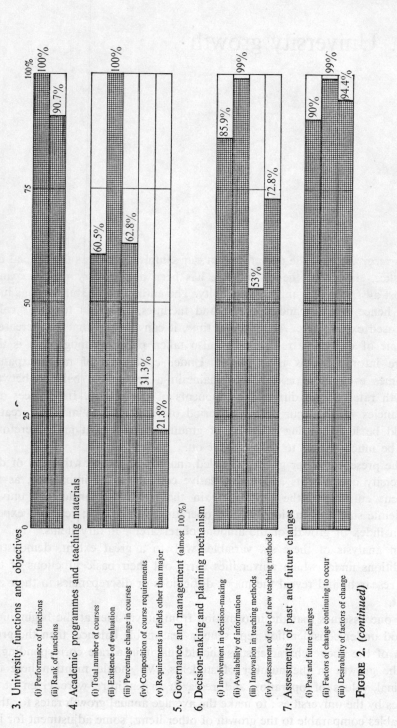

3. **University functions and objectives**
   (i) Performance of functions — 100%
   (ii) Rank of functions — 90.7%

4. **Academic programmes and teaching materials**
   (i) Total number of courses — 60.5%
   (ii) Existence of evaluation — 100%
   (iii) Percentage change in courses — 62.8%
   (iv) Composition of course requirements — 31.3%
   (v) Requirements in fields other than major — 21.8%

5. **Governance and management** (almost 100 %)

6. **Decision-making and planning mechanism**
   (i) Involvement in decision-making — 85.9%
   (ii) Availability of information — 99%
   (iii) Innovation in teaching methods — 53%
   (iv) Assessment of role of new teaching methods — 72.8%

7. **Assessments of past and future changes**
   (i) Past and future changes — 90%
   (ii) Factors of change continuing to occur — 99%
   (iii) Desirability of factors of change — 94.4%

FIGURE 2. (*continued*)

IV. University growth

Data received from the universities in our sample, as well as the official national statistics, show that the last decade has been one of very rapid expansion in almost all spheres of university activity. The enrolment of students has increased and, hence, the demand for staff and facilities, which in turn has called for increased expenditure. At the same time, it can be seen that an increase in the volume of university research has also taken place, although this is the area where information is most scarce. Under conditions of rapid expansion, it becomes even more essential to maintain a reasonable balance between the growth rates of the different components of the system. Imbalances and discrepancies which occur during a period of rapid growth may be greater than would be likely during a period of gradual development and, therefore, they will be much harder to correct later on.

The present chapter gives a detailed analysis of the growth rates of different university components and their relative consistency or imbalance, as follows: student enrolment—the key factor in the overall expansion of universities; academic staff; instructional space; operating expenditure; research expenditure as an index of growth of the amount of research ; library items.

An analysis of these six variables will, to a great extent, demonstrate the conditions under which universities carry out their basic functions of teaching and research, and reveal the major difficulties or discrepancies in their development.

If one assumes that the information from universities at the beginning of the period under consideration represents a reasonable balance, then the growth of each of the above characteristics should maintain a rate corresponding to that of the growth in the number of students. We should mention here that the original values of operating and research expenditure were given at current prices by the universities ; to make the average annual growth rates for these two variables comparable to the growth of other items, some adjustment for inflation had to be made. The year 1963 was considered as the base and deflation was computed according to the index numbers given in the United Nations Statistical Yearbooks for 1968 and 1970. However, we would also point out that we are not allowing for any effects which innovation might have had on instructional programmes and other aspects of university activity.

Our comparative analysis of growth rates (Table IV) is aimed at demonstrating one of the methods of analyzing university development and at revealing the actual situation in different groups of universities. We are aware that interpretation of the behaviour of different variables and of their interaction may be different at individual universities and in groups of universities. This also depends on the situation prevailing at the starting date of our analysis and on the types and rates of innovation which have had an influence on the different university characteristics. However, any future planning should allow for the growth of all university characteristics consistent with the growth in the number of students.

1. Overall sample

The average annual growth rate of the total number of students in the overall sample was 11.8 per cent during the period 1958-68, which is balanced quite well by a growth rate of full-time staff at 10.9 per cent. (Due to difficulties in collecting data on part-time teachers and in interpreting them correctly, the growth of staff was calculated from figures for full-time academic staff only.) Instructional space grew at almost the same rate with an average of 10.25 per cent, while operating expenditure is slightly ahead at 12.5 per cent each year. This leads us to wonder why universities as a whole have considered finance as their major problem, especially since the annual average growth rate of research funds was 17.6 per cent. Thus the greatest growth seems to be occurring in the field of research and is probably due to the fact that, to many universities during the mid-fifties, emphasis on research was quite new.

The one disturbing factor is the annual growth rate of 8.7 per cent for library items, which falls about one-quarter below the average annual growth rate of students and would seem to indicate that library budgets have not received the same increases and many universities must have difficulties in providing students with teaching materials and textbooks.

Control sample

In order to check the extent to which our overall sample is representative, because of the heterogeneity of the replies, we calculated growth rates for groups of universities who have either been able to give figures for all the variables (seven universities only) or for five of the variables (eleven universities), and so on. As one can see (Table IV.10) the behaviour of these variables and their interrelation is very similar to that in the overall sample, with the exception of the first group of seven universities who gave complete information. In this particular group, the weak points were space and operating expenditure.

2. Existence of a planning system

When the six variables are arranged according to existing planning systems, the growth rates for each sub-class over the ten-year period have their own characteristics. We were unable to consider the universities in countries with central planning only, since the rate of response was insufficient.

In this classification, most striking are those universities with both central and university planning or university-level planning only, who have maintained excellent research and operating expenditure growth rates compared to the increase in students. The rates for the former universities are 20 per cent for research and 10.9 per cent for operating expenditure as against 7.5 per cent for students, while for the latter, 25.6 per cent and 17.7 per cent as against 12.9 per cent for students. However, at the same time, universities with central und university planning increased their space at only half the rate of the increase in students and this may suggest a much greater use of existing facilities.

A low increase in space is to be found in all universities, indicating that efficient use of space is of major importance and has certainly been a factor contributing to the greater interest in planning and the use of computers shown over the decade.

Also of note are serious imbalances in those sub-groups with university planning only and no planning at all. The former, although receiving a significant increase in operating expenditure and balancing other factors quite well with its student growth rate at 12.9 per cent, has had a staff growth rate of only 7.7 per cent. The latter's growth rate in library items of 6.1 per cent is less than half the growth rate for students (14.4 per cent).

3. Level of economic development

It can be seen that, on average, among universities of the developing countries, the rate of growth of student enrolments was higher than any other factor. Table IV.3 shows that a 13.1 per cent annual increase in enrolments was met by an 11.6 per cent increase in staff, a 12.5 per cent increase in instructional space and a 13.8 per cent increase in research expenditure. However, the lowest increases were in operating expenditure (11.0 per cent) and library items (9.6 per cent) and these must certainly have created severe problems.

Overall sample *(base 1958 = 100)*

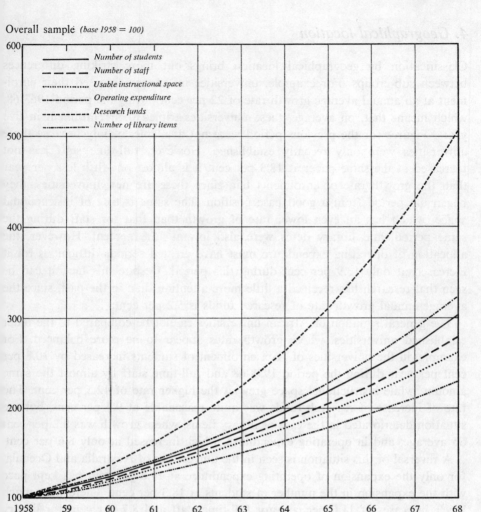

——————— Number of students
– – – – – – Number of staff
·················· Usable instructional space
·–·–·–·–·– Operating expenditure
– – – – – – – Research funds
·–··–··–·· Number of library items

ᶠIGURE 3. *Growth rates of selected university sub-systems over the period 1958-68*

These discrepancies become more marked when compared with universities in developed countries, where growth rates of students at 9.2 per cent were lower and consequently growth of staff (9.4 per cent) and operating expenditure (15.5 per cent) have been adequate. As can be seen, they devoted more of their effort to research than universities in the developing countries; the annual growth rate of funds spent on research was 20.8 per cent. However, the growth of space and library items at 7.3 and 7.5 per cent lagged behind the rate of growth of students and, apparently, at least in respect of physical expansion, the developing countries are in a more favourable position.

4. *Geographical location*

Classification by geographical location brings out more striking differences between sub-groups. For example, universities in Africa increased their enrolment at an annual average growth rate of 22 per cent during the period 1963-68, which means that, on average, these universities tripled their enrolment in five years. Figures for the previous period were not available, mainly because these universities were only recently established. However, full-time staff has not increased at the same pace; at 18.3 per cent it is almost one-fifth less per year than the growth rate of enrolments but, since these are new universities, they began the period from a good base position. The same is true of instructional space, which has an even lower rate of growth than that for staff during the same period, and library items were also low at 15.8 percent. However, the allocation of operating expenditure must have created serious difficulties for it increased at only 13.9 per cent during this period. Despite this fact, it can be seen that research has received a little more attention than in the past, since the average annual growth rate of research funds is 5.2 per cent.

The general situation of African universities cannot be compared to the older established universities, whose growth rates appear to be more balanced. For example, in the universities of Asia enrolment of students increased by 10.8 per cent per year during the period 1958-68 and full-time staff by almost the same amount, while instructional space grew at the higher rate of 12.5 per cent. The rate of increase of research funds was quite reasonable at 9.4 per cent, but the situation deteriorated in the case of library items, where growth was 8.2 per cent on average, and in operating expenditure, which increased at only 8.6 per cent.

A reversal of this situation is seen in the universities of Australia and Oceania, for only the expansion of operating expenditure at 19.8 per cent has kept pace with the expansion in the number of students at 18.3 per cent. There were much lower increases of 11.6 per cent for full-time staff and 8.7 per cent for library items. It would be interesting to study in detail the reasons for such unevenness. The increase in space at 15.2 per cent does not compare quite so badly, and the rate of growth of research funds (14 per cent) was also reasonable. The number of universities in our sample from this part of the world is, however, too small to lead us to any definite conclusions about the general situation.

Universities in Europe expanded their staff at almost the same rate as the number of students, although instructional space and library items grew at lower rates. Average annual growth rates of full-time staff, instructional space and library items were 10.4, 7.5 and 6.4 per cent respectively, during the period 1958-68 and the number of students grew at 10.3 per cent. Operating expenditure grew at the comparatively high rate of 13 per cent and the increase in the amount of research funds seems to have been satisfactory at 16.9 per cent. One can conclude that European universities pay more attention to the qualitative aspects of their activities but, nevertheless, the situation with regard to available physical facilities, books and other publications is worsening.

Universities in North America appear to be the most privileged when considering rates of expansion. Increases in all factors have been higher than the rate of increase in enrolments, which increased at an annual rate of 11 per cent, whereas the number of full-time staff increased by 17 per cent, instructional space by 12.5 per cent and library items by 17.8 per cent. Rates of increase in operating and research expenditure have been higher at 15.8 per cent and 47.1 per cent per year respectively. Seemingly, more and better paid staff are used for teaching and research and universities are buying more literature for their work.

Such a favourable situation is not found in Latin and Central American universities, where the number of students grew at an average annual rate of 14.5 per cent during the period 1963-68, with corresponding average rates of 12.2 per cent in instructional space and 13.3 per cent in the number of library items. The most disturbing factor is that full-time staff increased only at an average of 6.6 per cent—this is, however, partly explained by the fact that, in most Latin and Central American universities in our sample, there are a large number of part-time staff to take care of the increased teaching load. The growth of finance was also hardly satisfactory at 11.7 per cent for operating expenditure and 10 per cent for research funds during the period 1963-68.

5. University size by number of students

Classification by size reveals some interesting divergences and imbalances. The smaller universities have a high rate of growth for student numbers (16.4 per cent) which is not matched by the growth rate of other factors. This phenomenon can be partly explained by some of the universities in this group being newly established. Academic staff has a growth rate of 11.8 per cent only and available instructional space grew at 9.9 per cent. It is worth mentioning, however, that instructional space grew at a very fast rate over the period 1963-68. The growth rates of operating and research expenditures were well below that for students at 12 and 8 per cent respectively.

Medium-sized universities, with 5-10,000 student, have fairly integrated growth rates. All factors, with the exception of library items, have grown faster than the number of students over the past decade. The enrolment rate was 11.8 per cent, whereas staff and instructional space grew at 13.1 and 14.1 per cent respectively. Operating expenditure grew at a rate equal to the increase in students, but the most striking element was the growth of funds allocated to research which, over the ten-year period, was 26.4 per cent.

Universities with more than 10,000 students have steady balanced growth rates for students of 7.9, academic staff 8.2 and instructional space 7.9 per cent. Library items fall somewhat below the other factors with a growth rate of 5 per cent. The two highest rates of growth were for operating expenditure and research funds—the former was 13.7 and the latter 18.4 per cent.

We can thus conclude that in medium-sized and large universities better conditions for research exist than in small ones. However, overall, medium-sized universities were better balanced. Therefore, the optimum size of a university from the point of view of management and planning would seem to be one with 5-10,000 students.

6. Emphasis on the field of study

When we group the universities according to their fields of study, emphasis on social sciences has by far the higher rate of growth in the number of students (24.2 per cent), well ahead of humanities at 15.8, professional training at 14.5 and pure science at 12.7 per cent. All of them experienced serious discrepancies between the rates of growth of students and library items, but the worst situation in this respect was to be found at universities emphasizing social sciences. The staffing situation was also unsatisfactory for social sciences and pure science. As for operating expenditure, only those universities with no special emphasis seem to be in a good position—contrary to what one might expect, specialization seemed to attract less rather than more funds.

7. Emphasis on university function

When the universities were considered according to the emphasis they themselves gave to different functions, it was only possible to take the sub-groups of undergraduate and graduate teaching into account. The other two sub-groups did not have sufficient responses to give significant observations.

Universities emphasizing undergraduate teaching have fairly steady and integrated growth rates for all factors. The growth rate of student numbers over the decade was 13.2 per cent, while operating expenditure matched this growth and research funds were considerably higher at 19.4 per cent. Academic staff and instructional space have not expanded quite so fast at 11.2 and library items were even lower at 9.8 per cent.

Universities emphasizing graduate teaching also have reasonably balanced growth rates, except for library items. Student growth was 10 per cent (although this was for *all* students in this particular context) matched closely by operating expenditure and academic staff. Instructional space grew at the slightly lower rate of 9.4 per cent over the decade, but library items again were much lower at 6.8 per cent, which is rather difficult to understand. As with the under-graduate teaching universities, research funds had a high rate of increase at 15.7 per cent.

It is worth noting that, overall, universities emphasizing undergraduate teaching had higher growth rates than universities emphasizing graduate teaching for all factors.

8. *Type of control*

The public universities seem to have balanced all the factors quite well; an increase in students of 11.6 per cent has been met by increases in staff at 11.1, library items at 12.4, operating expenditure at 12.7 and research funds at 16.4 per cent. Instructional space at 9.9 per cent was out of step. The scarcity and high price of land in cities, where some of the large public universities are situated, is probably a contributory factor.

The private universities, although receiving a very favourable increase in research funds of 21.4 per cent, have not managed to balance their student increase (12.7 per cent) quite so well with the remaining factors—in particular, academic staff at 10.2 per cent.

9. *Type of admission system*

The average annual growth rate in the number of students for universities with open systems of admission is almost twice that for universities with a selective system. Such a rapid increase has meant that other factors have not kept pace. Enrolments, at 22.5 per cent, have had to be met by an increase of 17 per cent in staff, 14.3 per cent in instructional space and 11.4 per cent in library items—all of which reflect very serious inconsistencies.

Universities having a selective system of admission, however, have done much better. Increases in the number of students (11.9 per cent) have been met by almost equivalent increases, except for library items (8.4 per cent).

Universities with a mixed system of admission also appear to have done quite well in maintaining consistency between the growth of enrolments and different facilities. While the number of students increased at an annual rate of .8 per cent, full-time staff, instructional space and library items increased at 1.4, 10.5 and 10.8 per cent respectively. These universities also gave a great deal of emphasis to research judging from the funds spent, which had a growth rate of nearly 30 per cent. Operating expediture at 17.5 per cent is also very satisfactory.

10. Conclusions

The following general conclusions can be drawn from the analysis of growth rates of different university characteristics:

1. Growth rates vary considerably from one group of universities to another. This demonstrates that not only general problems common to all university development should be analysed in depth, but also that certain specific features of groups and even peculiarities of individual universities should be studied.
2. The most striking imbalances may be observed in all parts of the world, except the Americas, in the development of the university library, which is one of the most important bases of teaching. Growth rates were so often found to be very much lower than other factors that, obviously, this matter deserves very serious attention and investigation.
3. It was noticed in the developed countries and in public universities that space is proving to be a factor which cannot be increased at the same rate as the increase in students. It is therefore evident that planning methods and innovation are urgently needed in this area.
4. Universities with an open system of admission experienced much more serious imbalances and discrepancies than universities with a selective or mixed system.
5. Research activity developed much faster in the universities of industrialized countries in Europe and North America than in other countries. This may seriously influence the relative quality of the training of undergraduate and especially, graduate students in the developing countries and should be borne in mind when planning future development, particularly in view of the necessity to increase the university contribution to national economic and social development. However, over-emphasizing research work which is linked neither directly with improving the quality of teaching staff nor the training of graduate students may also be detrimental since it diverts resources and staff time from their main functions.

V. University autonomy
and the involvement of different bodies
in the internal decision-making process

A. University autonomy

The problem of university autonomy attracts much attention and has an important place in any discussion about university planning and management.

In our opinion, today, autonomy is only one of the instruments ensuring the fulfilment of a university's educational and socio-economic functions. The meaning of university autonomy has changed drastically even since the last century. It can now be considered as a measure of the division of functions and responsibilities between the university management and society, as represented by central and local governments. We decided, therefore, to try to measure the present degree of autonomy enjoyed by universities in order to provide a more or less objective basis for discussions on its role today.

Seven areas of activity were identified as being necessary for the fulfilment of the most commonly-held university objectives, as follows: finance; curriculum; selection of students; staff recruitment; setting of academic objectives; formulation of research policy; setting of general objectives.

The degree of autonomy enjoyed by universities in each of these areas has been calculated from the opinions given by university heads or their delegates. On a four-point scale (3, complete autonomy; 2, partial; 1, slight; and 0, none), average scores and standard deviations have been computed for the overall sample and for groups of universities of different classes and sub-classes. The results are set out in Figure 4 and in more detail in Table V.

For six activities (excepting finance) the average scores differ very little, varying only between 2.526 and 2.763. Finance, with an average score of 1.988, stands rather apart.

Each of the areas of decision-making is now considered in turn, by the different classification of universities.

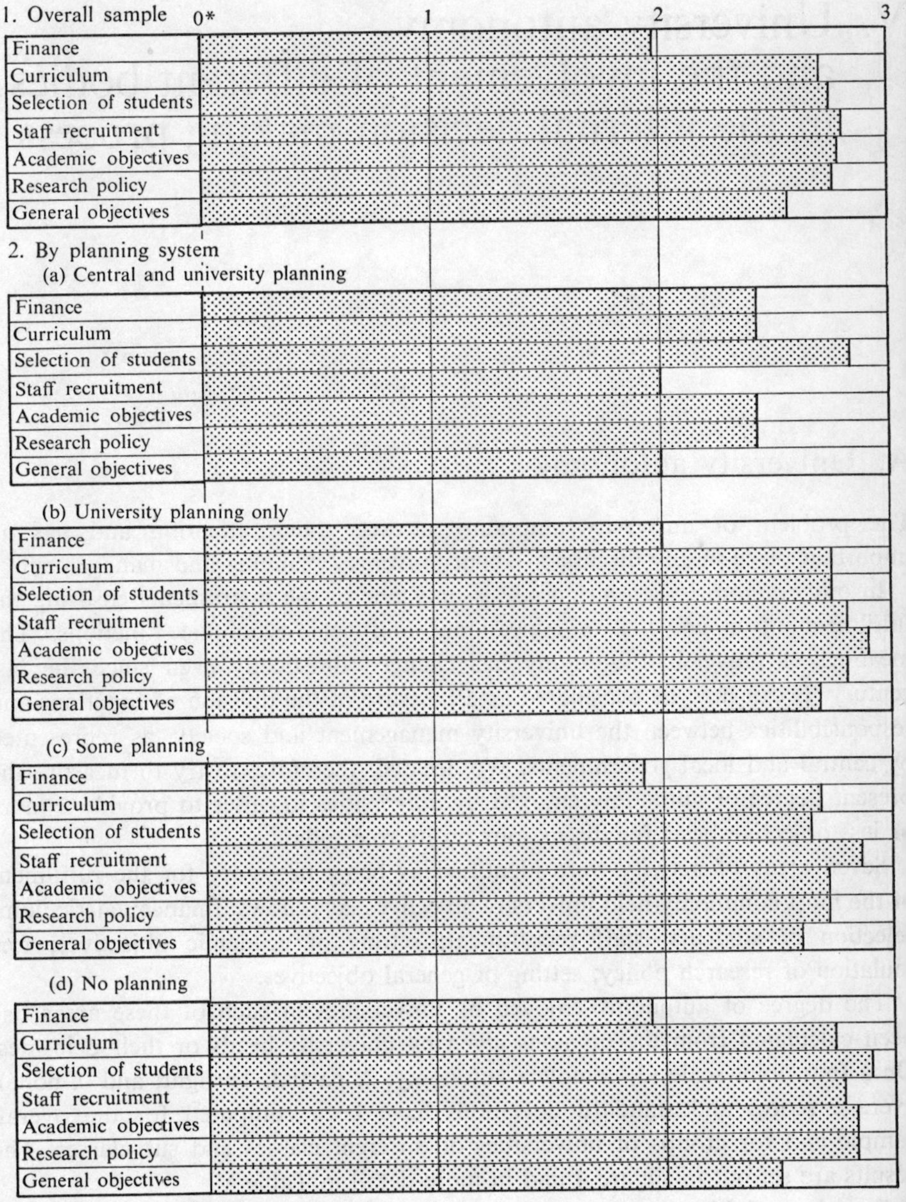

1. Overall sample

| Finance |
| Curriculum |
| Selection of students |
| Staff recruitment |
| Academic objectives |
| Research policy |
| General objectives |

2. By planning system
   (a) Central and university planning

| Finance |
| Curriculum |
| Selection of students |
| Staff recruitment |
| Academic objectives |
| Research policy |
| General objectives |

(b) University planning only

| Finance |
| Curriculum |
| Selection of students |
| Staff recruitment |
| Academic objectives |
| Research policy |
| General objectives |

(c) Some planning

| Finance |
| Curriculum |
| Selection of students |
| Staff recruitment |
| Academic objectives |
| Research policy |
| General objectives |

(d) No planning

| Finance |
| Curriculum |
| Selection of students |
| Staff recruitment |
| Academic objectives |
| Research policy |
| General objectives |

* Scale 0-3 : 0 = none ; 1 = slight ; 2 = partial ; 3 = complete

FIGURE 4. *Average degree of autonomy enjoyed by a university in different areas of decision-making*

1. Finance

In the overall sample, universities have the least degree of autonomy in this area. The average score of 1.988 means a degree of autonomy very close to partial and yet this seems remarkable considering that all universities are heavily dependent upon their governments for financial support. In our sample it was found that more than 70 per cent of university expenditure is financed by governments.

The classification of universities according to different types of planning systems brings out some differences in the average degree of autonomy for different sub-classes. For example, universities working to both a national and institutional plan have an average score of 2.400, those which have only their own institutional planning follow with an average score of 2.000, and very little difference exists between universities who have some sort of planning and those who have no planning at all; their average scores are 1.912 and 1.952 respectively.

However, analysis of the responses shows that size, geographical location, type of control, system of admission and emphasis on function do not, apparently, play a significant role, and even when grouped into developing and developed countries there is still no remarkable difference in autonomy with regard to financial decision-making. The only other classification which shows more varied average scores is the emphasis on the field of study. Universities concentrating on social sciences enjoy the highest degree of autonomy with an average score of 2.250 and humanities the least at 1.571. Pure science, professional training and no particular emphasis have average scores of 1.889, 2.087 and 2.000 respectively.

We can thus conclude that, with only a few exceptions, universities, according to their own estimation, have a rather high degree of autonomy with regard to financial decisions. Although the average response indicates 'partial' and is lower than in other areas, this reflects the situation where all universities are being financed from government sources to a greater and greater extent, which inevitably leads to some external control of their financial activity. One of the major directions of university effort should be, in our opinion, an active improvement of methods and techniques of financial planning and management, but obviously, in some cases, universities should have greater rights in the utilization of the limited financial resources allocated to them.

2. Curriculum

One of the most important factors in achieving academic objectives is the university's curriculum. Apparently, the universities in our sample enjoy a high degree of autonomy in this area, for the overall sample of eighty universities shows an average score of 2.675 with a standard deviation of 0.519. Therefore, almost complete autonomy exists in the average university as regards the design of the curriculum.

However, as one can see from Figure 4, the situation differs slightly in some of the sub-classes. The classification by different planning systems shows that universities which have a combination of central and institutional planning have a lower degree of autonomy (2.400) than the others, but even the lowest score in this classification is still fairly high. The degree of autonomy enjoyed by universities working only to their own plans has a score of 2.706, while universities having some sort of planning or no planning at all have averages of 2.647 and 2.714.

Although it can be observed that there are wider differences in degrees of autonomy in designing the curriculum when universities are classified by GNP per capita, the figures, nevertheless, reinforce the results of the classification by developing/developed countries. Universities in developing countries have an average score of 2.804 (standard deviation 0.397) while those in developed countries have an average of 2.375 (deviation 0.633). The difference here is greater than that observed for finance and may partly be explained by many developing countries possessing only one university, which is naturally considered to be the most expert body in deciding on the curriculum.

When geographical location is taken as the basis for classification, the average degree of autonomy enjoyed is highest in Asia (average score 2.826), followed by Latin and Central America (2.824), Africa (2.714), Australia and Oceania (2.667), North America (2.400) and Europe (2.389); standard deviations are all between 0.38 and 0.48.

Emphasis on the field of study appears to have some influence on the degree of autonomy enjoyed by universities in designing their curriculum, for those placing emphasis on social sciences enjoy complete autonomy, those having no particular emphasis average 2.811, those concentrating on the humanities 2.571, professional training 2.522 and the lowest is pure science at 2.444. When we turn to emphasis on functions, research apparently enjoys the maximum degree of autonomy, followed by undergraduate teaching (2.719), graduate teaching (2.556) and teacher training (2.333).

The other classifications do not show any important differences and, as a whole, those differences which can be observed are not very striking. Evidently, universities usually enjoy a very high degree of autonomy in that field of their activity where they are the experts and should make the decisions, and they do, in fact, have the greatest responsibility for working out curricula.

3. Selection of students

The universities in our sample have three types of admission system: open, selective and a mixture of the two, and from the overall sample it seems that they enjoy nearly complete autonomy (2.718) in the selection of students. The situation varies only slightly when we classify the universities into different categories.

For example, universities in the developing countries have a slightly higher degree of autonomy in this domain (average score 2.796, standard deviation 0.557) than those in the developed countries (2.542 with a deviation of 0.865). The difference is shown up more in the classification by GNP *per capita*. Complete autonomy is enjoyed by universities in the groups $200-300 and $300-400. The remainder of the sub-classes converge with averages of 2.692 to 2.556. Universities in the groups $500-1000 and $1000-2000 have the same score of 2.556 but the standard deviation varies—in the former it is 0.497 and in the latter 0.956 showing that the former group, although the same size, had a more stable opinion.

As to the emphasis on field of study and function, universities emphasizing the humanities enjoy complete autonomy, those emphasizing pure science and with no particular emphasis are fairly high at 2.778 and 2.750 respectively, and lower down come professional training and social sciences with 2.609 and 2.500 but their standard deviations are higher at about 0.870. Our tables show that universities emphasizing research enjoy complete autonomy on admission whereas undergraduate and graduate teaching have averages of almost 2.725. Teacher-training universities have the least degree of autonomy with 2.333.

Private universities enjoy more autonomy in this particular area (2.929) than public (2.672) which are, to some extent, controlled by the government.

Interestingly, universities with a selective system of admission consider that they enjoy more autonomy (2.804) than those with open systems (2.556) or mixed systems (2.462).

The remaining classifications do not provide a basis for any meaningful conclusions with regard to the degree of autonomy in this area.

4. Staff recruitment

The questions of teaching and research staff recruitment and subsequent utilization are of the highest priority in the activities of the university. The standards achieved here determine to a great extent the quality of the whole spectrum of university performance. We found that, although there is a lot of controversy today about the conditions of tenure and the evaluation of per-formance, recruitment of staff has the highest score (2.763) in the overall sample for the degree of autonomy.

When considering the classification according to planning systems, one can notice a rather important difference between the universities having both a national and institutional plan (average score 2.000) and the other groups of universities (2.762 and above). The lower degree of autonomy in the former group may be explained by the fact that these universities apply the same rather high standards in the recruitment of all staff, and recruitment is also subject to norms (student/staff ratio, teaching load, etc.) which are applicable throughout the system of higher education.

It appears from our analysis that universities in the developing countries have a higher degree of autonomy in this area of university activity, with an average of 2.857 as against 2.542 in the developed countries.

By geographical location, universities in Australia and Oceania enjoy complete autonomy for staff recruitment, while Latin and Central America (2.941), Africa (2.857) and Asia (2.783) follow closely. Universities in Europe have the lowest score (2.389)—a situation which is common to all their areas of activity, except finance.

There are no differences worthy of comment in the other classifications, but the analysis demonstrates that universities, whatever their situation, main function, etc., enjoy a very high degree of autonomy in this key field of their activity, the recruitment of staff.

5. Academic objectives

Academic objectives are defined here as the universities' targets in the field of teaching and training, including the standards and methods of teaching work. It seems from the overall sample that universities enjoy a high degree of autonomy in this area. The average score is 2.750 and ranks second after that for staff recruitment.

As in the field of staff recruitment, universities working under national and institutional planning have a slightly lower degree of autonomy (2.400) than the other sub-groups of this classification (2.667 to 2.882). This is to be expected since planning at different levels of their activity is more closely linked with the overall social and economic needs of the countries. This is reflected also in research policy and general objectives.

There is no significant difference in this area between developing and developed countries, but the classification by geographical location shows (as noted previously for the selection of students and staff) that universities in Australia and Oceania and North America enjoy a very high degree of autonomy with regard to academic objectives. The least degree is again found in European universities (2.611).

Here again, the size of the university does not appear to have any influence although the classification by fields of study produces some variations. Those universities which concentrate on the humanities enjoy complete autonomy and those with no particular emphasis almost complete autonomy, whereas emphasis on professional training has the least autonomy at 2.522. Emphasis on functions also produces some wider differences: universities emphasizing research enjoy complete autonomy and teacher training has the lowest score at 2.333.

The type of control causes little variation, and this is also the case with the admission system.

In conclusion, although all universities enjoy a very high degree of autonomy in formulating their academic objectives, those universities which are oriented to training people for practical jobs (professional training, teacher training) have less autonomy. This is quite natural as the demand for these specialists, as well as the standards and other requirements of potential employers, have to be taken into account.

6. Research policy

Here, universities in the overall sample have an average score of 2.737 for the degree of autonomy in formulating research policies, which is quite close to the score for academic objectives.

The difference between the scores of developing and developed countries is more significant at 2.804 and 2.583. Again, by geographical location, Australia and Oceania has complete autonomy, with North America and Europe coming at the bottom of the list (2.600 and 2.556).

Formulation of research policy is one of the two areas (the other being general objectives) where the number of students influences the degree of autonomy—it has been noted that differences are not significant in the other areas—and here the small universities have more autonomy than the large ones.

As to emphasis on the field of study, the least degree of autonomy exists for professional training, preceded closely by pure science. These universities are probably more dependent on outside sources for financing their research. With regard to function, it is interesting to note that universities emphasizing graduate teaching have less autonomy than undergraduate teaching (2.611 as against 2.789). Universities concentrating on teacher training have the least autonomy at 2.333.

The type of control again does not cause any significant variation, but classification by system of admission shows that universities with a mixed system have less autonomy (2.538) than selective or open (2.759 and 2.889). This situation might be explained by universities with open or selective systems having more clear-cut policies than universities with mixed systems, who are subject to various kinds of pressure.

7. General objectives

We defined general objectives as the objectives in the field of higher education as a whole, including its orientation towards the socio-economic and other needs of the country and, apparently, universities have slightly less autonomy in this respect than in the other areas mentioned so far, except for finance. Nevertheless, the average score of 2.526 in the overall sample is still rather high.

As mentioned already, universities with both central and institutional planning have a lower degree of autonomy in formulating their general objectives (2.000) than other sub-groups, which range between 2.476 and 2.647, and this might be accounted for by their integration into the overall planning in their countries.

Developing countries again enjoy a relatively higher degree of autonomy (2.636) compared to developed countries (2.261), a situation which is repeated in the classification by geographical location—Latin and Central American universities having the highest degree and North American and European the lowest. In developing countries, the opinion of the university (since in some cases there is only one) is probably decisive in formulating the general objectives of higher education.

Emphasis on the field of study shows that those universities with no particular emphasis enjoy more autonomy (the average scores range from 2.611 to 2.250) but, by function, universities concentrating on undergraduate teaching have a higher score (2.625) than graduate or teacher training, which are rather low at 2.278 and 2.000.

As might be expected, private universities have more autonomy than public ones, but there is not a large difference (2.625 as against 2.500). Again, by system of admission, universities with open and selective systems have higher scores (2.667 and 2.589) than mixed (2.154).

8. Inter-dependencies between degrees of autonomy in different areas of university activity

A correlation analysis was carried out to examine how the average scores achieved by universities in a particular area of activity relate to their scores in other areas (Table V.10). It appears that the degree of autonomy enjoyed by most of the universities in finance has little to do with either the selection of students, staff recruitment, academic objectives, curriculum or research. Only in the case of general objectives is there a closer correlation—those universities having a higher degree of autonomy in finance also have a higher degree of autonomy in setting their general objectives.

The degree of autonomy in formulating the curriculum is, however, relatively highly correlated with other areas, except for finance. Universities which have a higher degree of autonomy in the selection of students, also enjoy more autonomy in staff recruitment, setting general objectives and curricular design, but not in others. Universities having a higher degree of autonomy in academic objectives, curriculum, research policy and general objectives also have a higher degree of autonomy in the matter of staff recruitment.

9. *Some conclusions*

After having considered quantitatively our analysis of the different areas of university autonomy, the following conclusions can be drawn:

1. The universities in our sample, according to the opinion of their heads, enjoy a rather high degree of autonomy in all the most important areas of their activity. The lowest degree of autonomy is found in finance, which is to be expected since the basic source of university financing nowadays is the state budget, but even here the score indicates 'partial' autonomy.

2. From the classification according to planning systems, one can see that universities working under both national and institutional plans enjoy a more *balanced* autonomy, i.e. their degree of autonomy in all the areas of activity is similar. They have the highest degree of autonomy in finance but there is not a great difference between this and other areas. However, other sub-groups have a rather wide gap between high degrees of autonomy in the basic areas of their activity (curricular planning, staff recruitment, setting of academic objectives, etc.) and a lower financial autonomy. Presumably, a university can only really enjoy a high degree of autonomy in a particular field or area if it is supported by a similar degree of autonomy in other areas, especially finance. Balanced degrees of autonomy provide the basis for the balanced development of the university.

3. It will have been noted that universities in the developing countries have a higher degree of autonomy in all areas of activity than universities in industrialized countries. This finding is supported by the classification according to geographical location which shows that the highest degree of autonomy is enjoyed by universities in Latin America, followed by those in Africa and Asia. The lowest, but still a rather high degree of autonomy, is found in Europe. This can be accounted for by the fact that, in some developing countries, only one university exists and it is often master of its own affairs.

4. From our analysis, such characteristics of universities as their size, type of control and system of admission do not appear to have any important influence on the degree of autonomy. There is no unanimity among universities in the degree of autonomy by function or by field of study, but it would seem that universities emphasizing research activities enjoy a higher degree of

autonomy than other universities in the most important areas of their activity.

5. Thus it appears that the most important differences in the degree of autonomy are due to the socio-economic system of the country. University autonomy is generally considered to be important for university development; this might well be so, but in the present situation practically all universities enjoy a high degree of autonomy and, therefore, their most important problem is how to use it in the most effective way in accordance with the progressive social and economic trends of their respective countries. This being so, universities, in order to make a greater contribution to progressive national development, might sometimes have to sacrifice some of their autonomy.

B. The involvement of different bodies in the university's internal decision-making process

The problem of decision-making, and the participation of different agents (administrative bodies and other groups) in this process, is a crucial one in relation to the planning and management of the university. Very often it is merely interpreted or reduced to the problem of student participation in university affairs and to the question of the degree of university autonomy within the national context. We have attempted to go further and to measure the degree of participation in decision-making of several different bodies, including the students, in the most important fields of university activity. For this purpose the following ten possible participants in decision-making were defined: central government; regional government; Senate or University Council; university administration; faculty administration; department administration; individual professors; senior teaching staff; junior teaching staff; students.

Also, eight areas where decisions have to be taken were listed. Some of these areas are the same as those considered in the previous section and they can therefore be cross-checked, as follows: major allocation of funds; planning and development; decisions on student admissions; staff appointments; curriculum approval; research policy; innovation; extra-curricular activities.

On a five-point scale (giving 4 to authority for a final decision or veto, 3 to active participation, 2 to consultation, 1 to being informed about a decision and 0 to no involvement), average scores and standard deviations have been computed for the participation of the ten groups in the different areas of decision-making, both in an overall sample as well as in different classifications of universities. We have to point out at the very beginning of our analysis that we observed a greater diversity of opinion here than in the case of university autonomy—the standard deviations in almost all cases are much higher. Nevertheless, we believe the attempt to be valuable since it allows us to make some observations and draw conclusions which might be used to improve the university decision-making process. (See Table VA.).

In general, the four bodies which play the most decisive roles are, in order of importance: 1. the Senate or University Council; 2. university administration; 3. faculty administration; and 4. departmental administration. The regional government plays no real part and in most cases the role of the central government is no more than merely being informed. As for the different members of the university community, individual professors and the senior teaching staff are the most important, but, even so, in only one case (formulating research policy) are they involved to a degree which is higher than consultation. Other scores indicate that they are informed about decisions. Junior teaching staff and students have scores in the overall sample (with the exception of extra-curricular activities for students) which are either at the level of being informed or not involved.

This summarizes the general pattern of the analysis which varies somewhat within the different classifications. The most interesting of these variations are commented on by area of decision-making in the following sections.

1. Major allocation of funds

In the overall sample, the University Council appears to have almost complete authority for final decisions in this area (average score 3.403) with the university administration and faculties also playing a very significant role. It is interesting to note that the degree of involvement of the central government, although it is the major source of finance, is nevertheless less than that of any organized university group. This situation is similar in the classification by planning systems, even for those universities under both national and institutional planning. The involvement of the regional government is higher for universities under different forms of planning than for those having no definite plans, and we found it also to be higher in developed than in developing countries.

This classification also indicates that students in the developed countries take less part in this decision-making area than they do in developing countries, but by geographical location, students in Asian universities score only 0.045 whereas in the universities of Australia and Oceania and Latin and Central America they obtain scores which indicate that they are informed about decisions.

In large universities the importance of the Senate in this area is, in comparison with the university administration, much greater than that found in the smaller universities.

Government bodies do not play a noticeably different role between private and public universities in this area.

2. Planning and development

Responsibility for decision-making in the planning and development of the university follows the general pattern, but it can be observed that the degree of involvement of the central and regional governments has increased. In the classification by planning systems, this is most marked for those universities with central and university planning—here the score for the central government indicates the most decisive role of all the different bodies in the area of planning and development. Government involvement is less for those universities which do not follow definite plans.

The central government has a higher degree of involvement in African and European universities than in the other regions, but in North America the regional government plays a similarly important role.

As would be expected in this respect, the central government is more involved in public than in private universities.

3. Decision on student admissions

In decisions on student admission, the role of the university administration and faculties becomes relatively more prominent and the Senate takes less interest in this matter than in any of the other areas in the overall sample.

In the classification by planning systems, faculties have the most responsibility for decisions on admission in universities under both central and institutional planning, but university administration plays the leading role for those following central planning only, institutional planning or no planning. However, for those under central planning, the central government has a higher degree of involvement, equalling that of the Senate and faculties, while the institutional planning and no planning sub-groups also show a higher degree of involvement by departmental administration. It is also interesting to note that, in this area students have the greatest degree of involvement (1.400) in universities under central and institutional planning; their score is equal to those obtained by senior and junior teaching staff in this sub-group.

In this respect, there is a noticeably higher degree of participation by departments in the universities of the developing countries as compared to those in developed. This is also the one area where the involvement of the central government is also higher for universities in developing countries.

By geographical location, most of the sub-groups follow the general pattern with the Senate and administration as the leading decision-makers, but in Africa faculties take second place and, in Europe, administration takes the leading role with the students playing a much greater part as well (1.154).

4. Staff appointments

We have discussed the degree of autonomy enjoyed by universities in the matter of staff recruitment in the first part of this chapter and we find that several of the points are confirmed in this analysis. From the overall sample and different classifications, the degree of involvement of various bodies is quite varied but overall university administration is slightly ahead of the Senate, both having scores denoting active participation, with the faculties and departments following closely with scores indicating more than mere consultation.

Although the central government has very little involvement in this area in the overall sample, it has quite a high degree of involvement in those universities under central and institutional planning, equalling the Senate in this sub-group. For those universities following definite plans the university administration plays the leading role in staff appointments, whereas in those with little or no planning the Senate has priority.

Similarly in developed countries, the administration and faculties are to the fore, whereas the Senate takes first place in the developing countries. This trend is also seen in the classification by geographical location; in the universities of Europe, North America and Latin and Central America, for example, the university administration, faculties and departments have the major responsibility.

In the private universities the university administration has a much greater responsibility for staff appointments than the Senate and departments, whereas in the public universities, administration and the Senate are almost equal and there is a greater central government involvement.

5. Curriculum approval

Traditionally and as was confirmed in the analysis on autonomy, universities enjoy a great deal of freedom in the design of the curriculum. So far as involvement in decision-making is concerned, the overall sample shows that the Senate has the greatest responsibility, followed closely by the faculties and departments. As is to be expected, administration drops to a lower level—it is only a little higher than that accorded to senior teaching staff. Students are kept informed in this matter.

When classified by planning systems, the same general trend is seen. Again the central government has a prominent role in the case of universities under central and institutional planning. The classifications by developing/developed countries and geographical location reiterate the general situation, except that in the European universities faculties and departments have the major responsibility for curricula.

In private universities the Senate and faculties are involved almost to the same degree and departments follow closely after. However, students have a higher degree of involvement in public than in private universities on this question.

6. Research policy

In the overall sample the involvement of the Senate in formulating research policy is high in comparison with other bodies, although faculties and departments are next in line with almost identical scores. Apparently, students are little concerned in decisions on research.

The same situation can be seen in the classification by planning systems, except for those universities with no planning where the faculties and departments are the main decision-makers and for those under central and institutional planning where the central government has high priority with a score of 3.600.

It is interesting that, in the developed countries, individual professors have almost as great an importance in research decisions as the Senate or faculties and this is shown particularly in European universities where the senior staff and individual professors have a leading role. However, in Africa, it is the departments along with the faculties who have the most important role in research decision-making.

7. Innovation

The general pattern of responsibility for decisions (Senate, administration, faculties, departments), re-appears in the case of innovations in the university, although here the scores of the faculties and departments are more closely aligned with those of the other decision-makers. This pattern continues throughout the classification except that the involvement of students in innovation is much higher in the developed than in the developing countries.

Some variations occur in the classification by geographical location in that faculties have the major responsibility for innovation in European universities, while in North America the university administration comes to the fore.

8. Extra-curricular activities

Although one would think that the students would play a major part in decisions regarding extra-curricular activities in the universities, this does not appear to be the case in the overall sample, which shows that they are only consulted (1.985) along with the faculties. The major responsibility is taken by the university administration and Senate.

When classified by planning systems the situation varies considerably, faculties taking a more important role for those universities with central and institutional plans, and the Senate and administration occupying first and/or second places in the others. Varied situations are also seen in the classification by geographical location; there seems to be no common view as to who shall take major decisions on extra-curricular activities ; for example, in European universities it is shared equally by the faculty, Senate and administration and in North America by the administration, Senate and students.

9. Some conclusions

Analysis of the involvement of different bodies in decision-making shows a variety of situations in the various types of university. However, generally it does follow a more or less traditional pattern where students, teaching and research staff, especially at the junior level, are either playing no role or a less important role than they should if universities really want to democratize their decision-making process. The situation is better balanced in universities working under both central and university planning.

VI. Trends of change in university structure (1958-68)

Changes in the overall structure of universities, as well as in the organization and function of their planning and decision-making bodies, can be considered as an important indicator of efforts and attempts undertaken in different universities to adjust to the new developments taking place in society. We have therefore tried to measure these structural changes in our sample.

1. Basic structure of universities in the sample

On examining the questionnaires individually, it was possible to gain an idea of the general basic structures. First of all it must be said that a large number of universities (58 per cent) had faculties as their main administrative units. One should not assume that these were traditional faculties, as owing to the global nature of the sample there were variations and adaptations, but nevertheless they were the basic administrative and teaching units. The next largest section (19 per cent) was universities with schools as their basic teaching unit and it is worth while saying here that those who specified schools did not refer to them as administrative units. Departments were the basic teaching and administrative units in 18 per cent and only 7 per cent had institutes as their main constituent bodies.

2. Changes in the teaching units

Universities were asked in the questionnaire whether units had been added dropped and either significantly combined or reorganized. In cases where any of these were true, they were requested to give the date and a brief description of the change.

Looking at the purely quantitative results first of all (Table VI), the overall sample shows that there has been considerable structural change in that 92.5 per cent of universities have added units. It is also interesting to see that in 36.3 per cent units have been dropped, and since this was probably one of the most difficult operations to undertake, this is a significant figure. In terms of the improvement of existing units, 58.8 per cent of universities have reorganized or combined units, thereby involving considerable structural change. All these aspects will be looked at in greater detail further on.

When the sample is classified according to planning systems, it is worth noting that the amount of structural reorganization—whether it involves adding, dropping or reorganizing units—declines steadily as the degree of planning declines. In the group of universities in countries with both central and university level planning, 100 per cent have added units; this is also true of the next two groups, but thereafter it becomes 91.1 per cent of universities with some planning mechanisms and 85.7 per cent of those with no planning. In the first group, 60 per cent have dropped units and this percentage steadily declines (with the exception of universities under central planning only, but this is a very small group) to 28.6 per cent for universities with no planning. The same is true of the reorganization of existing units; percentages range from 100 down to 47 per cent.

When universities are classified by developing and developed countries, the similarities are more striking than the differences. However, by geographical location, it is possible to conclude that universities on the African continent have had somewhat less structural changes than universities elsewhere, but this is to be expected in newly created universities. Otherwise the distribution is fairly even, with North America standing out as the region where the greatest number of universities (60 per cent) have disbanded or dropped units.

Classification by emphasis on fields of study reveals, as might have been anticipated, that universities emphasizing pure science have the most marked tendency towards structural change and reorganization. In 100 per cent of these universities units have been added and in 77 per cent units have been dropped and reorganized.

3. *Reasons given for changes in teaching units*

We have already considered the form of the change, whether it was addition, reduction or reorganization, and now we must look at the reasons behind it. In the case of teaching units added, the main reasons given were the expansion of student numbers and the manpower demand. In the latter case, the universities stated clearly the existence of a demand for a certain type of graduate and the creation of a teaching unit to provide them.

The reasons given for dropping certain faculties or fields of study fall into three categories. The first of these, and the largest, was that the faculty or department in question had been absorbed elsewhere, either by a larger unit within the same university or by another university in the country, or it had been split off to form a separate institute. The second category was the straightforward reason of no demand, but, unfortunately, it is not always clear whether this refers to students or to manpower. Thirdly, a very small number were dropped due to lack of teachers or lack of suitable equipment and this obviously had little to do with voluntary reorganization.

The reorganization of existing faculties or teaching units showed two distinct tendencies. The first and the most marked was towards greater interdisciplinarity of study. This involved the incorporation of small departments into larger ones or the creation of centres of study combining allied subject matters. The reasons given for reorganization mainly fell into this category. The second tendency is almost directly opposed to the first, i.e. the splitting-up of unwieldy departments into smaller ones. Frequently this was true of universities which were developing rapidly and, perhaps, had originally grouped together subjects which were not really homogeneous. A very small number simply gave the reason of reforms introduced by the government of the country.

4. Reorganization and/or the need for new administrative and planning units

Moving from the structural reorganization of what are, essentially, teaching units to the reorganization of administrative and planning units, we asked the universities to answer three questions. The first was whether there had been any significant reorganization of major responsibilities for planning, management and decision-making. If the answer was affirmative, a description was asked for. The second question was whether the need was felt for new planning units and if so, what kind. The third question asked whether any of the existing planning methods were thought to be out of date and, if so, which ones.

If we look first of all at the replies, which can be easily quantified (Table VIA), we see that in the overall sample during the period 1958-68 responsibilities have been reorganized—this included the introduction of planning units or other consultative bodies—in 75 per cent of universities. An even higher percentage (78.8) felt the need for new planning or organizational units and 53.8 per cent thought that at least some part of their organizational structure was out of date.

When the universities are classified according to planning systems, it can be seen in the first instance that the percentage of universities where responsibilities have been reorganized declines as the degree of planning declines. All the universities in countries with both central and university planning have undertaken some reorganization of their structures during the period under review.

This percentage drops to 61.9 per cent in universities where there were no planning mechanisms. When it comes to the need for new planning units, once again all the universities in countries with both central and university planning expressed a need for some innovation. The other groups varied between 66.7 and 81 per cent—the latter being universities with no planning mechanisms. Eighty per cent of universities in countries with both central and university planning considered that some part of their structural organization was out of date. The other groups varied between 33.3 and 66.7 per cent—once again the latter were universities with no planning mechanisms.

Developing countries appear to have undertaken less reorganization than the developed, but a greater percentage of the former felt the need for new units. However, a smaller percentage in the developing countries felt that some part of their administration was out of date.

Looking at universities classified according to their geographical location, it can be seen that 100 per cent of the North American universities have undertaken reorganization of their administrative responsibilities and only 56.5 per cent of the Asian universities. Logically enough it is this latter group which has the highest percentage (86.9) of those wanting new planning mechanisms. The highest percentage of universities who consider some part of their administrative structure to be out of date was found in Europe (72.2) while the lowest (33) was in Australia and Oceania, but this was a very small sub-division.

When we come to look at the less easily quantifiable aspects of these three questions we nevertheless find that the response, although descriptive, falls into well defined groups. The principal group was composed of universities which have added planning units to their administrative structure. Among these were included two universities who have created the post of planning officer. Next comes a rather loosely defined group who describe an overall administrative reform, which has frequently been occasioned by a government decree affecting university organization. The third largest category was that of student and staff consultation. Nearly a quarter of the universities concerned describe the setting up of consultative committees to facilitate the expression of student and staff opinion in the running of the university. There are three other minor groups which are worth mentioning. Firstly, universities where there was a decentralization of decision-making from government to university level, involving re-organization of the decision-making structure in the university. Secondly, here were the universities who set up other forms of consultative committees, either with industry, the local community or other bodies, to counsel in the running of the university. Lastly, and this was a very small number, there are those universities which set up institutional research units.

Descriptions of the kind of new administrative or planning units needed fell into two large equal categories with some fairly minor ones following. The first

63

of the two large ones consisted of those universities who felt the need for a better information system. Here the words 'information system' were taken in their most generalized sense to describe needs varying from better record-keeping to a fully computerized information system. The second category is that of universities expressing the straightforward need for a planning unit. This included those who described, in general terms, the need for some kind of rational planning. The few minor categories include the need for an institutional research unit, the need for better-qualified administrative staff, and so on.

Similarly, descriptions of units or parts of the administration which were out of date fell into three main areas. In addition, there were less numerous (but very serious) views that the whole administrative system was unequal to its task. The greatest need for modernization was felt in general administration. Problems varied from inadequate liaison with the central government to insufficient means of communication with the teaching staff of the university. The two other important areas were more clearly defined: the first was that of the system of data collection and this tied in well with the need for an improved information system expressed in answer to the previous question; the second was a lack of efficiency in the budgeting system and this, perhaps, corresponded to the need expressed earlier for a planning unit.

5. Conclusions

From the foregoing, one may conclude:

1. There is a marked awareness in universities that serious changes in their organization should be made if they are to meet the social and economic needs of their countries and improve their management and planning. However, from the percentages of units dropped, added or re-organized, it seems that they are more inclined to add than to re-organize; the former does not necessarily bring any improvement in the structure and may bring new problems. Improved overall management and planning can only be brought about by a systematic and balanced approach to the whole university.

2. One may also notice that those universities which are already working under both national and institutional level planning are more innovatory in both teaching and administrative structures, and this is, no doubt, due to the fact that they know the overall socio-economic needs of their countries better.

3. Serious efforts were made during the decade under review towards the organization of greater interdisciplinarity of study and towards better co-operation among the different units inside the universities. Nevertheless the majority of universities feel there still exists a great need for further innovation in their management and planning and for the establishment of planning and institutional research units.

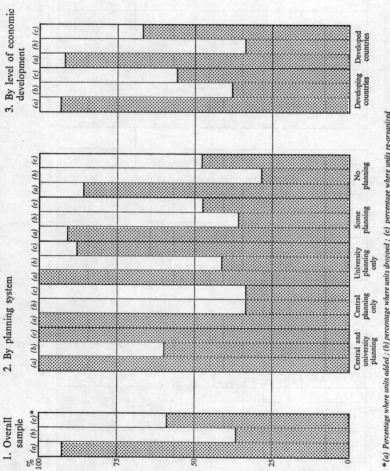

*(a) Percentage where units added ; (b) percentage where units dropped ; (c) percentage where units re-organized

FIGURE 5. *Trends of change in university structure, 1958-68*

65

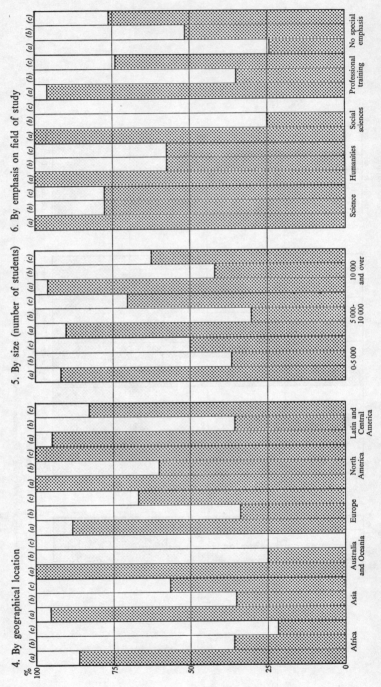

FIGURE 5. *(continued)*

VII. Structure of the student body

Analysis of the student body provides information on a very important aspect influencing university performance and characterizes to a great extent the social links of the university with different groups of the population and the social role of the university in the country. Growth rates of the total number of students have already been discussed in Chapter IV and in this section, therefore, we shall consider the growth rates for different kinds of students, both graduates and undergraduates, male and female, and then look at drop-out rates and the socio-economic background.

1. Growth rates of undergraduates and graduates

This section discusses the data given in Table VII. The overall sample shows that the growth rate for the number of graduate students (in the reduced number of universities having post-graduate programmes) is higher (13.8 per cent) than the growth rate for undergraduates (10.9 per cent) over the period 1958-68. (See Figure 6.) Analysis by the five-year periods would seem to indicate an overall tendency towards the development of graduate studies.

When the universities are classified according to planning systems (Table VII.2) it can be seen that in every sub-group, with one exception, the growth in the numbers of graduate students was greater than that for undergraduates over the ten-year period. The exception is universities with their own planning only, but even here graduate enrolment was considerably higher for 1963-68.

Classification by level of economic development shows the developing countries to have had a higher rate of expansion of undergraduate students (11.6 per cent) than the developed (8.7 per cent). These figures speak for themselves about university expansion in countries of differing levels of economic development. The developed countries on the other hand, even though they start from a highly developed base, have a higher growth rate of graduate students (15.2 percent) than the developing countries (12.8 per cent), although the latter figure is nevertheless impressive and is also slightly higher than the growth rate for undergraduate students.

By geographical regions, the figures again show the number of graduate students to be growing faster. The figures for Latin and Central America, and also to some extent Europe, should be treated with reserve since, here, because of differences in the systems of education, the classification of students into the undergraduate and graduate categories is not standard.

The highest growth rates for both types of students are to be found on the African continent and, similarly, the gap between the two rates is at its largest: 15.6 per cent for undergraduates as against 27.5 per cent for graduates. This would seem to indicate a fairly rapid change in the composition of the student body, although it must be remembered that these universities started from a much smaller base as far as graduate students are concerned. Universities in North America are also increasing their numbers of graduate students (20.7 per cent) very much faster than undergraduates (11.8). In Asia, Australia and Oceania and in Europe the difference in growth rates is not so large, which would seem to indicate the pressing need to expand undergraduate numbers.

Classification by university size tends to give trends which might be expected. The smaller universities have the highest rates of expansion for both types of students (14.4 and 19.2 per cent) while universities with more than 10,000 students have the lowest rates of expansion on both counts at 7.3 and 7.6 per cent. Medium-sized universities fall in between. Clearly, some large universities have reached a ceiling and are levelling off.

Emphasis on different fields of study shows that the highest increase in the rate of growth of undergraduate and graduate students was in universities emphasizing social sciences (21.8 and 35.9 per cent) but it should be noted that this is a very small sub-group. The second lowest growth rate of undergraduates is to be found among pure-science universities (8.6 per cent), but they have a considerably higher growth rate for graduates (16.5 per cent). Both here and in universities concentrating on the humanities, the growth rate of graduate students has been nearly double that of undergraduates over the ten years and this demonstrates a change in the composition of the student body and in the level of study. Professional-training universities have similar growth rates for the two types: 13.1 per cent for undergraduates and 12.7 per cent for graduates. The same is true of universities with no particular emphasis; they have the lowest growth rates of all the sub-groups at 7.5 and 9.1 per cent respectively. This perhaps indicates the preference given to the expansion and development of more specialized universities.

The classification by admission system gives predictable results. Universities with an 'open-door' system are the only sub-group to have a higher growth rate of undergraduates than of graduates (16.3 and 12.2 per cent), although it should be said that this sample is small. Nevertheless, this runs counter to the general tendency and it is clearly more difficult to control the student mix in an open system. Universities with a selective system, constituting the majority of the sample, have an undergraduate growth of 10.3 per cent and a graduate growth of 13.0. Universities with a mixed system have a very similar growth rate of undergraduates (10.7 per cent) but a higher one for graduates (17.4).

2. Growth rates of male and female students

The participation of women in higher education is an important indicator of social change (Table VIIA). The overall sample shows that the growth rate for women students (15.3 per cent) over the ten-year period is considerably higher than the growth rate for male students (11.1 per cent). Over the 1958-63 period the difference was even more marked (20.2 as against 14.8 per cent), but obviously the female students started from a rather poor base. Although absolute figures can only give an indication, it is worth noting that female students constituted only about 20 per cent of the student body in 1958 and about 30 per cent in 1968.

The classification according to planning systems shows a consistently higher growth for female students throughout the sub-groups. There is no great difference when classified by level of economic development, except in the rapidity of growth. Universities in developing countries have higher rates of growth for both male and female students (13.1 and 17.9 per cent) than developed countries (7.6 and 11.5 per cent).

Classification by geographical location again shows a higher growth rate in the number of female students throughout all the sub-groups. The region with the biggest difference in the two growth rates is the Asian continent with a growth rate for female students of 18.9 per cent as opposed to 10.1 for male students, which, according to the average number of students, gives a male/female ratio in 1968 close to those prevailing in more industrialized continents. The African region has a surprisingly small difference in the two growth rates (21.4 as against 20.1 per cent) even though the base from which the women started was the lowest of all, but the rate for 1963-68 was particularly high.

It is interesting to see in the classification by emphasis on the field of study that universities emphasizing pure science have a high growth rate of 16.4 per cent for female students, compared to 10.9 for male students, and here women students—in absolute figures—make up 40 per cent of the student body. Professional-training universities have rates of 16.9 and 12.5 per cent for female and male students respectively, similar to the overall sample, while universities with no special emphasis have lower growth rates at 12.6 and 5.8 per cent.

69

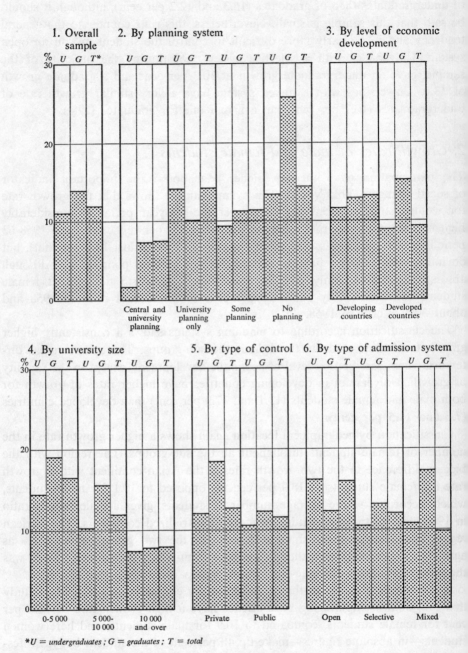

1. Overall sample
2. By planning system
3. By level of economic development
4. By university size
5. By type of control
6. By type of admission system

U = undergraduates ; G = graduates ; T = total

FIGURE 6. *Average annual growth rates of the numbers of students, 1958-68*

3. Student drop-out rates

Student drop-out has an effect not only on the composition of the student body but on many other aspects of university life (Table VIIB). It is an important indicator of the 'behaviour' of the student body under the conditions and demands of university environment, as well as an important factor in maximizing the utilization of resources.

Unfortunately data on this very important subject were not good. As can be seen in Chapter III on the state of the replies, we received only a 26 per cent response to this question. This has naturally had a serious effect when the universities were broken down into the different classifications. Another problem was the interpretation of the term 'drop-out', since we found there was no unanimity among universities on this.

One general conclusion which may be tentatively drawn from the overall sample is that there has been a decline in the drop-out of both graduate and undergraduate students over the ten-year period. This is necessarily tentative since a greater number of universities answered for 1968/69. For this year the drop-out rate for undergraduate students is 13 per cent and for graduate students 8.8 per cent, while the figures for 1958/59 are 17.4 and 10.2 per cent respectively.

It is difficult to analyse the information available for the different classifications due to the very low rate of response and it has therefore been possible to comment on only some of them. It is interesting to note that there is better reporting on these drop-out rates from the developing countries. Moreover, the latter have a lower drop-out rate for undergraduate students (12.8 per cent) than universities in the developed countries (14.0). The situation is reversed for graduate studies, where the developed countries have the lower drop-out rate (8.0 per cent compared with 9.3).

In the classification by geographical location, it is possible to consider the drop-out of undergraduates in Africa, Asia, Europe and Latin and Central America. The highest drop-out rate for the year 1968/69 is to be found in Latin and Central America with 21.3 per cent. African universities come close to this with 19.1 per cent. In Europe the rate does not change from 1963/64 to 1968/69—the same number of universities responding for the two periods—but remains constant at 12.8 per cent. The lowest drop-out is found on the Asian continent at 3.8 per cent and perhaps some supplementary information should be looked for here.

As far as graduate students are concerned, the response rate is so poor that only Africa, Asia and Europe can be considered. In the case of Africa and Europe the drop-out rate for graduate students is lower than that for undergraduates, being 18 and 6.3 per cent respectively. However, in Asia the graduate rate is higher at 7.8 per cent and this would tend to confirm the need for closer investigation here.

71

The classification by size of university gives a better response rate for the year 1968/69 than some of the other classifications, although even here it is by no means good. The smaller universities have the lowest drop-out rate for undergraduates (10.4 per cent) and the highest for graduates (11.4). This situation is reversed in universities with over 10,000 students; 5.0 per cent of their graduate students dropped out and 22.1 per cent of their undergraduates. Perhaps some conclusions as to the facilities and working conditions for graduate students in the large universities may be drawn here.

Classification by type of admission system allows us to study the selective universities only, given the very poor rate of response from the others. The drop-out rate for undergraduate students in these universities is 10.5 per cent and that for graduates 9.6 per cent.

The next question asked for the reasons for drop-out and the relevant numbers of students, but it was extremely difficult to obtain a clear picture as to why students abandoned their studies. First of all, the response rate to this question was again very low and, secondly, there was a problem concerning the three different areas into which the reasons might fall, namely, academic, financial or 'other'. Some universities attributed one reason only to all students who dropped out, others gave two reasons and yet others three. In order to surmount these difficulties, it was decided to consider, as a percentage of the total response, the number of universities giving any of the three reasons. This tends to put the emphasis on the frequency of causes for drop-out rather than on the frequency of actual numbers of students dropping out. However, as a measure of control, the average percentage of students abandoning their studies for each reason was calculated and this showed that the reasons most frequently given accounted for the largest percentage of drop-out. There is thus a link between the reason frequency and the drop-out frequency.

Table VIIC shows that, whether it is a question of undergraduate or graduate students, there is little difference between them as to the reasons for drop-out. In both cases, a greater number of universities quote 'other' reasons as the cause of drop-out and the percentage frequency remains constant at approximately 39 over the ten years. It can also be seen, for both undergraduate and graduate students, that as drop-out due to financial reasons declines, so the percentage for academic reasons climbs, which seems to indicate that financial pressure on students has eased somewhat due to greater availability of grants and other aid, but that academic standards are now beginning to be the major cause of drop-out from the university—the percentage for undergraduates in 1968/69 (39) equals that for 'other' reasons. This has rather worrying implications about the universities' ability to maintain the quality of their teaching and the level of their students while expanding rapidly.

4. *Socio-economic background of students*

The students' socio-economic background (Table VIID) was considered to be one of the most important aspects of the structure of the student body and an important indication of the type of links the university has with society as a whole. Several questions concerning both the income of parents, the source of students' support and parents' occupation were asked of the universities. Unfortunately, the data on all these questions were usually lacking. As can be seen from the state of replies, only a 17 per cent response was received on the varying economic levels from which students came. In actual fact, the percentage giving data which allow us to see the dynamics of the situation—i.e. for more than one year—is even lower. The universities were asked to state the number of their students coming from the upper, middle or lower-income group. These fairly general categories were chosen in order that they might be applicable to different levels of economic development.

As can be seen from the analysis of replies from the individual universities, the typical situation for the majority is that the percentage of students from the upper-income group increased fastest, followed by students from the middle-income group. In only two universities (of the nine analysed) has the proportion of students from the lower-income group grown faster than the other two groups. In two universities where the percentage of students from the upper-income group was declining, this would appear to be to the advantage of students from the middle-income group.

The occupation of the parents of university students was another piece of information asked for in building up the socio-economic background. The categories for response were professional, owner/manager, white-collar worker, blue-collar skilled worker, blue-collar unskilled worker, farm worker/labourer, and others. Once again the data were very poor and the most we are able to do is to make some general comments on the small number of universities who did respond with sufficient data over the later five-year period. For the majority, with the exception of two universities only, the situation in 1968 shows that between 63 and 90 per cent of students have parents who are in the first three categories. In four cases, the ratios reveal that it is these three categories which have grown the fastest over the past ten years. The exception, in terms of ratios, is a technical university where the participation of students whose parents are in the categories from blue-collar skilled workers to farm workers has increased by far the largest proportion over the last ten years. The other exception, a university in eastern Europe, has no students from the professional or owner/manager categories, but has 88 per cent of its students from the next three categories.

Another aspect of the socio-economic background, which we had hoped to study, was the varying sources of student support. This gives some indication not only of the provenance of the students themselves, but also of the contribution made by governments to student maintenance in the form of grants. Once again, the data were extremely poor and it is impossible to discern any trends as far as student support is concerned from the very small number of universities responding.

5. Percentage of foreign students in the university

The percentage of foreign students in universities throughout the world is interesting from several points of view. It shows up poles of attraction for university students and to a certain extent their mobility. We may also assume that students studying in countries other than their own are in a position to do much towards furthering international co-operation and understanding. The data were available in sufficient quantity to be of interest only for 1968/69 (Table VIIE).

The overall sample shows that within the responding universities the average percentage of foreign students was 5.5. This is fairly high, but it must not be forgotten that it includes both graduate and undergraduate students.

The classification into developing and developed countries reveals, much as might be expected, that the developed countries have a higher percentage of foreign students (7) than the developing (4.5). The difference is not, however, very large and the percentage for developing countries would seem to indicate a fairly large measure of mobility.

Classification by geographical location reveals the strong pull of the North American continent for students from other regions (10.2 per cent). The universities of Australia and Oceania (although this is a very small sub-group) have an average of 8.1 per cent of foreign students. European universities, with the highest response rate for this classification, come next with 6.1 per cent; this, perhaps somewhat surprisingly, is only a little above the average for the overall sample. Both Asia and Latin America have low averages at 2.1 and 1.99 per cent respectively. As regards Africa, there is one extreme case in this region which influences the figure.

6. Some conclusions

Some conclusions can be drawn from the foregoing analysis of data relating to the structure of the student body:

1. Despite the fact that students form one of the most important components of a university and influence all the aspects of its activity, the first general conclusion from the data collected from the questionnaires is that information

concerning the composition of the student body and its dynamics is inadequate in most of the universities in our sample and cannot provide a basis for a serious and thorough analysis.

This is especially true when we consider the qualitative and social aspects and one can only conclude that it is therefore not surprising that very often university administrators and students have difficulties in understanding one another.

2. The available data show that, during the decade under review, a very rapid growth took place in the number of students, which was, in general, higher in the developing than in the industrialized countries but was, nevertheless, very uneven from country to country.

3. A very important phenomenon which should be noticed is the higher growth of graduate students in comparison with undergraduates. This tendency was much stronger in the developed than in the developing countries.

4. A very clear social tendency in the composition of the student body is the higher annual growth rate for female students, especially at the undergraduate level. However, this tendency did not bring them to parity with the male students, although their proportion of the student body is now much higher than a decade ago. Much remains to be done in this direction in many countries.

5. When we turn to the analysis of drop-out rates we find that in the overall sample for the total student population there were no serious changes during the decade. The percentage of drop-out remained rather high and there was no serious attempt to investigate the reasons reported in the questionnaire. It is clear that much more attention should be paid to this problem.

. Analysis of the small amount of data on the socio-economic background of students shows a very alarming situation where, for the majority of the responding universities, the basic tendency is for the number and proportion of students from the upper and middle-level income groups to increase. The number of students from the lower income group is increasing in absolute terms, but their proportion remains low. It should be noted that most of the information received came from the developing countries and this shows that they, at least, pay some attention to this matter. This very important social problem has, or will have, a great influence on planning the development of universities.

. Thorough analysis of the composition and dynamics of the student body is one of the most important prerequisites for improving university planning and management, but serious efforts are still to be undertaken in this respect.

VIII. Teaching staff

Teaching staff is one of the most important components determining the quality of a university's performance and, to a great extent, the amount and quality of the university contribution to the social and economic development of the country. Therefore, the proper planning and management of teaching staff formation, and the continuous evaluation of its quality and most efficient utilization is, or should be, one of the most important tasks undertaken by the heads of universities.

We have tried to make an analysis of the staff in different types of universities including expansion, qualifications and the percentage of foreigners.

1. Expansion of the teaching staff

As observed in Chapter IV, overall, the average annual growth rate of teaching staff almost balanced the increase in the number of students but, since this comparison does not indicate the situation prevailing in 1958, an analysis of the compound index student/teacher ratio will give more information. We computed this ratio on the basis of the total number of full-time undergraduate and graduate students and the total number of full-time staff in 1958, 1963 and 1968. Figures relate only to those universities where data were available for all three years. Therefore, the response rate is somewhat reduced and the result will not be exactly comparable to trends observed in the growth rates (Table VIII and VIIIA).

The overall sample shows that the student/teacher ratio increased slightly from 9.9:1 in 1958 to 10.5:1 in 1968, but this was not a steady rise and the ratio of 11.2:1 for the year 1963 suggests that the early 'sixties was a difficult period for the recruitment of university staff.

The classification by planning systems shows that only universities under central and university planning experienced a decline in student/teacher ratio rom 8.0 to 6.8:1. However, these universities organized a greater variety of courses; correspondence, evening, part-time and short courses as well as day courses are usually held. Universities with institutional planning have the highest ratio at 12.7:1 in 1968 which had increased steadily from 10.9 in 1958, whereas those universities with some planning dropped back in 1968 to almost he same ratio (11.3:1) with which they had started the decade. Universities with no planning at all began the period with a low ratio of 6.9:1 but this has now increased to 8.4:1.

The classification by level of economic development shows, for both sub-groups, a rise in the student/teacher ratio for 1963 and a decline in 1968 as has been seen in the overall sample, although the developed countries increased their ratio slightly more (from 9.5 to 10.4:1) than the developing countries 10.1 to 10.6:1). Thus, on average, ratios in the developing and developed countries are now similar.

By geographical location, all the sub-groups show an increase in their ratios over the decade (except Africa, but this sub-group consists of only four universities); North America shows the least movement, from 12.8 to 13.3:1, but this s higher than the other regions and has perhaps been influenced by the greater use of new teaching aids and techniques. The greatest increase in the ratio is o be found in Latin and Central America; their figure for 1958 was 7.3:1, which rose to 10.2 by 1968. In all, the 1968 figures show much less variety than those for 1958—Africa, Asia, Europe and Latin and Central America all have ratio of approximately 10:1, North America being the exception at 13.3. This might be interpreted as the result of more attention being paid to student/staff atios by universities.

We had also asked in the questionnaire for information on part-time staff since it is known that universities generally make use of them in one form or another. However, from the information we have received it appears that it is nly in those universities where substantial use is made of part-time staff that adequate records are kept. Therefore, for most universities, use of part-time staff would seem to be an unplanned activity on which few data are available and this would indicate that universities have not paid enough attention to the effective use of such staff.

Of the eighty universities in our sample, only seventeen gave information regarding the numbers of part-time staff. Of these, we found that the ratios of part-time to full-time staff declined in nine cases, increased in five and remained static in three and there would seem to be a tendency to make proportionately ess use of part-time staff. There was no difference between the developing and developed countries or between different regions in this respect.

Overall the situation with regard to the numbers of staff would seem to have improved in 1968 as compared to 1963, although the ratio increased slightly over the decade. It was the opinion of university heads that the problem of expanding the number of staff was not so serious in the period under review as it is expected to be during the next. They have a similar opinion about the quality of staff.

2. Foreign citizens on the teaching staff

From the number of universities reporting on the percentage of foreign citizens on the teaching staff, it appears that there is an increasing tendency for universities to recruit staff from abroad; the percentage of the overall sample rose from 15.2 in 1958 to 22.7 in 1968 (Table VIIIB).

It will be seen from the classification by level of economic development that as might be expected, the developing countries have more foreign staff—27.7 per cent as against 12.3 per cent. But the developing countries' rate of increase has been much less, moving from 21 per cent in 1958 to 27.7 per cent in 1968 whereas the developed countries increased from 2 to 12.3 per cent.

This lower rate of increase in the developing countries is accounted for by the Asian universities who have reduced their percentage from 15 to 10 over the ten-year period, while both Africa and Latin America show a marked slackening off during the period 1963-68. It is apparent that the availability of local graduates is now having a significant effect in the developing countries.

In Europe the figures remain static for the period 1958-63 but show a slight upturn for 1968 at 6 per cent. Australia and Africa have by far the highest percentage of foreign staff at 65 and 60 per cent respectively in 1968. North America at 35 per cent still seems to attract many foreign staff.

3. Composition of the staff body

In order to make the different types of teaching staff more or less comparable on a world-wide basis, we asked the universities in our sample to group their staff into three main categories: senior, middle and junior level, in accordance with their own existing classifications, so that we might gain an idea of the varying proportions of such staff within the different types of universities.

If we look at the overall sample (Table VIIIC), we find that the proportion of junior, middle and senior-level staff in 1958 were 39/32/29, whereas in 1968 they are 41/35/24. It is thus evident that universities are making more use of middle and junior-level staff, but university expansion, in most cases, has probably meant a greater increase at this level than at the senior level.

In the classification by planning systems, the greatest change in the level of teaching staff is to be found among those universities with no planning. The proportions of junior, middle and senior-level staff were 21/39/39 in 1958 but in 1968 are 43/37/20, showing a rapid decline in senior-level staff. It may be that the reason for the deterioration in quality has been, in part, a lack of proper management, since the universities under planning systems of any kind have increased their proportions of senior-level staff. (The figures for those universities with institutional planning are valid for 1963 and 1968 only,[1] and show a fairly stable situation.)

The situation has deteriorated somewhat in universities in the developing countries where the proportion of senior teachers has gone down from 31 to 23 per cent but, if this is due to greater use of young nationals, this represents an improvement from the local point of view and quality should rise over time. The proportions in developed countries have remained much the same at approximately 43/30/27 for junior/middle/senior staff, but the tendency was very uneven from country to country and some European universities show quite opposing trends.

This can also be observed in the geographical classification. In all regions, except for Africa and Australia and Oceania, junior-level staff in 1968 represented the greatest proportion of the three levels, and in Europe and North America it is approximately 50 per cent. This meant for Europe an increase from 39 to 46 per cent over the decade, whereas in North America the percentage declined from 62 per cent in 1963 to 51 per cent in 1968.

African universities increased their proportion of junior-level staff from 22 to 32 per cent, whereas Asia declined from 51 to 44 per cent, middle-level staff taking up a greater proportion (40 per cent) in 1968. Latin and Central American universities—for which the response rate in 1958 is very low—have almost equal proportions of the three levels of staff in 1968.

Emphasis on university function reveals that graduate teaching universities have a high proportion of junior-level staff (probably due to the provision of assistantships and research posts); the ratio of junior/middle/senior staff was 60/27/13 in 1958 which had become 52/31/17 by 1968, showing a general increase in the level of staff. On the other hand, undergraduate teaching universities show a general decline in levels from 28/33/36 to 38/35/26.

Classified by admission systems, universities with a selective system have retained much the same proportions over the ten years at 38/38/23, whereas the mixed system shows a significant decline in senior-level staff from 47 to 33 per cent, most of this decrease being taken up by junior-level staff. The figures for 1968 show that universities with an open system of admission have a high proportion (51 per cent) of junior-level staff.

1. Only two universities replied for 1958.

4. *Academic qualifications of the staff*

We also asked for information on the percentages of staff in the university holding first, second, higher-than-second degrees and other types of certificates or diplomas, in order to try to ascertain more closely the situation with regard to the quality of staff and the kind of balances which exist in different types of universities. It can be seen from the overall sample that the situation has changed very little over the ten-year period: those staff members with first degrees comprised 25 per cent of the total; those with second degrees 38 per cent; higher-than-second degrees 34 per cent; and other types of diploma 3 per cent. (Table VIIID.)

However, universities under central and university planning have, over the period, reduced the number of staff with first degrees from 13.0 to 8.6 per cent and this percentage has been replaced by staff with higher-than-second degrees (43 per cent in 1968). Universities with institutional planning have also reduced their percentage of first-degree staff from 49 to 33 per cent and increased their numbers with higher-than-second degrees. The percentages for universities with some planning and no planning mechanisms remained fairly static, although their percentages of staff with higher-than-second degrees were much greater in 1958 than the other sub-groups, but in 1968 universities with central and university planning and those with no planning had much the same percentages, which suggests that the former universities have made a conscious effort to improve the quality of their staff.

When comparing countries by level of economic development, it is clear that the developing countries have a larger percentage of staff with first degrees but despite the fact that the ten-year period has been one in which they have employed many more local staff, percentages have remained at approximately 29/38/31/2 for the four categories. The developed countries have increased their percentage of staff with higher-than-second degrees but the pattern has not changed much; in 1968 the figures were 15/37/43/5.

Regionally, Latin and Central American universities have by far the greatest percentage of first-degree staff at 53 per cent, which is much the same as that prevailing in 1958. Africa has approximately one-third of its staff each with first, second and higher-than-second degrees, while in Asia there is a tendency to employ more staff with second degrees, the figures being 20/43/35 in 1968. The percentages for Europe have remained fairly constant at 14/45/37, but those for North America show a sharp increase in staff with high qualifications; in 1958 the figures for first/second/higher-than-second were 8/34/52 and in 1968 they were 7/27/65.

It would seem that, as regards the academic qualifications of the staff, most universities are maintaining their standards and that those universities in countries which are making rapid scientific and technological advances are increasing the number of staff holding high qualifications. However, it is obvious that those universities who teach only at the undergraduate level or who give basic courses, would require a different balance of staff to those whose main objective is, say, research. This can be seen in the geographical classification and also in that for university function. In this classification, universities emphasizing undergraduate teaching have a much higher proportion of their staff with first degrees (33 per cent) whereas universities emphasizing graduate teaching and research have more staff with second degrees (54 and 61 per cent).

5. *Teaching loads*

Data on teaching loads were available for one year only so that we were unable to measure any dynamics in this area, but it may be useful to gain an idea of the conditions existing in various types of universities which, in turn, have a bearing on the ability of the university to attract staff and to carry out its functions adequately (Table VIIIE). However, it should be noted that universities had different methods of calculating the teaching load and that, in some cases, it seems that not only direct contact hours were included. Nevertheless, the data give an indication of the distribution of the teaching load and it can be seen that senior-level staff are not expected to take such a large share of the teaching load (two to three hours less) as middle and junior-level staff. This is obviously due to their greater involvement in administration and research. This is true throughout the classifications, except for Latin and Central America where for all three levels of staff the teaching load is much the same.

Staff in the developing countries are expected to carry a greater teaching load than those in the developed countries and this relates particularly to Asia and Latin and Central America. In Africa the teaching load for senior-level staff is similar to that in Europe, but the hours for middle and junior-level staff are longer. In European universities the teaching load is lightest at approximately three hours less per week for all levels of staff than the overall sample.

6. *Some conclusions*

Analysis of the information available on the tendencies of development of the teaching staff demonstrates that the decade under review has been one of very rapid growth, which seems to have met the expansion in numbers of students in most parts of the world. However, the question of teaching staff seems to have posed a particularly difficult problem for African and Latin and Central American universities.

According to our data, expansion of the teaching staff has resulted in the proportion of junior-level staff rising in comparison with the situation which existed in 1958. However, it is reassuring to see that this has not meant any decline in the level of academic qualifications and in some cases our figures would indicate that junior-level staff were more highly qualified in 1968 than in 1958.

One particular problem which has come to light in this area is the lack of information on part-time staff, suggesting ineffective use of a valuable resource, and universities might do well to investigate their own organization in this respect.

IX. Innovation in the teaching work

In attempting to evaluate the development of universities, it is also necessary to try to find out what kind of innovation has taken place, especially in a basic field of activity such as teaching. Statistical analysis of innovation in teaching is a rather difficult task, but we have made some attempts to measure it by asking the universities to state whether they were using any of seven relatively new teaching techniques or methods, either at an experimental or at an already systematized level. The seven methods were: instructional television; instructional radio; computer-assisted instruction; independent study courses; programmed instruction; team teaching; and a central service for the production of teaching materials. A space was also given for any others to be mentioned. The universities were also asked to estimate the role played by new teaching techniques and methods and the use made of them during the two five-year periods under review and also during the 1970s. This question was analysed in the overall sample only, and we shall look at this first of all to see the general trend.

1. Use of new media

Overall, a clear trend can be seen over the ten-year period towards the use of new media for new methods of instruction (Table IX). In 1958, 84 per cent of the responding universities did not use any new media, 14 per cent were using them principally for traditional methods of instruction and the remaining 2 per cent used them partly for traditional and partly for new methods of instruction. None of the responding universities used new media entirely for new methods of instruction.

The situation had changed considerably by 1963, although, even then, by far the greatest proportion of the new media were used for traditional methods of instruction (23 per cent). However, 3.6 per cent were used entirely for new

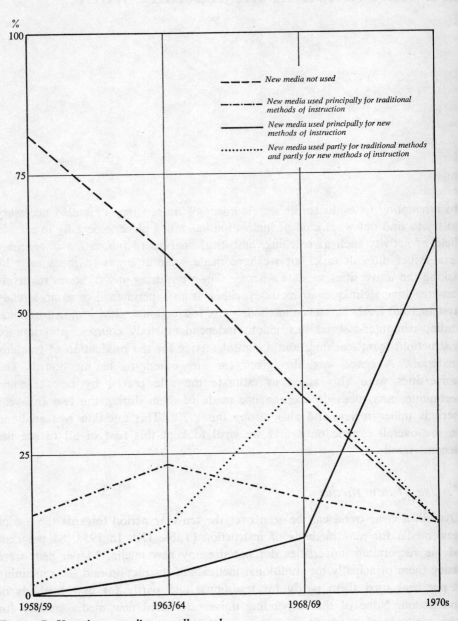

FIGURE 7. *Use of new media: overall sample*

methods of instruction. The intervening percentage—and this has increased to 12.5 per cent—used the new media for a mixture of traditional and new instructional methods. There remains, however, 61 per cent who made no use whatsoever of new media in 1963.

In 1968/69 the picture changes once again as those not using new media are now only 35 per cent. At the same time the percentage of universities using new media for traditional methods of instruction also drops (17 per cent). New media for new methods of instruction makes up 10 per cent and new media used with a mixture of new and traditional methods becomes 38 per cent.

Universities expect this trend to continue in the 1970s, when by far the largest percentage (63 per cent) expect to be using new media together with new methods. A decrease is foreseen both in the percentage expecting to use new media with traditional methods and in the percentage expecting to use them with a mixture of traditional and new methods. The percentage of universities who do not use new media at all has dropped over the period from 83 per cent in 1958/59 to an expected 12 per cent for the 1970s.

2. Innovation in instructional methods and techniques

It should be noted first of all that the innovations mentioned by the universities, even when they are used systematically, do not apply to the whole university. From the information available to us, it is apparent that innovation took place in individual fields of study. Thus, if one were to consider the use made of these techniques and methods, taking into account the number of departments within the universities, the percentages would be very small indeed. As has been seen in the previous section, the period under review is one in which many of these innovations were first introduced to the universities and their general use, where appropriate, is yet to be instituted (Table IXA).

From our overall sample, we find that of the seven types of new techniques and methods of instruction, team teaching was the most widely used in 1968/69; 26.4 per cent of the responding universities have systematized this method of instruction, while 12.5 per cent are at the experimental stage. As might be expected, it has also had the broadest application within the university, since the departments of education, medicine, dentistry, architecture, engineering and humanities were mentioned by different universities as being units in which team teaching was used.

Instructional television, independent study courses and a central service for the production of teaching materials are the next most widely used by 18, 17 and 15 per cent of universities respectively, although 13.9 per cent of universities are experimenting with television while 9.7 per cent are experimenting with the two other innovations. The majority of universities who make systematic use of instructional television stated that medicine and dentistry were the fields in which it was most used, but teacher training and languages were also mentioned. It seems that independent study courses are used mainly for languages and for courses at the graduate level.

Computer-assisted instruction and programmed instruction have been the least adopted by universities at 11.1 and 9.7 per cent, but it is obvious that these techniques are at an earlier stage of development and are being widely experimented with at 19.4 and 27.8 per cent of universities. These innovations have particular relevance in scientific fields and equal mention was made of science, mathematics and research, and also psychology in connexion with programmed instruction.

Radio does not seem to be widely used—8.3 per cent for systematic and 5.6 per cent for experimental use—it has probably been superseded by television. The replies to our questionnaire indicate that radio is used for language teaching and correspondence courses.

Under the heading 'others', 8 per cent of the universities replied that they had language laboratories and 8 per cent that they used audio-visual aids.

The classification by planning systems shows that universities in countries with both central and university planning make the greatest systematized use of all types of innovation, except for instructional radio and computer-assisted instruction. The latter are more widely used by universities with planning at the institutional level. It is interesting to note that, as the degree of planning decreases down to those universities with no planning, so the percentage of systematic use of new media declines. For example, independent study courses are used by 40 per cent of the universities in the sub-group 'central and university planning', by 29 per cent of 'university planning only', by 13 per cent of 'some planning' and by 6 per cent of 'no planning'. The most widely systematically adopted technique throughout all the sub-groups, except for universities with planning at the institutional level, is team teaching, followed by independent study courses. At the experimental level programmed instruction has, with one exception, the highest percentage, with computer-assisted instruction following closely, particularly in those sub-groups where it is not yet established at the systematized level.

Classification by level of economic development shows that, on the whole, the developed countries have a much more extensive use of new methods. At the moment, the method most widely used at the systematic level in the developing countries is team teaching (25 per cent) which is almost equal to the percentage for the developed countries, but in all other cases the amount of innovation is approximately one-third of the developed countries. The availability of resources and facilities is obviously important, since in the developed countries instructional television at 43 per cent is the most widely used, followed by independent study courses (used more at the graduate level), computer-assisted instruction and a central service for producing teaching materials.

Geographical location supports the general conclusions drawn from the classification by level of economic development.

On the African and Asian continents, there has not been a great deal of innovation (ranging from 5-15 per cent), although there is some systematic use of team teaching and of a central service for the production of teaching materials. However, on the African continent systematic use is also made of the radio which does not seem to be used in Asia, while, in turn, there is more interest both at the systematic and experimental levels in independent study courses and programmed instruction in Asia.

Moving from Africa and Asia to Latin America, it is at once apparent that the new methods are much more widely used, whether it is a question of the experimental or the systematized level. The method most widely used here in a systematized way is team teaching (47 per cent), but it is interesting to note also the spread of a central service for the production of teaching materials, which has been established by 20 per cent of the responding universities. The use of instructional television is equally developed. Independent study courses, which tend to be popular in the other sub-groups in this classification, are used by only 13 per cent of the universities in Latin America but, while only 7 per cent are already using programmed instruction, 40 per cent of universities are experimenting with the method.

The percentages for Europe show that, with two exceptions, the techniques are used to a greater extent at the systematized than at the experimental level. The two exceptions, programmed instruction and computer-assisted instruction, show differing stages of introduction and potential use: the latter is in systematic use by 28 per cent and at the experimental stage in 33 per cent, whereas the former is being used systematically by only 17 per cent and is at the experimental stage in 56 per cent of universities.

3. Conclusions

Analysis of the above data shows that the years from 1958 to 1968 have been a period of intensive review of new means to meet the growing demand for higher education and to adapt the teaching work accordingly. It marked, however, only the beginning of substantial changes in this field at universities, the rate of innovation commencing relatively slowly but increasing gradually over the period.

The trends in innovation were similar in both developing and developed countries, although the gap between them is rather wide. However, it can be seen that universities in the developing countries have adopted team teaching to the same extent as the developed countries, which suggests that, where feasible, they are ready to innovate in their teaching work. It is realized that the difficulties to be overcome in using new techniques are greater in the developing countries; finance, expertise and equipment are not so readily available, but in view of the problems posed by expansion, it might prove worth while making a greater effort in this area.

In the expectations of the universities, the 1970s will be a period of much more rapid innovation. It will also be a period when important theoretical and practical problems will need to be solved to incorporate the results of scientific and technological progress into university planning and management. University planning will be an increasingly important instrument of innovation in the teaching work.

X. Evaluation of teaching programmes

Evaluation of teaching programmes should include all aspects of the teaching activity: content of courses; methods of instruction; teachers' and students' achievements; to mention only a few. However, here we are concerned with trying to establish growth and change in the curricula of different universities during the decade under review. We also attempted to find out if there was any continuous evaluation of the content of courses and, if so, which organizations or groups inside and outside the university were involved.

1. Average annual growth rates in the number of courses

Growth rates of the number of courses would indicate development of the university in the instructional sphere, whether the courses are devoted to new technological subjects or just add to the normal range of subjects, and we find that, overall, there has been an increase of 7 per cent each year over the period 1958-68 (Table X). It can be observed that the five-year period 1963-68 has been, in most cases, one of higher expansion in the number of courses with a growth rate of 9.6 per cent compared with 8 per cent for the period 1958-63. This might be interpreted as an attempt on the part of the universities to diversify instruction and to incorporate new knowledge and developments in the fields of pure science, social sciences and the humanities, but expansion in the number of students could also be a contributory factor. The growth rate does not, of course, indicate how many courses have been withdrawn from the curricula.

When classified by the various types of planning systems, it can be seen that universities with no planning or only some elements of planning increased their number of courses at a much faster rate than those with institutional plans or under both central and university planning—the rates of growth range from 10 per cent in the first case to 3.5 per cent in the last. This might indicate that in some of the universities, the number of courses increased in an unbalanced way, but this would become clearer when compared with the growth rates of staff, expenditure and so on.

The classification by level of economic development shows that the developing countries are increasing their number of courses at an annual rate of 8 per cent, while the corresponding figure for the developed countries is 5 per cent. However, while the African and Asian universities have increase rates of approximately 8-9 per cent, that for the Latin and Central American universities is 5.6 per cent—a rate which is equal to universities in Australia and Oceania and slightly lower than that in European universities (6 per cent). However, there was a very much higher rate of growth in African universities during the period 1963-68 (21 per cent), but most of these universities were only recently established, while Asia's growth rate decreased slightly in this period. It is rather strange to note that European and North American universities show a different timing in their spurts of growth; the higher growth rate in European universities occurred during the period 1958-63 (9.5 per cent) and that in North American universities in 1963-68 (11 per cent).

Universities having an open system of admission expanded their number of courses at a slightly higher rate than those with selective or mixed systems of admission (8 per cent as against 7 and 6 per cent), but their growth occurred mainly during the second five-year period (21 per cent).

These growth rates can, of course, only indicate the relative increase over a period in the number of courses at different types of university.

2. Changes in the content of courses offered in 1958/59 and still offered in 1968/69

To gain some idea as to how the universities have reacted to scientific and other developments in modifying the content of their courses, the heads of universities were asked to report on the percentage of courses offered in 1958, still offered in 1968 and which may have changed very little, moderately, substantially or drastically (Table X).

In response to this question, the overall sample shows that universities consider that 25 per cent of their courses have, on average, changed very little and a further 25 per cent only moderately; about 21 per cent changed substantially and 29 per cent drastically. The degree of change differs for the various types of universities and it appears that the planning system of a university has an important connexion. Whereas the universities with central and university planning have, on the whole, changed their courses only moderately (18 per cent very little and 46 per cent moderately), universities with planning at the institutional level have made major changes to their courses (24 per cent

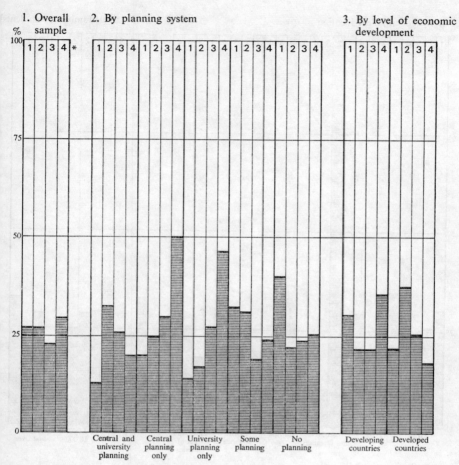

1 = very little ; 2 = moderately ; 3 = substantially ; 4 = drastically

FIGURE 8. *Average percentage of courses changed in content in different degrees over the period 1958-68*

91

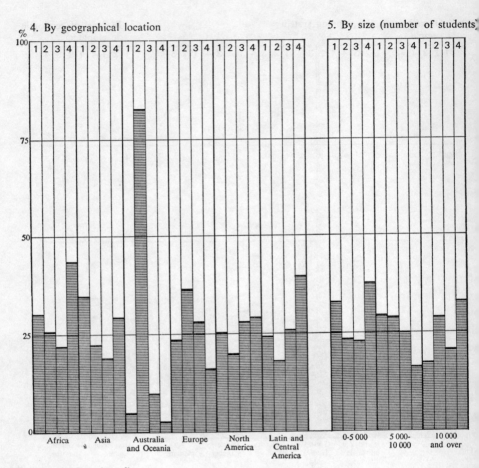

FIGURE 8. *(continued)*

substantially and 46 per cent drastically). Universities with some elements of planning or no planning at all have a much higher percentage of courses which have changed very little (30 per cent and 36 per cent respectively) but, at the other end of the scale, they have changed approximately 24 per cent of their courses drastically.

There seems to be more moderation in the amount of change in courses at universities in the developed countries and this is particularly true for Europe (37 per cent) and Australia (83 per cent). The greatest degree of drastic change can be seen in Latin and Central America (40 per cent) and Africa (37 per cent).

It is also interesting to note that the large universities have changed their courses to a greater extent than the small and medium-sized; only 16 per cent of the former's courses have not changed much, whereas the percentage is approximately 28 per cent for the other two sub-groups.

The above analysis gives a rough idea as to how universities of different types have reacted to the changing demands of society by adjusting the content of their courses. One can assume that some attempts were made to balance existing content with the necessary changes, but only a careful and deep analysis of the situation in individual universities and their departments can show if these changes were really sufficient and responded to the changing social and economic needs of the countries.

3. Existence of continuous evaluation of courses

While it is important that the number of courses should grow and that the content should meet the changing demands of society and the expanding number of students, it is also important that growth and change should occur on a rational basis. It is therefore imperative for the universities to have some sort of continuous evaluation, and it would seem from the responses received that the universities themselves have found this to be so, since 85 per cent in the overall sample report that they have such evaluation mechanisms (Table X).

The greater the extent of planning in the university, the more likely it is to have course evaluation mechanisms; all of those under central and institutional planning carry out evaluation, while the figure for those universities without any planning at all is 81 per cent. In the former case, there is a lower growth rate in the number of courses and the content has changed moderately. In the latter case, there is a relatively high growth rate in the number of courses and most of the courses have changed very little. This indicates that continuous evaluation ensures that changes are made on a regular basis and avoids drastic action.

The level of economic development shows that slightly more universities in the developed countries (88 per cent) have an evaluation mechanism as against 84 per cent in the developing countries, but here the percentage of courses which have changed drastically is very much higher. Considered by geographical location, an evaluation mechanism is to be found in 94 per cent of Latin and Central American universities, while their growth of new courses is the lowest (5.6 per cent). Inversely, the lowest percentage of universities with an evaluation mechanism (79 per cent) found in Africa shows the highest growth rate in courses (9 per cent). However, both African and Latin American universities have high percentages of courses which have changed drastically. Generally the existence of an evaluation mechanism cannot be seen to have had any particular effect on the change in content of courses.

It would seem that the small universities are more likely to have an evaluation mechanism than the large, and public more than private universities, but the differences are not great. However, a much smaller percentage of universities with an open admission system (67 per cent) have an evaluation mechanism than those with a selective system (88 per cent) and the effects of this can be seen in the uneven growth rates of the number of courses in the open admission universities—4 per cent in the first five-year period and 21 per cent in the second.

4. Persons involved in the evaluation of courses

Replies to this question indicate that, in 1968, members of the teaching and research staff were involved in the evaluation of existing courses and in establishing the need for new ones in all the universities who responded, except one (Table XA). In 76 per cent the university administration were also concerned. It is interesting to see that 46 per cent report that undergraduate students were involved, whereas only 33 per cent of them stated that graduate students were consulted; these questions are, after all, of more concern to the undergraduates. In 35 per cent of the universities representatives of the Ministry of Education, and in 38 per cent business and industry, help in the evaluation process.

It is clear that most of the universities under central and institutional planning have a representative from the Ministry of Education, and from business and industry, on their evaluation committees, but of those universities which do not have any planning or only institutional plans, only a small percentage involve representatives from business and industry.

The question of participation by business and industry in the evaluation of courses is directly related to manpower planning and is necessary if higher education is to be responsive to the demands of the economy. It is therefore interesting to note the degree of such participation in the sub-classifications: 35 per cent of universities in the developing countries involve business and industry as against 43 per cent in the developed. However, regionally the situation is vastly different; in Africa and Europe the figures are 60 and 53 per cent, while in Latin and Central America it is 30 and in Asia 26 per cent.

Business and industry are involved in 20 per cent of private universities compared to 38 per cent of the public universities.

If these figures are compared with those of 1958, it can be seen that a slightly greater percentage of universities reported participation of graduates, under-graduates, and business and industry in course evaluation in 1968; the per-centages for the other participants remain the same.

5. Conclusions

This very general analysis of the situation with regard to the evaluation of teaching programmes in the universities of our sample reveals that efforts were undertaken by the majority to up-date and develop their curricula according to changes in knowledge and to social and economic demands.

It can be seen that the situation is very diverse in the different universities around the world, but it would appear that more serious efforts are being made by the universities under central and institutional planning to carry out evaluation and adjust their teaching programmes to actual demands.

However, with regard to those without planning, the absence of representatives from society at large would mean that overall evaluation procedures are far from satisfactory and energetic efforts should be made by each university to work out a permanent and reliable mechanism to link its basic activities to the rapidly changing national social and economic needs.

XI. Research in the universities

From our analysis of the questionnaires, two findings are particularly striking with regard to research in the universities. The first is that, according to the opinions of the heads of universities, research has a high priority among the various functions (it is ranked third in the overall sample) and second, that in the majority of universities no concrete facts or statistics are available.

The questions asked by us with regard to research included the amount of money spent, and the number of projects and graduates involved. In this connexion too, the number of monographs, articles and research reports published by the staff and the number of research institutes established are of interest.

Research funds have already been discussed in Chapter IV, where it was seen that for those universities able to answer this question for all three points of time (27 per cent), increases in research funds had generally been higher than increases in the number of students, although the situation was not so favourable in the developing countries. As regards research projects and the number of graduates involved in them, only 12.5 per cent of our sample were able to give adequate information and therefore analyses by the various sub-classification are not meaningful. However, in this small number of universities, the number of research projects increased at a rate of 13.7 per cent each year, while the sub-classification by level of economic development shows a higher figure (17.2 per cent) in the developing than in the developed countries (10.2 per cent) (Table XI). University research projects thus tend to be smaller in the developing countries and according to our analysis of functions, are more likely to be applied research, since this is ranked third and theoretical research is seventh. Both developing and developed countries show higher growth rates for the period 1963-68 than during 1958-63, particularly in the developed countries which show an increase of 19.8 per cent for the later period as against 13.3 per cent for the earlier.

This small amount of information is hardly sufficient to show that research s a major university function, but more information could be obtained from ur enquiries about the type of units added to the university over the decade. Here we found that 28 per cent of our sample had added research institutes 26 per cent in the developing countries and 33 per cent in the developed). It was nteresting to look closer at the replies by region: in Africa 36 per cent nentioned setting up research institutes for particularly pressing problems— ceanographic, statistical and educational research were among them; while in Asia, 30 per cent of the universities had established new institutes for applied esearch in such subjects as food technology, water and energy, demography and conomics, to name a few.

The percentage in European universities was not so high ; 22 per cent had cquired new units for studies into such areas as energetics, building methods nd cancer. Latin American universities showed an equal interest in applied and heoretical research—20 per cent established units for oceanographic, population nd pure science studies.

Turning to the number of monographs, articles and research reports published y members of the university, 44 per cent of our sample replied to this uestion and we found that overall the number of publications in 1968 was ouble that for 1958. The average number of staff had also doubled over the ecade, but the figures for publications would seem to indicate that this rapid ncrease in staff has not brought with it any proportional decline in interest in esearch. Classifications by level of economic development or by geographical cation do not show any significant variations with regard to publications.

The above findings with regard to research funds, number of projects, nsitutes and publications do demonstrate that there is an increasing amount of esearch being carried out by the universities and, particularly in the case of niversities in the developing countries, shows their participation in solving ational problems. However, the lack of information also demonstrates that esearch is generally not planned or well managed within the university. In fact ome universities stated that they would need to make enquiries of individual aff members in order to obtain responses to our questionnaire. How then does ie university ensure that research receives top priority? In this connexion, we in give the example of the European region which accords top priority to ieoretical research, yet only 39 per cent gave some kind of reply to the uestion on the number of projects and 27 per cent to that on the number of raduates engaged. Of the 61 per cent unable to answer the first question, 4 per cent ranked theoretical research as university function number one.

It is true that, for many universities, major decision-making (see Chapter V) ith regard to research is at the faculty/department/individual professor level, et research requires the utilization of scarce university resources, such as space

97

and staff time, and the university should be able to assure itself that these are efficiently used and that there is an adequate return on their investment. Quantity and quality of research need to be evaluated since information of this nature is vital to any university concerned about its role within the social and economic framework of its country. Opinions, however right they may be in some cases, are not sufficient. In fact the opinions of the universities do agree with the above findings as regards the increase in research and their ability to cope with the problem, as is shown by the following analysis of research as a factor of change.

1. Research as a factor of change

In order to be able to obtain more details on the varying kinds of research, the first half of our question was split into five parts: the universities were asked whether there had been changes in the amount and type of research and, if the response was positive, whether it took the form of an increase or decrease in research. This last part was asked for all research together, for basic and applied research and for development. The same question was asked with regard to the future (Table XIA).

The overall sample in the past shows that the majority of universities (81 per cent) consider research to have been subject to change. Of those believing it to have changed, the tendency is towards an increase in all types of research; 95 per cent saw an increase both in overall research and in applied research; slightly less (88.5 per cent) saw an increase in basic research; and 79.5 per cent an increase in development. Therefore the area where the largest percentage noted a decrease (20 per cent) is that of development. However, it will be seen in Chapter XV that development is not generally considered to be an important university function.

The reaction to the problems arising from changes in research in the past was not estimated as being very good; it is ranked fourteenth out of the fifteen problems.

A look at the overall sample for the future shows that a larger percentage (95 per cent) consider that the amount and type of research will change in the future and that the overall amount of research will increase. Thus, when the question of increase or decrease is asked separately for different types of research, only very small percentages (1.7 and 3.5 per cent) think that basic and applied research will decrease. These percentages are too small to be significant and the 28.6 per cent of universities who see development research decreasing in the future is much more striking.

The estimated reaction to this problem in the future is somewhat more optimistic than the reaction for the past in that it has moved up to ninth position

Table XIA also includes classifications according to the planning system, level of economic development and geographical location. The main points of significance are that the universities in the sub-group under central and university planning all state that research has been a factor of change, whereas, in the other sub-groups with some planning or no planning, approximately one-third to one-fifth have stated that research has not changed. Looking ahead, this attitude is found for those universities under institutional planning only.

Exactly one-third of the universities in developing countries thought that research activities had not been subject to change whereas practically all those in developed countries found that there had been changes; for instance, half of the African and Latin American universities had not noted any change in research. The situation is expected to be very different in the future with nearly all universities anticipating increases in all types of research, the developing regions of the world particularly foreseeing increases in applied research.

XII. Source of university finance

As was seen in Chapter IV on growth rates, the increases in operating expenditure of a great many universities have kept pace with the increases in the number of students. However, we must emphasize that this analysis is of only relative importance because of the differences in the structures of university budgets, in national currencies and in rates of inflation. An attempt was made to deflate the figures, but there are peculiarities of university expenditure which are not directly reflected in the indices of inflation. This analysis thus gives an idea of tendencies but not of exact information. However, we have found (Chapter XV) that the universities are not at all satisfied with the rate of increase of finance and consider this as one of their major problems and an obstacle to development. Even where the rate of increase in finance is much higher than the increase in students, in most cases the universities have still indicated that this is a serious problem for them. An example is the universities in North America, who were able to finance the highest increases in operating expenditure, but whose mean score for seriousness of the problem is also the highest—although their reaction was good.

1. Source of university finance

Our analysis of the source of university finance shows that, overall, 77 per cent of the universities' budgets are received from the government and here is the probable reason for the seriousness of the problem for this entails the university making difficult decisions about priorities, the justification of extra expenditure for new courses, special teachers and so on. Therefore, even if the fund eventually received suffice, the question of finance still presents considerable work and anxiety for the universities each year.

It can be seen (Table XIIA) that other sources of support are usually small; 7 per cent is derived from tuition fees, 5 per cent from 'own funds', 4 per cent

100

from foreign aid, and just 1.5 and 1 per cent from private and industrial donations. The percentages for government support, private donations and 'own funds' have declined slightly over the decade while foreign aid has risen.

Those universities under central and university planning receive practically all their funds from government sources—tuition fees are just 0.2 per cent. Universities under other types of planning or no planning have larger percentages for funds derived from their own assets or tuition fees—sometimes as much as 14 per cent.

The developed countries rely to a greater extent on government funds (86 per cent) than the developing countries (73 per cent), while the latter depend more on foreign aid, tuition fees and 'own funds'. This can be seen particularly in the classification by geographical location, where Asian universities receive 71 per cent of their budgets from the government and 12 per cent from 'own funds', as against figures of 88 and 0.5 per cent in European universities. African universities receive the highest amount of foreign aid at 17 per cent and only small amounts from other than government sources. While the share of the budget from government funds has declined in Africa, Australia, Europe and Latin America—particularly so in the latter countries from 92 to 73 per cent, which has meant an increase in the percentage derived from tuition—North American universities' support from the government rose during the ten-year period from 35 to 77 per cent. The change in sources of support is really very striking in this continent. In 1958 40 per cent of the budget was received from tuition fees, while that share is now only 16 per cent. 'Other' kinds of support also fell from 14 to 0.3 per cent. The sources of support for North American universities are now very similar to those in other regions of the world, apart from a somewhat higher percentage from tuition fees.

2. Conclusions

The relative decline of the government share of university budgets over the ten years suggests that universities have had to do a certain amount of fund-raising to obtain finance for projects which the government were not prepared to assist. This probably relates to research, since the percentage given by industry has risen slightly in both developed and developing countries. Finance from 'other' sources has also risen slightly. This trend suggests that the universities, while receiving their basic finance from the government, will need to continue their search in future for funds for any extra projects which they wish to undertake.

XIII. Use of indices
for university planning

In order to cope with the very serious problems of their development, universitie need more attention and help from society, as well as to make better use o their internal resources. The experience of most advanced universities show that an important contribution can be made by better planning and management But the question is, how well are they equipped to implement this; do they hav the necessary tools for improving planning and management? One of th sections of our questionnaire was specifically formulated to find out how wel universities are equipped to solve both strategical and current planning and managerial problems which arise in the process of their development; on wha quantity and quality of information do they base their planning and decision making?

The increasing size and complexity of university activities has meant that th heads of universities feel a growing necessity for rapid and efficient quantitativ methods for planning development. Platitudes and appeals to inherited pro cedures and rules of thumb are not sufficient today. To move forward, one mus identify and quantify the inputs and outputs of the various components of university, define the relevant boundaries of its systems and sub-systems, an specify the interactions among the different components and programmes. T avoid crippling maladjustments the universities require a 'systems approach to self-diagnosis and planning. The multitude of links between a moder university and its environment makes such an approach difficult, but by n means impossible.

A system of indices can be worked out as a start, but to develop a set o indices for use in planning one needs adequate and up-to-date statistica information. These items should be accurate enough to be useful both fo decision-making at the different levels of university activity and for the contro of implementation. Information may be of two types: quantitative and qualitative Some qualitative aspects of university characteristics are also approximatel quantifiable. The construction of quantitative indices, though less difficult than that of qualitative ones, needs a lot of care if they are to be meaningful. These indices can help in the balanced expansion of university activities and also serve as a warning signal for any imbalance or maladjustments. It must be remembered that each index is dependent on all or some of the other indices, and no one taken in isolation can be usefully employed for forward planning. The student/teacher ratio, for example, has to be taken together with the proportion of new courses in the curricula, and the availability of instructional space. It will equally need to be considered in relation to unit costs and availability of teaching and research equipment. In the same way, inter-relationships for each of the other indices can be worked out.

The following list of useful indices, covering both qualitative and quantitative characteristics of university functions, was drawn up for planning purposes in the universities:

1. Ratio of acceptances to applications;
2. Number of graduates in relation to demand;
3. Student/teaching staff ratio;
4. Rate of drop-out—student wastage;
5. Proportion of graduate students in the student body;
6. Proportion of new courses in the curricula;
7. Ratio of available books per student;
8. Availability of teaching and research equipment;
9. Availability of instructional space;
10. Availability of other space;
11. Unit costs per graduating student;
12. Proportion of research that is of a high professional calibre;
13. Number of hours per week instructional space is fully utilized;
14. Distribution of staff time among teaching, research and other activities.[1]

A request was sent to all the universities asking them to let us know what other indices, not included in our list, might be useful or were in fact used by them for planning activities. None of the universities suggested any additional items. Table XIII shows that a great many universities either do not have a sufficient number of these indices or do not use them to their full capacity. All indices should be used, taking into account interdependence.

The utilization of indices, such as these, runs through each level of university planning and management. They can, for instance, be used to identify areas where resources are under-utilized and subsequently be used for a better

1. Not all the universities were asked this question, and it is, therefore, not included in Figures 9, 10 and 11.

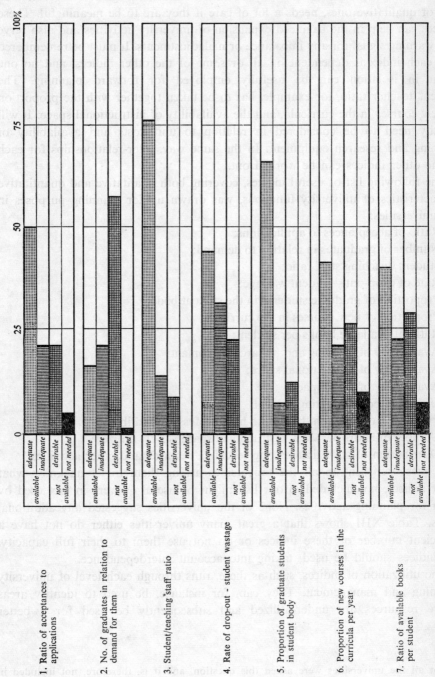

FIGURE 9. *Availability and desirability of different types of information for planning and management: overall sample*

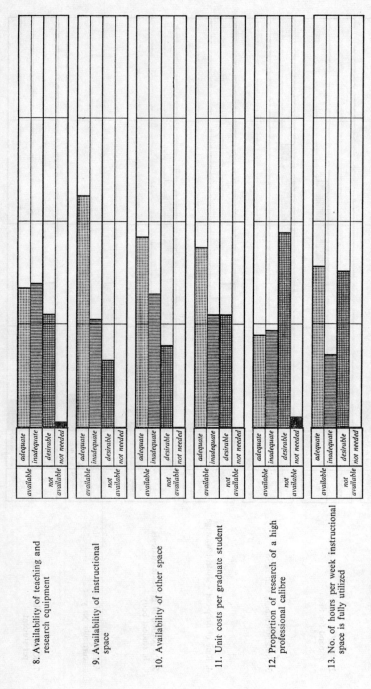

FIGURE 9. *(continued)*

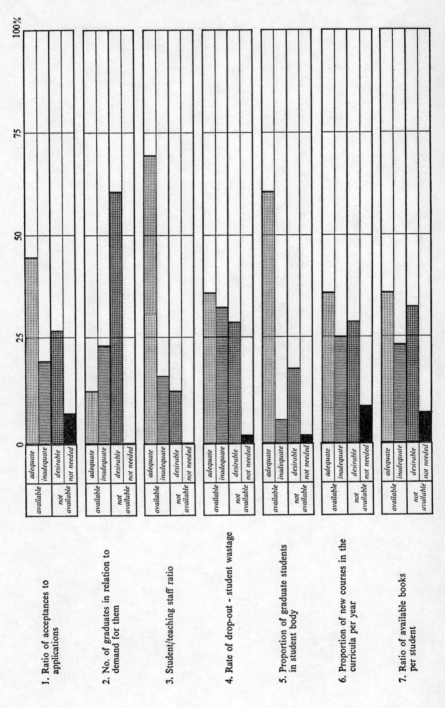

FIGURE 10. *Availability and desirability of different types of information for planning and management: level of economic development*

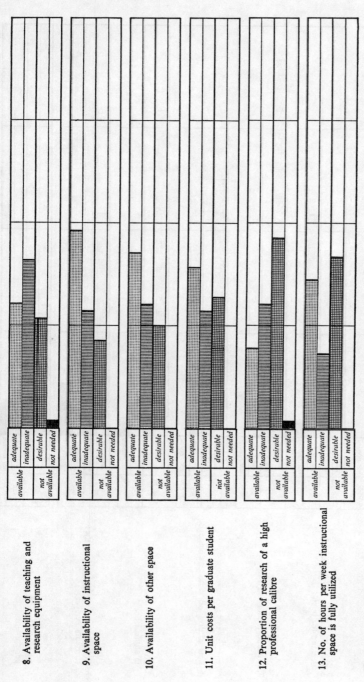

8. Availability of teaching and research equipment

9. Availability of instructional space

10. Availability of other space

11. Unit costs per graduate student

12. Proportion of research of a high professional calibre

13. No. of hours per week instructional space is fully utilized

FIGURE 10. *(continued)*

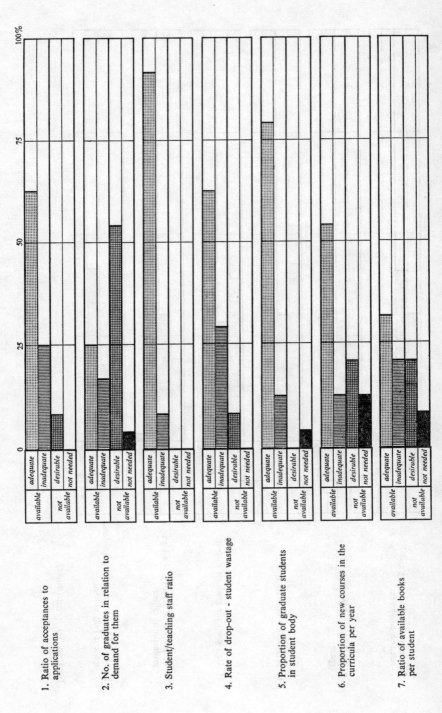

FIGURE 11. *Availability and desirability of different types of information for planning and management: level of economic development (b) developed countries*

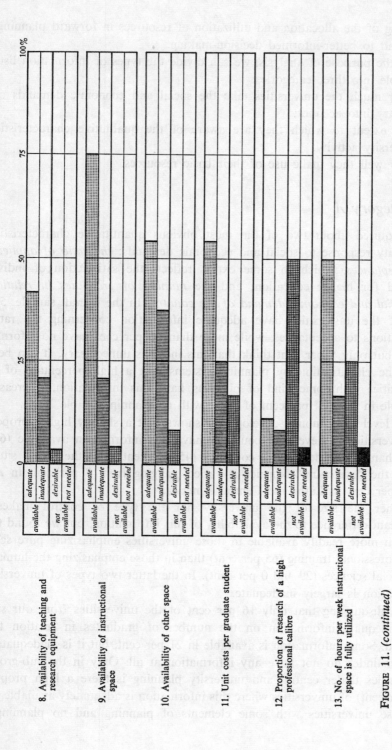

FIGURE 11. (*continued*)

planning of the allocation and utilization of resources in forward planning and thus lead to better-informed decision-making.

For the purpose of analysis, we can divide the types of information listed in our table into three categories:

A. How much the universities take the social and economic demands of the country into account;
B. The extent to which they are aware of the qualitative characteristics of university activity;
C. How well they make use of their basic resources.

1. Category A

We enquired about two of the most obvious quantitative characteristics of university response to social and economic demands: *the ratio of applications to acceptances,* which to some extent reflects the satisfaction of individual demand for higher education; and the *number of graduates in relation to the social and economic demand of the country.* In the overall sample, 50 per cent of the universities have adequate information concerning the ratio of applications to acceptances, while more than 26 per cent have no information at all, but only 5 per cent think that this index is unnecessary. It can be seen from the classification by planning systems that a high percentage of those universities with some kind of planning have this information, whereas it is available in only 24 per cent of those with no planning (Table XIII).

The level of economic development shows that a slightly higher proportion of universities in developed countries have this information available (63 per cent) than in the developing countries (45 per cent), but the actual situation within the developing countries is varied, ranging from 7 per cent in Africa to 82 per cent in Latin and Central America.

Neither the size of the university nor the type of control makes any significant difference to the availability of this information, but we found that it is much more readily available in those universities emphasizing pure science and professional training (65 per cent) than in those emphasizing the humanities and social sciences (29 and 0 per cent). In the latter two types of university the information is largely inadequate.

It is disquieting that only 16 per cent of the universities from our sample have adequate information on the number of graduates in relation to the demand. Some information is available in 21 per cent, but it is inadequate, and the remainder do not have any information at all. Only in the sub-group of universities under central and university planning is there a high proportion (80 per cent) of universities where this information is adequately available, while in those universities with some elements of planning and no planning, the percentage sinks to under 10. The availability of this information is not good in either developed (25 per cent) or developing countries (13 per cent) and is particularly bad (8.7 per cent) in Asia.

The remarks made about the ratio of applications to acceptances apply to the other classifications, except that the private universities have noticeably less information (6 per cent) than the public (19 per cent). However, almost all of the universities agreed that this information is very important for their future development and, therefore, work in this direction should be one of the major preoccupations of university and national planners.

. Category B

The qualitative aspect of university activities is the most important and should be the continuous concern of university administration, but in some cases the availability of statistical information characterising this aspect is very poor. We have considered only some of these as follows:

PROPORTION OF RESEARCH OF A HIGH PROFESSIONAL CALIBRE

Only 23 per cent of the universities in the overall sample have adequate information on this index and nearly 50 per cent have no information at all. This high proportion having no information at all can be noticed in all sub-groups, except for universities under central and institutional planning. In the developed countries only 9 per cent claimed that this information was adequately available (but there was a high non-response rate of 28 per cent for this question), while in the developing countries the percentage is 20.

When classified by regions, differences in the availability of this index became more marked; none of the North American universities had such information and only 7 per cent of the African universities, whereas 35 per cent in Latin and Central America responded affirmatively. Twenty-nine per cent of universities with 10,000 students and over record this information, which is more than was found in medium-sized and small universities. Classifications by emphasis on field of study and university function revealed that this index is recorded more by universities emphasizing pure science, social sciences and graduate teaching than in the others.

It can also be seen that none of the private universities have this information whereas 28 per cent of public universities record it.

RATE OF DROP-OUT—STUDENT WASTAGE

In our sample, 44 per cent of the universities stated that this information was adequately available and a further 31 per cent that it was available but

111

inadequate. Again, a high percentage of those universities following definite plans have this information available, whereas only 10 per cent of those with no planning could reply that this index was adequate.

Although the developing countries have a lower percentage than the developed for this index (36 as against 63 per cent), half of the African and Latin and Central American universities replied that their information was adequate, but in Asia this was only 22 per cent. Other classifications do not show significant differences.

PROPORTION OF NEW COURSES IN THE CURRICULA PER YEAR

Although 41 per cent of our sample had adequate information on this index it is one of the few which we listed that some universities felt was not needed—10 per cent stated that they did not think it necessary for planning purposes. In fact, more universities in the developed countries (13 per cent) felt this than in the developing (9 per cent), although their respective percentages for information adequately available were 54 and 36 per cent. In Africa 14 per cent of the universities had recorded this information and 29 per cent thought it was not needed, but it can be seen that other regions attach more importance to it.

Universities emphasizing pure science in particular think it valuable since 78 per cent replied affirmatively, but a much smaller percentage of universities with no special emphasis had adequate information.

PROPORTION OF GRADUATE STUDENTS IN STUDENT BODY
AND STUDENT/TEACHING STAFF RATIO

Of all the types of indices listed under Category B, the most satisfactory with regard to availability are the proportion of graduates in the student body and the student/teaching staff ratio, but even in these cases adequate information available is just 66 and 76 per cent respectively. The developed countries particularly make use of these indices—the figures are 79 and 92 per cent, and in North America all the universities have this information.

3. Category C

As for the information concerning the utilization of basic university resources the results of the analysis are very surprising. One of the basic resources is teaching and research staff and it is obvious that proper utilization of their time can make a major contribution to the amount and quality of university activity ut only 27 per cent of the universities have adequate information available on 1e distribution of staff time among teaching, research and other activities, and 8 per cent do not have such information at all. It is interesting to note that 1e situation in the developing countries seems to be better than in the eveloped, since 33 per cent in the developing countries responded that they ave adequate information, and only 13 per cent in the developed.

As for information on other basic resources, the situation is similar. For xample, only 39 per cent of universities have adequate information about the umber of hours per week instructional space is used, but approximately 6 per cent have information about the availability of other space. What is ven more striking is that only 34 per cent have information about the vailability of teaching and research equipment and just 40 per cent know the 1tio of books per student. Forty-four per cent of universities say they have 1e unit costs per graduating student. It is worth while noting that the 1formation situation is very similar in both developed and developing countries, /ith only one exception—the developed countries have better information about 1e availability of instructional space (75 per cent) and other space (54 per cent) 1an the developing countries (48 and 42 per cent respectively).

It is thus apparent that many universities do not have adequate means of 1alysing their resources and, consequently, they do not pay enough attention) the problem of improving the efficiency of their utilization. Probably some f these resources are lying idle, which, if identified and used, might help to lleviate the seriousness of the problems they are facing, including financing, :aching-staff formation, etc. However, one can observe that the availability of 1formation is better in those countries where higher educational planning xists at both the institutional and national levels. Likewise, it tends to be etter in public than private universities and better in those concentrating on ure science and graduate teaching than in those universities with no special mphasis.

. *Actual ratios and norms used by universities*

)ne of our questions asked for the norms which universities were using in their 1anning and management. Unfortunately, the rate of response to this question 'as extremely low, which can only be interpreted as non-utilization of norms 1 most of the universities in our sample. Only eight of them gave any norms t all.

An attempt was made to calculate the actual ratios of students/teaching staff, 1te of drop-out, proportion of graduate students in the student body, proportion f new courses in the curricula per year, available books and instructional space er student. These ratios were compared with the norms used in the same

113

universities (Table XIIIA). Our results show an important difference between the actual situation and the prescribed norms, especially for such ratios a student/teaching staff (actual 13.4 against the norm of 9.5) and instructiona space per student (actual 1.4 sq. m. as against the norm of 5.0). The situation seems to have got more out of control in the universities with no planning a all (25.8 students per teacher against the norm of 10.7) than in universitie where there is planning.

Classification by level of economic development shows a greater differenc between the actual and the prescribed student/staff ratios in the developing than in the developed countries. Surprisingly, in both groups of countries, th proportion of graduate students in the student body is lower than prescribed We should also point out the ratio of books available per student in th developing countries, which is more than three times less than in the developer countries.

Although these particular universities have had to disregard some of thei norms, a comparative analysis of these norms with the actual ratios in th university would have been a help in identifying the weak points in thei development.

5. Conclusions

The major conclusion one can draw from this analysis is that the universities although facing very serious problems in their development, do not hav reliable information and mechanisms to analyze it. This does not mean the are not concerned about their problems and are not doing anything to solv them, but rather, that they are not taking advantage of modern planning an management techniques and are neglecting to make efficient use of method which are available.

We are far from thinking that the availability of data on different activitie in the university and an information system are one and the same thing. Not a data are informative. This is why it is extremely important to have method and criteria for selecting data, the analysis of which will be significant and o which a university information system can be built. In other words, informatio gives the basis for decisions but not the decisions themselves. It is very importan to have adequate methods of analysis, adequate criteria for evaluation anc also, an adequate mechanism for decision-making on the basis of tha information.

The indices which we have mentioned in this chapter, when analyse separately and inter-related, may be used for identifying the most crucial point in university development. Certainly the list is not exhaustive but helps in th identification of problems, after which a deeper quantitative and qualitativ analysis with more detailed indices should be undertaken. It is interesting to mention that, after receiving our questionnaire, several universities started to develop an information system and to improve their managerial mechanisms and this can be considered as the first encouraging practical result of our project.

XIV. Past and future factors of change in the university

To ascertain the present situation at universities, we considered it very important to study the past and foreseeable future tendencies of university development as seen by the universities themselves. A large part of our questionnaire was devoted to this. We sought the opinions of the heads of universities on the major tendencies influencing development, their evaluation of the importance of the problems and their ability to cope with them. We were aware of certain limitations in this approach and did our best to overcome them.

In order to give the problems as wide a range as possible, they were formulated on the basis of discussions at the international seminar on higher education held at the IIEP in July 1969. Fifteen factors of change which might create problems were considered and an item was left for the universities to add any other factor which they felt we had overlooked.

For each factor, the universities were asked to reply to a composite question having six parts. They were asked whether they considered the given factor had created problems in the past. If the answer was positive, they were asked to grade the seriousness of the problem on a five-point scale, ranging from 'very serious' (1) to 'not serious' (5), and subsequently to grade the way in which the university reacted to the problem on a five-point scale, ranging from 'very well' to 'badly'. The question was asked in the same way for the future. If it was not considered to have been a factor of change, it was given a score of 6.

1. Importance of factors in the past and the university's reaction

OVERALL SAMPLE (Table XIV.1)

Analysis shows that the most crucial problems, in order of seriousness, which universities faced during the past ten years were: increase in enrolments; the need to increase the volume of sources of financing; the need to expand facilities; increase in applications; and the need to expand the numbers of teaching and research staff. In sixth place was the need to change the curriculum to fit changing social and economic needs, which was followed by the need to improve the quality of staff.

As one can see, the importance of qualitative changes followed closely after quantitative developments, but accent was given to the former. In the universities' view, these were well managed, except for the two most serious problems of finance and facilities. However, there were other problems which had not been considered as serious but which were coped with very poorly—the increase in applications relative to the number of available places was one of these, as well as several aspects of university activity which are influenced by socio-economic needs. The latter, consisting of the differences between the distribution of graduates by field and manpower needs, refresher courses and continuing education, are ranked ninth, twelfth and fifteenth for the universities' reaction to them.

Interestingly, despite the great attention which the participation of students in university governance attracted during the decade under review, most of the universities reacted promptly to this problem.

The question on research as a factor of change was set out rather differently and has already been discussed in Chapter XI.

EXISTENCE OF PLANNING SYSTEM (Table XIV.2)

There are some startling differences in the problems which universities have considered as important when our sample is classified into the different planning systems. Generally, those universities with some elements of planning or no planning follow much the same pattern as the overall sample, but those universities under central and institutional planning place the increase in applications, the need to change the curricula and the structure of the university in equal first place, and, although they coped with the applications and structural changes well, their reaction to changes in the curricula is ranked as thirteenth. Finance and facilities are not seen as such serious problems by them, although again, facilities has had a poor past reaction (15th). It is interesting that these universities ranked their past reaction to the demand for continuing education very high at fourth, whereas the other universities all rank it either fourteenth or fifteenth.

LEVEL OF ECONOMIC DEVELOPMENT (Table XIV.3)

The only major difference to be observed in the relative seriousness of past problems in the two sub-groups of this classification is the increased participation of students in university governance, which the developed countries considered as rather more serious (7th) than the developing countries (12th), although both groups thought they had kept pace with this problem.

However, reactions to the problems have been more varied. Rankings show that the developing countries feel they have dealt well with the problem of expanding numbers of teaching and research staff (1st), whereas the developed countries place their reaction to the increase in applications in first place and that for the problem of staff numbers fifth. Another variation in the rankings is between the developing countries' past reactions to changes in the curriculum and structure (seventh and sixth), and the developed countries' (twelfth and eleventh). It is obvious that the developed countries found other problems, such as improving the quality of incoming students and changes in research, much easier to deal with than the developing countries and, therefore, their reactions to structural and curricular changes are ranked lower—the mean scores are not in fact very different.

GEOGRAPHICAL LOCATION (Table XIV.4)

The classification by geographical location also shows some interesting differences in the seriousness of the problems encountered by the universities Australia and Oceania show the greatest divergence from the rankings in the overall sample, but this is rather a small sub-group of relatively new universities who, it seems, have been able to accommodate the problems of facilities, the demand for continuing education, and changes in the curricula and the number of applications relative to the number of places available—all of which are in opposition to the majority of the universities.

African and Asian universities were generally in agreement with regard to the importance of the problems and with the overall sample, but the reaction of African universities to expanding the numbers of staff and the increased participation of students in university governance had been poorer than in the other regions. However, their reaction to the distribution of graduates by manpower needs is ranked unusually high (3rd) and is probably due to the fact, that their countries can still make use of practically all the available graduates.

Asian universities deviate from the overall sample only because they have a high ranking for their reaction to changes in the curriculum, but we would point out that for the African, Asian and Latin American universities past reactions have mean scores of between, approximately, 2.00 and 3.57 whereas those in Europe ranged between 2.00 and 2.83, which would indicate that the latter's reactions on average were slightly better than in the other continents In particular, the European universities felt they had met the need for refresher courses (4th) to a much greater extent than can be seen in the other regions.

Latin American universities thought they had done badly with regard to the distribution of graduates by manpower needs (14th), although their ability to change the university structure to meet present needs is ranked second.

OTHER CLASSIFICATIONS (Table XIV.5 and 6)

Mean scores and rankings have also been calculated for the classifications by university size and type of control, but the only points worthy of comment are: the large universities felt their reaction was particularly poor with regard to improving the quality of incoming students; and the lowest ranking for reaction by the private universities is for the distribution of graduates by manpower needs—the public universities have a much higher mean score and place it sixth.

A brief analysis of the past importance and university reaction to our list of problems shows there is a need for more long-term planning, especially relating to links between the university and society. Here, in the past, although the problems were not considered as serious, the universities have felt their reactions were among the poorest. This would seem to indicate that little has actually been done in this sphere and the universities have, in fact, been caught napping'. But their opinions for the future show that they consider this situation will change.

2. Importance of factors in the future and the university's reaction

OVERALL SAMPLE

As for the future importance of these problems and the reaction to them, the conclusion can be drawn from Table XIV.1 that, generally, universities consider their problems will be more serious than in the past—the mean score indicating the least seriousness here is 2.93, as against 4.64 in the past. Qualitative aspects of university life will be given more attention in the next ten years, but this does not mean they think the quantitative problems have been solved—for example, in the opinions of the heads of universities, the need to increase the volume and sources of financing will be the most crucial problem (1st), but it is one that, at the university level, they do not feel able to do much about (15th); their opinion suggests the situation will be even worse than it was during the period 1958-68. It would seem more difficult to deal with the problem of expanding facilities, which is ranked second in importance and twelfth for solution.

Also, universities consider the qualitative aspects of their activities, such as the need to change the curriculum and university structure to meet changing needs, to expand numbers and to improve the quality of teaching and research staff, as more serious problems in the future than they were in the past. As can be seen from the table, the universities consider they will be better able to deal with these problems (ranked 3rd, 5th and 1st) and this is in accordance with our analyses of changes in structure, courses and growth of staff, where we have seen that the universities were very active in these areas.

Since qualitative aspects have taken some of the more important ranking for the future, the increase in applications and enrolments fall to sixth and seventh place, but the mean scores are not very different and the estimated ability to react remains much the same.

The gap between the distribution of graduates by field and manpower need is foreseen as being much more serious (mean scores 3.84 in the past and 2.57 in the future) but again estimated reaction will be no better. However, it is thought that the need for refresher courses will be met to a greater extent since it is ranked sixth for the future as against twelfth in the past, but, at the same time, the situation with regard to continuing education for persons in all walks of life looks as if it will remain much the same as in the past.

EXISTENCE OF A PLANNING SYSTEM (Table XIV.2)

While universities with some elements of planning or no planning generally follow the trends observed in the overall sample for the future, those universities under central and university planning show they will be pre-occupied with quite different problems. Changes in the curriculum and university structure were ranked first in importance in the past, but for the future the need for refresher courses and improving the quality of teachers and incoming students are seen as being of equal importance with finance and facilities. Where they had poor reactions in the past for facilities and curriculum, they expect to manage much better in the future (equal third), and their estimated ability to meet the demand for continuing education and manpower needs (equal third) is unusually high.

LEVEL OF ECONOMIC DEVELOPMENT (Table XIV.3)

The main difference between the developed and developing countries in the seriousness of the problems which the universities will face in the future, as shown by analysis, will be that the developed countries consider the need for refresher courses to be much more important and also (since it is ranked fourteenth for reaction), they will not be able to cope with it. The questions of changes in the curriculum and university structure are also areas in which the developed countries feel less confident (ranked seventh and tenth) than the developing (first and sixth). Perhaps this is because these are problems which the developing countries feel they can deal with, given their resources, much better than the increases in applications and enrolments (ranked tenth and thirteenth). The latter are ranked second and fifth for reaction by the developed countries.

GEOGRAPHICAL LOCATION (Table XIV.4)

Opinions about the future vary considerably in the different continents; Latin American universities are much more confident of their ability to react to their problems (mean scores range between 1.53 and 2.41), while universities in Australia and Oceania are by far the most pessimistic with mean scores of between 1.33 and 4.50—the reverse of the situation in the past.

The Latin American universities are particularly optimistic about some of the qualitative aspects (quality of incoming students and staff, changes in the curriculum and university structure) but, apart from finance and manpower needs, feel that balancing applications and enrolments will be among their worst reactions. African universities (apart from manpower needs) feel much the same, but those in Asia do not appear to be so concerned about increases in applications and enrolments and they follow the trend for the overall sample quite closely.

In contrast, the European universities foresee themselves dealing better with manpower needs, facilities and the participation of students in university governance, which is no longer considered as a serious problem since it has dropped from seventh to fourteenth place. However, in this region as opposed to the other continents, some of the qualitative aspects (quality of staff and students, university structure and refresher courses) will not, in the universities' opinion, be so well managed in the future.

Although the North American universities think they will have fewer problems on the increase in applications relative to the number of places available—which the other regions have expressed grave doubts about—they show a low ranking for their ability to meet manpower needs (this has fallen from fifth to fourteenth place for the future) and also low rankings for changes in the curriculum and research.

7. General comments

Therefore, the seriousness of the problems universities face depends to a great extent on the level of economic development and on the existence of planning.

121

A high level of development and planning would seem to bring with them a greater pre-occupation with the qualitative aspects, although finance and facilities remain as the main limiting factors.

Overall, the analysis also shows another interesting aspect: while the universities consider changes in the curriculum to be a serious problem, which will be dealt with quite well in the future, manpower needs, refresher courses and continuing education are not seen to be so important, although these are, of course, directly linked with the curriculum of the university if it is to be relevant to national needs. Furthermore, the majority of the universities expect this situation to remain much the same for the future as in the past, and they will react poorly. As already noticed in the chapters on university autonomy and evaluation of teaching programmes (Chapters V and X), the universities do not have sufficient links with industry, commerce or the government and it seems they do not foresee any changes.

4. Obstacles to change encountered by the university

Although, in the question on past and future problems, extra space was available for the universities to list any other factor influencing change, this was completed in only three instances. However, the following two questions asking the universities to list the most important past and future obstacles to necessary or desirable changes, elicited a number of extra comments. These have been ranked according to the frequency with which they were mentioned (Table XIVA). It will be seen that the universities have sometimes considered this question in much the same way as the previous one in that some of the obstacles listed are areas in which it has been difficult to achieve the desired change and which the universities thus feel are hindering development. We have grouped together those factors which have already been considered in the previous question and then listed the other obstacles which were put forward by the universities. The first group is thus mainly composed of the usual areas of university activity—teaching, administration and research—and generally confirms that the universities consider that the major obstacles to university development are insufficient financial support and facilities. The second group seems to give some of the reasons why the universities have not achieved desired changes and, in total, these items were mentioned almost as many times as those in the first group.

Foremost among them are tradition and resistance to change within the university, which came third in the past. Very closely behind, in fifth place, are politics and other external influences. It was not clear whether this is a question of an unstable socio-economic background or whether the universities felt themselves hampered by government interference. In any event, both of these obstacles will continue to be important in the future.

Obviously, the universities have felt keenly the lack of planning, of an adequate administration and/or long-term goals and statistics since these are ranked fifth, seventh and tenth. However, having become aware of these shortcomings, the universities are dealing with them and the majority expect to have removed these obstacles in the future.

There is one other significant change in the past and future rankings; the need to lessen the gap between university work and the socio-economic needs of the country climbs from eleventh to sixth place. From the responses received it was clear that the universities felt they would not be making sufficient changes to meet such socio-economic needs and that this situation will become more critical. This is in accordance with their previous opinions on manpower needs and continuing education.

Classification by level of economic development shows the developing countries have more often encountered obstacles in political/external influences, student unrest and lack of university planning than the developed countries. They also mentioned a greater number and a much wider variety of problems, some particular to their own country, such as the frequent changes of staff, changes in the language of instruction and systems of staff promotion and evaluation. There is no difference in the resistance to change within the university in both developing and developed countries. The developed countries did not take socio-economic needs into account in the past but it is ranked fourth in the future and their specific problems have some connexion with this, including insufficient numbers of science students, redeployment of staff, etc.

Conclusions

Analysis of the obstacles facing the universities shows they are more aware of external influences and necessities than has been shown by responses to previous questions. It seems to be a common situation that, while it is felt that socio-economic needs should be met and the university should change and develop accordingly, tradition and resistance encountered from both staff and students have delayed reforms. The universities consider themselves to have almost complete autonomy, except in the field of finance, so it would seem that they alone can resolve this problem. However, national needs cannot wait indefinitely and the universities, if they are unable to find a solution to internal resistance, must be prepared to lose some of their autonomy in order to be better linked with progressive social and economic developments in their countries.

XV. University functions and their priorities

Clear definition of the priorities in university activities is a very importan
prerequisite for planning development, but it is well-known that the question o
priorities is now the subject of much debate in view of the different direction
which the development of higher education can take and the increasing role o
the university in society.

We attempted, therefore, to gain an idea of the prevailing opinion of head
of universities on this question and for this purpose listed seventeen activitie
which are typical for the majority of universities. The list included suc
obvious university functions as the different aspects of teaching and researcl
including the preparation of instructional materials, organization of refreshe
courses, etc. Physical and financial planning and working with industry and th
local community were also mentioned. The universities were asked first whethe
the function was performed and second, if the answer was in the affirmative
the relative importance of that activity, 1 being top priority and 5 low priorit
The responses were analysed and the importance of the various functions wer
ranked according to their mean scores (Table XV).

1. Overall sample

In the overall sample, the teaching of undergraduate students and th
preparation of graduate students are ranked first and second respectively. Th
is hardly surprising since these two may be considered as the major functior
of any university. There is, however, a fairly considerable difference in th
mean scores, which indicates that teaching undergraduates has far and awa
the first priority in the majority of universities in the sample, although it
interesting to note that 92 per cent of those responding also prepare gradua
students.

Theoretical research and applied research, ranked third and fourth, follo ery closely on the preparation of graduate students. These high rankings show hat universities continue to consider research as one of their basic functions, lthough our analysis of information on research (Chapter XI) reveals that, in act, it probably receives a much lower priority in university planning and nanagement.

Physical planning and financial planning are ranked fifth and seventh, but vith similar scores. This would seem to reflect a growing concern among the niversities with the organized planning and management of their affairs, since hese two support functions follow directly upon the teaching and research unctions of the universities. It should also be pointed out that 12 per cent of hose responding do not consider themselves to have any physical planning and 3 per cent do not have financial planning.

Working with government organizations is ranked sixth. This reasonably igh ranking underlines the tendencies of universities to establish firmer links vith their environment, and working with the government is possibly becoming ne of the more important secondary functions of universities.

Training teachers for second-level education is ranked eighth. This is not a igh ranking and is perhaps explained by the fact that, in many countries, aere are other institutions which train teachers for the second level. However, aining of teachers for higher education has an even lower ranking (eleventh) nd since these teachers are unlikely to be produced anywhere other than t the universities, this is somewhat surprising. This may simply reflect a tuation where those who are subsequently to teach in the universities do ot, for the most part, receive special pedagogical training. In addition, it rould be noted that only 61 per cent of the responding universities consider aat they perform this function.

Working with industry and the local community are ranked ninth and tenth, ith scores which are not very different. Here again, we can see the relative nportance given to these functions, which may not rank among the primary inctions of a university.

Development research is ranked twelfth, although ninth to twelfth positions re all very closely grouped so that the difference in actual priority given to ae functions is not of great significance.

Extension work and refresher courses which mobilize very much the same nds of resources, and which frequently spring from similar motivations and .titudes, are grouped together at thirteenth and fourteenth. The relatively low riority given to these two extremely important functions of the modern niversity seems to indicate their importance very much as secondary functions.

The last three functions in the priority ranking are all concerned with the reparation of teaching materials. Preparation of teaching materials for higher lucation is ranked fifteenth, for second-level education sixteenth and for a complete system of education seventeenth. One may wonder who is to give the lead in the preparation of such materials if it is not the universities?

As can be seen here, 60 per cent of the responding universities prepare materials for higher education, but only 39 per cent prepare materials for second-level education and a mere 17 per cent for a complete system of education.

The universities were not asked simply to give a straightforward order of priorities among seventeen generally important functions. We would stress that, in our question, 1 denoted top priority, 5 low priority and 6 that the function was not performed, so the difference between the mean score for teaching undergraduates (1.54) and that for the preparation of materials for a complete system of education (5.48) is very significant.

2. Existence of planning systems

When universities are considered according to existing planning systems, there is not a great deal of variation with respect to the major functions of teaching and research as a whole. There are, however, differences as far as types of research and levels of students are concerned. Universities under both central and institutional planning give first priority to graduate students, whereas universities under other types of planning emphasize undergraduates. Graduate teaching in these sub-groups varies from second to thirteenth. This last position is a notable exception and was given by the extremely small sample of universities under central planning only. In effect, the variation in the ranking of graduate student preparation can be considered to be from second to seventh.

As far as research is concerned, all the sub-classes rank some form of it as second, third or fourth. The overall emphasis tends to be on theoretical research where the variance is from second to fourth, if the very small sample of central planning only is again ignored. Applied research has a ranking which varies from second in universities where there is no planning to eighth in universities with central and university planning. The ranking of development research does not differ widely from tenth to fifteenth, once again leaving aside the smallest sub-class.

When the two major support functions of physical and financial planning are considered, the differences in ranking tend to be somewhat larger. The range is from second, where there is planning only at the university level, to eleventh, where there is both central and university planning. The other two sub-classes rank this function seventh. This would indicate that universities with institutional planning only are, nowadays, necessarily much pre-occupied by this function. The same conclusion may be drawn for financial planning, which has similar divergences (from third to eleventh). Those systems where there is institutional planning only rank this function third and systems where there is both central and university planning rank it eleventh.

The training of teachers for second-level and higher education shows some variance. The sub-class according them the highest priority is central and university planning, which ranks them fifth and seventh. The lowest priority is given by those universities with institutional planning only, which ranks second-level teacher training eighth and higher teacher training thirteenth. This last ranking is remarkably low, but it should also be pointed out that only 17 per cent of this sample considered themselves as training teachers for higher education.

The preparation of instructional materials shows one variation. Materials for second-level education are ranked universally low at sixteenth and materials for higher education only slightly higher at fourteenth and fifteenth. The exception for the latter is the system with central and university planning which ranks this function third. The preparation of teaching materials for a complete system of education is ranked low by all, varying between sixteenth and seventeenth. This may well be because it has already been covered by the two preceding activities for most universities.

Working with the government and working with industry show very little variation from system to system, if the small sample of central planning only is not included. The former is ranked high varying only from fifth to sixth and the latter has a middle ranking from eighth to eleventh. Working with the local community has one notable variation: planning at the university level ranks this fairly high at seventh, whereas the ranking varies from tenth to thirteenth in the other planning systems.

Extension work and refresher courses are both ranked universally low. Taking both functions together, the variation is only between tenth and sixteenth. It is possibly surprising to find that universities, in general, accord little importance to these two functions, which may be considered to be of great importance among the secondary functions if the university is to fulfil its obligations to the community competently.

Level of economic development

There is a clear tendency, as far as the primary functions of teaching and research are concerned, for universities in developed countries to consider research as their main interest. Together with this there is a second priority given to the preparation of graduate students, with undergraduate students third. The universities in developing countries give the first priority to undergraduate teaching; preparation of graduates comes second, while theoretical research is ranked only seventh. It is interesting to note, however, that these universities rank applied research third. In both of these sub-classes, development research has a low ranking.

As far as the support functions of planning are concerned, there is no great difference between universities in developing and developed countries. The majority of universities, it would seem, are now much concerned with the problems of planning and management.

There are some variations in the priorities accorded to the training of teachers between developing and developed countries. A high priority is given to the training of teachers for second-level education by universities in developing countries. This function is ranked fourth. Training of teachers for higher education is however ranked considerably lower at twelfth. The situation is as it were, reversed for universities in developed countries, where the training of teachers for higher education takes precedence in sixth position, whereas the training of teachers for second-level education is ninth.

The preparation of instructional materials is not sensitive to the division into developing and developed countries. Taking the three functions together, i.e. six rankings, the variation is from fourteenth to seventeenth.

Universities in developing countries give a higher ranking to co-operation with the government than those in developed countries. The difference, from fifth to eighth, is fairly marked. Both sub-classes, on the other hand, give tenth position to the function of working with industry. As far as working with the local community is concerned, the universities in the developing countries give a slightly higher ranking than the developed countries. The two rankings are ninth and twelfth respectively.

Extension work and refresher courses have about the same priority in developing and developed countries. There is a slight variation in that universities in the developed countries tend to accord a little more importance to refresher courses. They are ranked eleventh, whereas in the developing countries they are ranked fifteenth. This is not a particularly high ranking in either case but is consistent with other classifications.

4. Geographical location

When the universities are considered according to geographical distribution the two principal functions of teaching and research tend to be the top priorities, with two exceptions and some slight variations in the order of priority. Universities in Africa and Latin America place the teaching of undergraduate students as first priority, but graduate students are ranked seventh in both cases. Consistently, research has a lower ranking than in the other geographical regions. The sub-class Australia and Oceania is left aside since

he sample is rather too small to be significant. The variations within the order
f priority appear in European universities, where theoretical research is ranked
op priority, the preparation of graduate students second and undergraduates
hird. Once again, this underlines the fact that the universities in economically
ighly-developed countries are able to concentrate on two principal interests:
raduate teaching and research. In the less economically developed regions, the
rincipal aims of the universities tend to be bound up with undergraduate
tudents, and research has not yet found its way into the very top priorities.

The support functions of physical and financial planning do not seem to vary
ignificantly with geographical distribution. They are consistently ranked fairly
igh.

The training of teachers for second-level and higher education is not par-
cularly sensitive to geographical distribution. In all the sub-classes, but one,
aining of teachers for second-level education takes priority over higher
ducation. The exception is Europe. One other ranking which is worthy of
ote is that given to second-level teacher training in Africa. This function
; ranked second by the African universities and is clearly considered to be
ne of their principal roles, whereas the highest ranking this function receives
mong the other sub-groups is sixth for Latin America.

The preparation of teaching materials, whether it is for the whole or for
part of the education system, is not particularly sensitive to geographical
ariations. Taking all three of the functions together, the ranking varies from
hirteenth to seventeeth, with one exception, namely, higher education materials
re ranked eleventh in Europe.

The three functions related to co-operation with outside organizations show
onsistently that working with governments takes precedence over working with
ndustry and the local community. There is one notable exception here. Working
vith the local community is ranked third in the Latin American continent.
his is very high, particularly when seen against the ranking for other regions,
vhich varies from tenth to fourteenth.

. *University size by number of students*

he number of students in a university appears to have some effect on the
riorities given to teaching and research. The bigger the university, the more
mphasis is placed on the teaching of graduate students and on theoretical
esearch. These two functions are ranked first and second by universities with
ver 10,000 students. The ranking declines slightly for universities with
,000-10,000 students; teaching of undergraduates takes first place here, with
raduates second and theoretical research third. The decline is even more clear
1 universities with less than 5,000 students; undergraduate teaching is first,

and graduate teaching is ranked only seventh, although theoretical research i fourth.

Smaller universities, however, rank the two support functions of physical an financial planning second and third respectively, whereas the other two sub classes rank them seventh and eighth.

It is somewhat difficult to isolate any significance in the training of teacher for second-level and higher education. The two sub-classes with over 5,00(students rank second-level teacher training sixth and, therefore, consider i among their first priorities. The sub-class 0-5,000 ranks this lower in eightl position. As far as training teachers for higher education is concerned universities with 10,000 students and over rank it fifth, medium-sized universitie tenth and smaller universities thirteenth.

Other classifications do not reveal any unexpected or important tendencies in the priority of university functions and activities.

6. Functions which the universities would most like to develop and obstacles to their implementation

As a follow-up to the statement of the functions they perform and thei relative importance, the universities were asked to state which of eight majo functions they would like to see developed and to give them a priority rankin; from 1 to 8. The average score for each function was calculated and the rankings for the overall sample and sub-groups given (Table XVA). Thi question, it was hoped, would show up universities' objectives for the future A subsequent question asked the universities to check, not in order of priority a list of reasons why it had not been possible to develop these functions a much as they would have liked to in the past. The percentage of universitie checking each reason was calculated to estimate the importance of eacl difficulty (Table XVB).

The overall sample shows that undergraduate teaching, graduate teachin; and research stay in the first three ranks, as they do in the priority accordec to existing functions, but research, as a whole, is ranked as the first priorit for development followed by the preparation of graduate students. The desir on the part of the universities to develop research and concurrently graduat studies is, once again, clearly discernible here, with the emphasis for the futur slipping slightly away from undergraduate studies.

Training teachers and continuing education (ranked fourth and fifth) ar functions to which the universities would like to give more attention than the do at present. This is a particularly significant change in regard to continuin; education since extension work and refresher courses are, in present estimations

130

almost last on the list of university priorities. However, this change in priorities is the only indication the universities give of a desire to integrate more fully into the socio-economic life, for working with outside organizations takes the last ranking of functions which they would like to develop in the overall sample and in practically all the sub-groups. Planning too, it seems, is to be given a lower priority if the university's wishes are put into practice. It is ranked high for present functions whereas, for the functions which the university would like to develop, the score is about the same as that accorded to preparing instructional materials (sixth and seventh). With respect to the latter, the low priority given to this function at present accords with the university's wishes.

Thus, generally, it is apparent that the universities would prefer to devote their attention to higher academic and research activities and, secondly, under-graduate teaching, and this tendency can be seen throughout most of the sub-classifications. Exceptions are the group of universities under central and institutional planning which would give third place to continuing education, and Latin American and African universities which would give second and third priorities to teacher training. The African universities, by the way, would continue to give top priority to undergraduates.

The principal reason for not developing these functions as much as the universities would like is, or was, the shortage of funds: 85 per cent of the universities gave this reason. Following on from this comes the shortage of professional personnel and, since 67 per cent gave this reason, we may assume that there are real difficulties in recruiting suitable staff for the development and expansion which universities would like to undertake. The next two reasons, each given by 52 per cent of the universities, are shortages of space and physical facilities. Administrative difficulties are cited by 25 per cent and 'other' reasons by 23 per cent.

The developing countries are hampered by shortages in all the areas, except for space, to a greater extent than the developed countries; in particular, funds, physical facilities and administration.

The above analysis clearly shows that the universities still hold much the same traditional view of the kind of activities to which they should give priority; teaching and research are high while planning and working with outside organizations are low. However, looking at the rankings of priorities actually prevailing in the universities, planning and working with the government follow immediately after teaching and research activities. One can draw the conclusion that this order of priorities is due to the encroachment of the outside world (government finance is an important factor) into the university rather than to the desire of many universities to play an active role in the socio-economic life of the country. This is largely confirmed by an analysis of the final opinion which we requested from the universities in our questionnaire.

7. *The university as a factor of political and social change*

Our question was: 'To what extent does your university see itself as a factor of political and social change within your country?' Although opinion questions were usually answered by all the universities, in this case 14 per cent of our sample were not able to reply—in fact, some of them stated that, within the university, opinions were divided on this matter.

In the figures for the overall sample, 48 per cent of the universities felt they were a limited or indirect factor of change, mainly by educating students and by research, and 5 per cent did not think they had any influence at all. Just 34 per cent considered themselves as an important factor. In all cases, they were a factor more of social than of political or economic change.

There is not a great deal of difference in the opinions expressed by the universities in the classification by level of economic development, although a slightly larger percentage (9) of the developed countries answered 'none at all', as against 4 per cent in the developing countries. However, considered by continents, only 21 per cent of the African universities thought they were an important factor, whereas 44 per cent in Europe and 37 per cent in Asia felt they had an important role to play.

It can be seen, therefore, that there is a wide range of views on this subject, but the majority (66 per cent) are very hesitant as to the part the university should take in social, economic and political affairs. In the past, universities were certain their activities were largely confined to the academic world but, today, this is not so; they have many more links with society and its economy. However, these links are tenuous and the influence of the university is uncertain, whereas external influences upon the university are becoming more pronounced. Apparently, the universities, generally, are resisting this change (see also Chapter V on university autonomy) instead of endeavouring to take up an active role in national socio-economic affairs.

The tables

TABLE IV.[1] University growth: average annual growth rates of principal university characteristics, 1958-68

	No. of students		No. of staff		Instructional space		Operating expenditure		Research funds		Total no. library items	
	%	Sample	%	Sample	%	Sample	%	Sample	%	Sample	%	Sample
1. Overall sample	11.82	(56)	10.9	(47)	10.25	(39)	12.5	(37)	17.6	(22)	8.67	(33)
2. Existence of a planning system												
Central & univ. plan.	7.47	(5)	6.9	(5)	3.38	(5)	10.9	(4)	20.0	(4)	5.51	(5)
Central planning only	34.89	(1)	—	—	—	—	—	—	-0.5	(1)	—	—
Univ. planning only	12.92	(12)	7.7	(9)	12.50	(8)	17.7	(6)	25.6[2]	(6)	12.99	(5)
Some planning	11.14	(24)	10.9	(20)	9.79	(17)	10.0	(18)	17.3	(8)	9.64	(15)
No planning	14.36	(14)	14.6	(13)	12.91	(9)	15.0	(9)	16.3	(7)	6.13	(8)
3. Level of economic development												
Developing	13.15	(37)	11.6	(31)	12.52	(22)	11.0	(24)	13.8	(10)	9.62	(18)
Developed	9.23	(19)	9.4	(16)	7.30	(17)	15.5	(13)	20.8	(12)	7.53	(15)
4. Geographical location												
Africa[2]	22.15	(11)	18.3	(10)	15.49	(5)	13.9	(7)	5.2	(3)	15.78	(4)
Asia	10.77	(18)	10.4	(18)	12.51	(9)	8.5	(12)	9.4	(5)	8.23	(10)
Australia & Oceania	18.34	(1)	11.6	(1)	15.20	(1)	19.8	(1)	14.3	(2)	8.70	(1)
Europe	10.26	(14)	10.4	(13)	7.45	(13)	13.0	(10)	16.9	(9)	6.35	(11)
North America[2]	11.05	(5)	17.0	(5)	12.46	(4)	25.8	(4)	47.6	(3)	17.77	(5)
Latin & Cent. America[2]	14.52	(17)	6.6	(12)	12.17	(10)	11.7	(14)	9.7	(6)	13.34	(12)
5. University size by number of students												
-5,000	16.44	(18)	11.8	(16)	9.91	(9)	11.9	(10)	8.1	(6)	11.34	(13)
5,000-10,000	11.82	(17)	13.1	(14)	14.09	(12)	11.2	(11)	26.4	(5)	10.57	(7)
10,000 and over	7.87	(21)	8.2	(17)	7.85	(18)	13.7	(16)	18.4	(11)	4.98	(13)
6. Emphasis on the field of study												
Pure science	12.66	(8)	8.1	(7)	14.13	(4)	8.5	(4)	11.7	(2)	7.99	(6)
Humanities	15.75	(6)	16.7	(6)	12.53	(3)	11.4[2]	(7)	41.4	(3)	11.84	(4)
Social sciences	24.16	(2)	15.6	(2)	14.12	(2)	10.5	(1)	14.3	(2)	7.57	(2)
Professional training	14.48	(17)	13.5	(11)	9.89	(17)	12.4	(10)	11.8	(5)	9.68	(8)
No special emphasis	7.47	(23)	8.4	(21)	8.38	(13)	12.2	(18)	15.2	(10)	7.55	(13)
7. Emphasis on university function												
Undergraduate teaching	13.19	(37)	11.2	(31)	11.19	(24)	13.0	(25)	19.4	(12)	9.80	(23)
Graduate teaching	10.02	(16)	10.2	(14)	9.40	(13)	10.15	(10)	15.7	(7)	6.77	(7)
Research	2.97	(2)	4.2	(1)	3.93	(1)	16.0	(1)	8.2	(2)	4.37	(1)
Teacher training	7.65	(1)	17.4	(1)	4.81	(1)	22.0	(1)	28.0	(1)	2.11	(1)
8. Type of control												
Private	12.69	(13)	10.2	(12)	11.83	(7)	11.7	(5)	21.4	(5)	11.70	(7)
Public	11.56	(43)	11.1	(35)	9.90	(32)	12.7	(32)	16.4	(17)	12.36[2]	(39)

135

TABLE IV.[1] (*continued*)

	No. of students		No. of staff		Instructional space		Operating expenditure		Research funds		Total no. library items	
	%	Sample	%	Sample	%	Sample	%	Sample	%	Sample	%	Samp
9. Type of admission system												
Open[2]	22.52	(7)	17.0	(5)	14.26	(4)	15.6	(2)	4.8	(2)	11.42	(1
Selective	11.94	(41)	10.8	(37)	10.32	(27)	11.5	(28)	13.9	(16)	8.42	(26
Mixed	9.83	(11)	11.4	(10)	10.49	(8)	17.48	(7)	29.7	(5)	10.83	(6
10. Control groups												
7 universities	11.03		9.97		8.01		9.87		21.57		10.19	
11 universities	13.04		12.05		9.70		12.27		—		10.78	
13 universities	11.92		10.99		8.65		—		—		9.46	
28 universities	12.06		10.36		—		—		—		9.64	
45 universities	12.39		11.00		—		—		—		—	

1. The table numbers relate to the relevant chapters.
2. For the period 1963-68 only.

TABLE V. University autonomy: average degree of autonomy enjoyed by universities in different areas of decision-making

		Finance[1]	Curri-culum	Selection students	Staff recruit-ment	Academic object.	Research policy	General object.	Sample
1. Overall sample									
Average score		1.988	2.675	2.718	2.763	2.750	2.737	2.526	(80)[2]
Standard deviation		0.766	0.519	0.677	0.426	0.461	0.494	0.524	
2. Existence of a planning system									
Cent. & univ.	av.	2.400	2.400	2.800	2.000	2.400	2.400	2.000	(7)
planning	s.d.	0.490	0.490	0.400	—	0.490	0.490	—	
Central planning	av.	2.333	3.000	2.667	3.000	2.667	3.000	2.500	(3)
	s.d.	0.471	—	0.471	—	0.471	—	0.500	
University planning	av.	2.000	2.706	2.706	2.765	2.882	2.765	2.647	(15)
	s.d.	0.686	0.456	0.570	0.424	0.322	0.424	0.478	
Some planning	av.	1.912	2.647	2.606	2.853	2.706	2.706	2.576	(34)
	s.d.	0.742	0.536	0.886	0.354	0.516	0.516	0.494	
No planning	av.	1.952	2.714	2.900	2.762	2.810	2.810	2.476	(21)
	s.d.	0.898	0.547	0.300	0.426	0.393	0.499	0.587	
3. Level of economic development									
Developing	av.	2.000	2.804	2.796	2.857	2.768	2.804	2.636	(56)
	s.d.	0.802	0.397	0.557	0.350	0.463	0.440	0.481	
Developed	av.	1.958	2.375	2.542	2.542	2.780	2.583	2.261	(24)
	s.d.	0.676	0.633	0.865	0.498	0.455	0.571	0.529	
3a. GNP per capita in $									
0-100	av.	2.077	3.000	2.692	2.846	2.923	2.846	2.750	(13)
	s.d.	0.730	—	0.606	0.361	0.266	0.361	0.433	
100-200	av.	1.769	2.615	2.583	2.846	2.615	2.692	2.385	(13)
	s.d.	0.890	0.487	0.862	0.361	0.487	0.462	0.487	
200-300	av.	2.118	2.706	3.000	2.882	2.706	2.706	2.706	(17)
	s.d.	0.758	0.456	—	0.322	0.570	0.570	0.456	
300-400	av.	2.333	3.000	3.000	3.000	3.000	3.000	2.667	(6)
	s.d.	0.745	—	—	—	—	—	0.471	
400-500		—	—	—	—	—	—	—	
500-1,000	av.	1.556	2.667	2.556	2.667	2.667	2.667	2.556	(9)
	s.d.	0.831	0.667	0.497	0.471	0.471	0.667	0.685	
1,000-2,000	av.	2.111	2.556	2.556	2.333	2.444	2.667	2.222	(9)
	s.d.	0.567	0.497	0.956	0.471	0.497	0.471	0.416	
2,000 +	av.	2.000	2.308	2.815	2.692	2.923	2.692	2.333	(13)
	s.d.	0.555	0.606	0.836	0.462	0.266	0.462	0.471	
4. Geographical location									
Africa	av.	2.000	2.714	2.462	2.857	2.786	2.786	2.500	(14)
	s.d.	0.926	0.452	0.929	0.350	0.410	0.410	0.500	
Asia	av.	1.826	2.826	2.864	2.783	2.696	2.739	2.591	(23)
	s.d.	0.761	0.379	0.343	0.412	0.547	0.529	0.492	
Australia &	av.	2.333	2.667	3.000	3.000	3.000	3.000	2.667	(3)
Oceania	s.d.	0.471	0.471	—	—	—	—	0.471	

. 0=none; 1=slight; 2=partial; 3=complete.
. Seventy-eight universities for information on the selection of students and general objectives.

TABLE V. (*continued*)

		Finance[1]	Curri-culum	Selection students	Staff recruit-ment	Academic object.	Research policy	General object.	Sample
Europe	av.	2.111	2.389	2.389	2.389	2.611	2.556	2.176	(18)
	s.d.	0.737	0.678	0.951	0.487	0.487	0.598	0.513	
North America	av.	1.800	2.400	3.000	3.000	3.000	2.600	2.400	(5)
	s.d.	0.748	0.480	—	—	—	0.490	0.490	
Latin & Cent.	av.	2.059	2.824	2.941	2.941	2.824	2.882	2.824	(17)
America	s.d.	0.639	0.381	0.235	0.235	0.381	0.322	0.381	
5. University size by number of students									
0-5,000	av.	1.972	2.694	2.706	2.861	2.750	2.861	2.686	(36)
	s.d.	0.866	0.517	0.666	0.346	0.493	0.419	0.464	
5,000-10,000	av.	2.050	2.650	2.750	2.650	2.700	2.700	2.368	(20)
	s.d.	0.497	0.477	0.698	0.477	0.458	0.458	0.482	
10,000 and over	av.	1.958	2.667	2.708	2.708	2.792	2.583	2.417	(24)
	s.d.	0.789	0.553	0.676	0.455	0.406	0.571	0.571	
6. Emphasis on field of study									
Pure science	av.	1.889	2.444	2.778	2.556	2.667	2.667	2.556	(9)
	s.d.	0.314	0.497	0.416	0.497	0.471	0.471	0.497	
Humanities	av.	1.571	2.571	3.000	2.857	3.000	2.714	2.429	(7)
	s.d.	0.728	0.495	—	0.350	—	0.452	0.495	
Social sciences	av.	2.250	3.000	2.500	2.750	2.750	3.000	2.250	(4)
	s.d.	0.433	—	0.866	0.433	0.433	—	0.433	
Professional	av.	2.087	2.522	2.609	2.652	2.522	2.652	2.455	(23)
training	s.d.	0.717	0.580	0.872	0.476	0.580	0.560	0.498	
No special	av.	2.000	2.811	2.750	2.865	2.865	2.784	2.611	(37)
emphasis	s.d.	0.870	0.455	0.595	0.342	0.342	0.473	0.541	
7. Emphasis on university function									
Undergraduate	av.	1.965	2.719	2.727	2.825	2.789	2.789	2.625	(57)
teaching	s.d.	0.772	0.449	0.673	0.380	0.449	0.449	0.484	
Graduate teaching	av.	2.056	2.556	2.722	2.556	2.667	2.611	2.278	(18)
	s.d.	0.621	0.598	0.731	0.497	0.471	0.487	0.448	
Research	av.	2.000	3.000	3.000	3.000	3.000	3.000	3.000	(2)
	s.d.	—	—	—	—	—	—	—	
Teacher training	av.	2.000	2.333	2.333	2.667	2.333	2.333	2.000	(3)
	s.d.	1.414	0.943	0.471	0.471	0.471	0.943	0.816	
8. Type of control									
Private	av.	2.000	2.687	2.929	2.812	2.812	2.750	2.625	(16)
	s.d.	0.791	0.464	0.258	0.390	0.527	0.559	0.484	
Public	av.	1.984	2.672	2.672	2.750	2.734	2.734	2.500	(64)
	s.d.	0.760	0.532	0.730	0.433	0.442	0.476	0.531	
9. Type of admission system									
Open	av.	2.111	2.667	2.556	2.778	2.778	2.889	2.667	(9)
	s.d.	0.875	0.471	0.956	0.416	0.416	0.314	0.471	
Selective	av.	2.000	2.741	2.804	2.793	2.741	2.759	2.589	(58)
	s.d.	0.743	0.438	0.515	0.405	0.476	0.466	0.492	
Mixed	av.	1.846	2.385	2.462	2.615	2.769	2.538	2.154	(13)
	s.d.	0.769	0.738	0.929	0.487	0.421	0.634	0.533	

1. 0=none; 1=slight; 2=partial; 3=complete.

ᴛABLE **V.** (*continued*)

	Finance[1]	Curri-culum	Selection students	Staff recruit-ment	Academic object.	Research policy	General object.	Sample
D. Matrix of correlation coefficients between scores obtained by universities in different areas of decision-making								
Ɪ̲inance	1.00	0.210	0.117	0.144	0.027	0.223	0.336	
ᴄurriculum		1.00	0.410	0.386	0.392	0.448	0.361	
ᴇlection of students			1.00	0.295	0.149	0.118	0.335	
ᴛaff recruitment				1.00	0.462	0.417	0.459	
ᴀcademic objectives					1.00	0.426	0.345	
ᴙesearch						1.00	0.349	
ᴇeneral objectives							1.00	

0=none; 1=slight; 2=partial; 3=complete.

TABLE VA. The involvement of different bodies in the internal decision-making process: average score and standard deviation of the relative importance of decision-making bodies in different areas

Areas of decision-making	Central govt. Av.[1]	s.d.	Regional govt. Av.	s.d.	Senate or univ. council Av.	s.d.	Univ. admin. Av.	s.d.	Decision-making bodies — Faculty Av.	s.d.	Department Av.	s.d.	Individual professors Av.	s.d.	Senior teach. staff Av.	s.d.	Junior teach. staff Av.	s.d.	Students Av.	s.d.
1. Overall sample																				
Major alloc. of funds	1.434	1.665 (76)[2]	0.672	1.209 (58)	3.403	1.084 (77)	3.000	0.796 (79)	1.986	1.020 (74)	1.806	0.844 (72)	0.826	0.947 (69)	0.942	0.946 (69)	0.443	0.824 (70)	0.375	0.735 (72)
Planning and development	2.054	1.635 (74)	1.089	1.491 (56)	3.467	0.806 (75)	3.053	0.776 (76)	2.041	0.942 (75)	2.041	0.943 (73)	1.157	0.995 (70)	1.174	1.021 (69)	0.783	0.849 (69)	0.783	1.020 (69)
Decision on stud. admissions	0.900	1.375 (70)	0.364	0.881 (55)	2.808	1.576 (73)	2.767	1.530 (75)	2.438	1.227 (73)	1.901	1.177 (71)	0.841	1.072 (69)	0.794	1.008 (68)	0.544	0.848 (68)	0.783	0.757 (68)
Staff appointments	0.822	1.474 (73)	0.232	0.906 (56)	2.921	1.511 (76)	2.960	1.183 (75)	2.361	1.194 (72)	2.289	0.984 (76)	1.123	1.216 (73)	0.915	1.097 (71)	0.441	0.811 (68)	0.254	0.706 (71)
Curriculum approval	0.861	1.548 (72)	0.218	0.802 (55)	3.316	1.300 (76)	2.192	1.421 (75)	2.945	0.680 (72)	2.773	0.704 (76)	1.761	1.156 (73)	1.803	1.121 (71)	1.232	1.169 (68)	0.863	0.997 (73)
Research policy	0.914	1.432 (70)	0.455	1.076 (55)	3.027	1.479 (74)	2.408	1.459 (71)	2.638	1.049 (69)	2.639	0.838 (72)	2.137	1.077 (73)	2.278	1.096 (72)	1.420	1.172 (69)	0.382	0.687 (68)
Innovation	1.062	1.356 (64)	0.472	1.002 (53)	3.408	1.145 (71)	2.915	1.123 (71)	2.631	0.869 (65)	2.308	0.943 (65)	1.562	1.130 (64)	1.646	1.143 (65)	1.097	1.132 (62)	0.800	1.041 (65)
Extra-curricular activities	0.435	1.026 (62)	0.294	0.847 (51)	2.924	1.460 (66)	3.015	1.234 (65)	2.065	1.401 (62)	1.787	1.243 (61)	1.238	1.164 (63)	1.375	1.205 (64)	1.111	1.142 (63)	1.985	1.191 (67)
2A. Existence of a planning system: central and university planning																				
Major alloc. of funds	1.600	1.356	1.000	1.225	4.000	—	2.750	1.090	2.800	0.400	2.200	0.748	1.400	0.490	1.200	0.748	0.800	0.748	0.400	0.490
Planning and development	3.400	1.200	3.250	1.299	3.200	0.400	3.250	0.433	2.200	0.400	2.000	0.632	1.800	0.748	1.400	1.020	1.400	1.020	1.000	1.095
Decision on stud. admissions	1.000	1.549	0.250	0.433	2.000	1.673	3.000	1.732	3.400	0.490	1.000	1.095	1.800	1.470	1.400	1.356	1.400	1.356	1.400	1.356
Staff appointments	2.400	1.960	1.500	1.658	2.400	1.356	2.000	1.581	3.000	0.632	2.800	0.748	1.800	1.166	1.200	1.166	0.800	1.166	0.600	1.200
Curriculum approval	2.400	1.960	1.500	1.785	3.200	1.166	2.000	1.500	3.000	0.632	2.400	0.490	1.600	1.020	1.600	1.020	1.200	1.166	1.000	1.095
Research policy	3.600	0.800	2.250	1.785	3.200	0.748	2.500	1.500	3.000	0.632	2.400	0.490	2.000	0.632	1.800	0.748	1.000	1.095	0.600	1.200
Innovation	2.250	1.785	1.750	1.299	4.000	—	3.250	0.829	3.000	0.707	2.500	0.500	2.000	0.707	2.000	0.707	1.250	1.090	1.250	1.090
Extra-curricular activities	1.250	1.639	1.500	1.118	3.500	0.866	3.250	0.433	3.250	0.433	2.750	0.433	2.000	0.707	2.000	0.707	1.250	1.090	1.250	1.090

1. 0 = no involvement; 1 = informed; 2 = consulted; 3 = active participation; 4 = final decision or veto.
2. Figures in brackets indicate number of responding universities.

Areas of decision-making	Central govt.		Regional govt.		Senate or univ. council		Univ. admin.		Faculty		Department		Individual professors		Senior teach. staff		Junior teach. staff		Students	
	Av.[1]	s.d.	Av.	s.d.	Av.	s.d.	Av.	s.d.	Av.	s.d.	Av.	s.d.	Av.	s.d.	Av.	s.d.	Av.	s.d.	Av.	s.d.
2B. *Existence of a planning system: central planning only*																				
Major alloc. of funds	1.333	1.886	1.333	1.886	2.333	1.700	3.667	0.471	2.500	0.500	2.667	0.471	—	—	0.667	0.943	—	—	—	—
Planning and development	4.000	—	1.333	1.886	2.333	1.247	3.333	0.471	2.500	0.500	1.667	0.247	1.000	0.816	0.667	0.471	0.333	0.471	0.333	0.471
Decision on stud. admissions	2.000	1.633	0.667	0.943	2.000	1.633	3.667	0.471	2.000	1.000	1.333	1.267	0.333	0.471	0.333	0.471	0.333	0.471	0.333	0.471
Staff appointments	0.667	0.471	—	—	2.667	1.886	3.667	0.471	2.500	0.500	1.667	1.247	1.667	1.247	—	—	—	—	—	—
Curriculum approval	0.667	0.471	—	—	2.667	1.886	3.333	0.471	3.000	—	3.000	—	0.667	0.943	1.333	0.943	0.333	0.471	0.667	0.471
Research policy	0.667	0.943	—	—	2.333	1.700	2.667	1.247	2.500	0.500	1.667	1.247	2.333	0.943	2.333	1.247	2.000	0.816	0.667	0.471
Innovation	1.333	0.943	0.667	0.943	2.333	1.700	3.667	0.471	2.000	—	2.333	0.471	1.333	0.471	1.667	0.471	1.667	0.943	1.333	0.471
Extra-curricular activities	0.333	0.471	—	—	1.667	1.700	3.667	0.471	3.000	—	3.000	—	1.000	0.816	1.333	0.943	1.333	0.943	2.667	0.471
2C. *Existence of a planning system: university planning only*																				
Major alloc. of funds	1.467	1.668	1.100	1.513	3.375	1.111	3.294	0.570	2.312	0.845	2.133	0.806	1.000	1.038	1.286	1.097	0.786	0.773	0.643	0.895
Planning and development	1.643	1.288	1.778	1.685	3.312	0.982	3.294	0.570	2.333	0.699	2.133	0.884	1.429	0.904	1.667	1.011	1.000	0.816	1.071	0.961
Decision on stud. admissions	0.857	1.355	0.667	1.247	3.214	1.145	3.500	0.612	2.733	0.680	2.000	1.000	0.923	1.141	0.769	1.049	0.538	0.746	0.692	0.821
Staff appointments	0.571	1.178	0.556	1.257	2.867	1.408	3.235	1.002	2.800	0.748	2.588	0.844	0.857	1.059	1.214	1.206	0.417	0.640	0.385	0.625
Curriculum approval	0.714	1.436	0.556	1.257	3.750	0.661	3.267	0.680	3.000	0.516	2.750	0.661	1.571	1.116	1.857	0.990	1.286	1.097	1.375	1.166
Research policy	0.538	1.151	1.222	1.474	3.467	1.087	3.133	1.087	2.667	1.011	2.647	0.588	2.062	1.088	2.375	1.111	1.500	1.180	0.643	0.811
Innovation	0.769	1.120	0.800	1.249	3.333	1.247	3.375	0.599	2.786	0.674	2.533	0.718	1.692	1.136	1.846	1.167	1.167	1.143	1.083	1.187
Extra-curricular activities	0.091	0.287	0.500	1.323	3.000	1.414	3.429	0.623	2.429	1.178	1.917	1.320	1.167	0.986	1.615	1.332	1.083	1.037	2.143	1.187
2D. *Existence of a planning system: some planning*																				
Major alloc. of funds	1.273	1.601	0.385	0.788	3.455	1.047	2.824	0.923	1.812	1.044	1.781	0.739	0.935	1.014	0.967	0.912	0.400	0.554	0.375	0.696
Planning and development	1.750	1.620	0.760	1.176	3.677	0.590	2.879	0.977	2.121	1.122	2.187	0.808	1.167	1.067	1.250	0.987	0.750	0.829	0.897	1.185
Decision on stud. admissions	0.900	1.422	0.208	0.576	2.969	1.610	2.219	1.473	2.161	1.393	1.903	1.228	0.700	0.900	0.724	0.943	0.483	0.725	0.310	0.463
Staff appointments	0.613	1.336	—	—	2.758	1.634	2.625	1.317	1.933	1.289	2.182	1.058	1.212	1.225	0.800	1.013	0.467	0.846	0.219	0.739
Curriculum approval	0.935	1.664	—	—	3.281	1.375	1.687	1.379	3.031	0.585	2.727	0.750	1.903	1.088	1.903	1.174	1.345	1.239	0.806	0.858
Research policy	0.724	1.257	0.125	0.439	3.133	1.522	1.933	1.548	2.357	1.042	2.690	0.835	2.000	1.183	2.300	1.215	1.414	1.190	0.321	0.601
Innovation	1.040	1.399	0.182	0.649	3.552	0.932	2.663	1.278	2.444	0.994	2.000	1.155	1.370	1.191	1.481	1.192	1.038	1.192	0.786	1.113
Extra-curricular activities	0.444	1.165	0.043	0.204	3.000	1.509	2.714	1.411	1.440	1.329	1.192	1.177	1.071	1.193	1.179	1.255	1.107	1.205	1.800	1.137

Decision-making bodies

1. 0 = no involvement; 1 = informed; 2 = consulted; 3 = active participation; 4 = final decision or veto.

TABLE V.A. *(continued)*

Areas of decision-making	Decision-making bodies																			
	Central govt.		Regional govt.		Senate or univ. council		Univ. admin.		Faculty		Department		Individual professors		Senior teach. staff		Junior teach. staff		Students	
	Av.[1]	s.d.	Av.	s.d.	Av.	s.d.	Av.	s.d.	Av.	s.d.	Av.	s.d.	Av.	s.d.	Av.	s.d.	Av.	s.d.	Av.	s.d.
2E. Existence of a planning system: no planning																				
Major alloc. of funds	1.650	1.768	0.667	1.247	3.350	1.014	3.000	0.535	1.737	1.068	1.294	0.824	0.471	0.696	0.588	0.771	0.222	0.416	0.222	0.711
Planning and development	2.200	1.691	0.600	1.083	3.500	0.742	3.053	0.510	2.250	0.887	1.778	1.133	0.778	0.853	0.667	0.882	0.556	0.762	0.389	0.591
Decision on stud. admissions	0.722	1.096	0.400	1.020	2.579	1.600	2.990	1.071	2.450	1.244	2.167	1.067	0.633	1.067	0.833	0.957	0.444	0.831	0.500	0.687
Staff appointments	0.950	1.564	0.267	0.998	3.400	1.200	3.053	1.099	2.500	1.245	2.167	0.833	0.889	1.197	0.947	1.099	0.389	0.756	0.167	0.500
Curriculum approval	0.474	1.094	0.067	0.249	3.150	1.388	2.053	1.432	2.737	0.909	2.944	0.705	1.889	1.242	1.722	1.145	1.167	1.118	0.500	0.898
Research policy	0.800	1.327	0.133	0.499	2.619	1.618	2.526	1.313	2.947	1.099	2.778	0.916	2.421	0.936	2.278	0.870	1.389	1.161	1.706	0.373
Innovation	1.000	1.257	0.286	0.795	3.300	1.229	2.778	1.133	2.778	0.786	2.562	0.704	1.706	1.125	1.667	1.054	1.000	1.085	0.444	0.685
Extra-curricular activities	0.471	0.848	0.308	0.821	2.824	1.339	3.000	1.369	2.294	1.486	2.187	1.014	1.437	1.273	1.375	1.053	1.062	1.144	2.250	1.250
3A. Level of economic development: developing																				
Major alloc. of funds	1.352	1.612	0.500	0.982	3.418	1.056	2.982	0.790	2.000	0.991	1.788	0.840	0.745	0.946	0.941	1.018	0.385	0.625	0.407	0.806
Planning and development	1.887	1.500	0.825	1.282	3.556	0.786	3.019	0.828	2.241	0.961	2.039	0.928	1.096	0.986	1.154	1.026	0.654	0.757	0.731	1.058
Decision on stud. admissions	1.075	1.439	0.250	0.698	2.943	1.472	2.743	1.324	2.396	1.234	2.173	1.087	0.733	0.989	0.712	0.947	0.385	0.655	0.327	0.469
Staff appointments	0.660	1.331	—	—	3.125	1.377	2.944	1.096	2.176	1.183	2.283	0.855	0.923	1.007	0.745	1.007	0.280	0.531	0.154	0.411
Curriculum approval	0.755	1.465	—	—	3.429	1.208	2.151	1.379	2.925	0.578	2.759	0.768	1.712	1.149	1.745	1.135	1.157	1.127	0.704	0.936
Research policy	0.706	1.209	0.175	0.543	3.111	1.461	2.451	1.473	2.608	1.011	2.706	0.799	1.923	1.107	2.173	1.069	1.260	1.092	0.294	0.570
Innovation	0.958	1.258	0.359	0.800	3.346	1.207	2.804	1.221	2.520	0.900	2.245	1.041	1.375	1.166	1.437	1.206	0.894	1.096	0.612	0.965
Extra-curricular activities	0.362	0.885	0.135	0.528	2.816	1.534	3.021	1.283	1.979	1.407	1.787	1.202	1.065	1.168	1.167	1.230	0.915	1.127	1.833	1.230
3B. Level of economic development: developed																				
Major alloc. of funds	1.636	1.772	1.125	1.576	3.364	1.130	3.043	0.806	1.952	1.090	1.850	0.853	1.056	0.911	0.944	0.705	0.611	0.591	0.278	0.448
Planning and development	2.476	1.867	1.750	1.750	3.238	0.811	3.136	0.625	2.143	0.886	2.045	0.976	1.333	1.000	1.235	1.002	1.176	0.984	0.941	0.672
Decision on stud. admissions	0.353	0.967	0.667	1.193	2.450	1.774	2.900	1.338	2.550	1.203	1.156	1.089	1.123	1.269	1.062	1.144	1.062	1.144	1.125	1.111
Staff appointments	1.250	1.728	0.813	1.550	2.350	1.711	3.000	1.380	2.810	1.096	2.304	1.231	1.619	1.327	1.350	1.195	0.889	1.197	0.526	1.141
Curriculum approval	1.158	1.725	0.800	1.376	3.000	1.483	2.300	1.520	3.000	0.894	2.810	0.499	1.895	1.165	1.950	1.071	1.444	1.257	1.316	1.029
Research policy	1.474	1.788	0.800	1.641	2.800	1.503	2.300	1.148	2.722	1.145	2.476	0.906	2.617	0.777	2.550	1.117	1.842	1.268	0.647	0.904
Innovation	1.375	1.576	0.786	1.372	3.579	0.936	3.200	0.748	3.000	0.632	2.500	0.500	2.125	0.781	2.235	0.644	1.733	0.998	1.375	1.053
Extra-curricular activities	0.667	1.350	0.717	1.278	3.235	1.165	3.000	1.085	2.357	1.342	1.786	1.372	1.706	1.015	2.000	0.866	1.687	0.982	2.368	0.985

1. 0 = no involvement; 1 = informed; 2 = consulted; 3 = active participation; 4 = final decision or veto.

	Decision-making bodies																			
Areas of decision-making	Central govt.		Regional govt.		Senate or univ. council		Univ. admin.		Faculty		Department		Individual professors		Senior teach. staff		Junior teach. staff		Students	
	Av.¹	s.d.	Av.	s.d.	Av.	s.d.	Av.	s.d.	Av.	s.d.	Av.	s.d.	Av.	s.d.	Av.	s.d.	Av.	s.d.	Av.	s.d.
4A. Geographical location: Africa																				
Major alloc. of funds	1.846	1.657	0.444	1.257	3.357	0.895	3.000	1.000	2.571	0.495	1.909	0.514	0.833	1.067	1.308	1.202	0.500	0.732	0.286	0.589
Planning and development	2.786	1.319	0.444	1.257	3.357	0.895	2.929	0.961	2.643	0.479	2.167	0.553	1.154	1.026	1.143	0.990	0.714	0.795	0.786	1.145
Decision on stud. admissions	1.786	1.612	0.222	0.629	2.692	1.488	2.786	1.206	2.500	0.982	2.182	1.029	0.769	0.890	0.462	0.634	0.385	0.487	0.250	0.433
Staff appointments	1.357	1.757	—	—	3.214	1.372	2.385	1.077	2.500	0.824	2.462	0.499	1.385	1.211	0.643	0.972	0.231	0.421	0.077	0.266
Curriculum approval	1.077	1.639	—	—	3.286	1.385	2.417	1.382	3.071	0.258	2.923	0.266	1.750	1.299	1.923	1.141	1.538	1.216	0.571	0.821
Research policy	1.167	1.462	—	—	2.692	1.682	2.417	1.081	2.786	1.081	2.833	0.553	2.333	1.027	2.308	0.821	1.417	0.954	0.083	0.276
Innovation	1.583	1.441	0.222	0.629	2.929	1.437	2.929	1.033	2.643	0.811	2.500	0.764	1.833	1.143	1.846	1.099	1.231	1.120	0.846	1.099
Extra-curricular activities	0.545	1.157	—	—	2.333	1.700	2.917	1.115	2.417	1.320	2.167	1.280	1.455	1.373	1.500	1.258	1.250	1.233	1.917	1.320
4B. Geographical location: Asia																				
Major alloc. of funds	1.182	1.585	0.813	1.073	3.500	1.077	2.696	0.748	1.381	1.045	1.545	0.839	0.591	0.887	0.500	0.783	0.182	0.386	0.045	0.208
Planning and development	1.905	1.630	1.600	1.356	3.524	0.852	2.762	0.750	1.727	1.135	1.857	1.037	0.810	0.906	0.762	1.019	0.381	0.722	0.333	0.714
Decision on stud. admissions	0.818	1.370	0.438	0.933	2.364	1.720	2.348	1.521	2.286	1.485	2.136	1.217	0.545	0.838	0.591	0.834	0.273	0.538	0.136	0.343
Staff appointments	0.636	1.263	—	—	3.174	1.403	2.714	1.201	1.526	1.352	2.000	0.976	0.714	1.030	0.400	0.735	0.200	0.510	0.048	0.213
Curriculum approval	0.545	1.269	—	—	3.478	1.016	1.773	1.505	2.952	0.653	2.636	0.979	1.864	1.057	1.524	1.180	0.905	0.971	0.364	0.643
Research policy	0.455	1.157	0.125	0.484	3.130	1.483	2.182	1.641	2.650	1.014	2.810	0.794	2.000	1.087	1.773	1.165	1.091	1.083	0.136	0.343
Innovation	0.800	1.166	0.467	1.024	3.619	0.785	2.550	1.244	2.211	1.055	1.650	1.108	1.050	1.023	0.950	0.973	0.450	0.740	0.150	0.477
Extra-curricular activities	0.409	0.937	0.250	0.750	2.636	1.524	2.810	1.531	1.286	1.485	1.286	1.119	0.810	1.139	0.864	1.140	0.909	1.203	2.045	1.147
4C. Geographical location: Australia and Oceania																				
Major alloc. of funds	2.500	0.500	—	—	4.000	—	3.000	—	3.000	—	2.500	0.500	2.500	0.500	2.000	—	1.500	0.500	1.500	0.500
Planning and development	2.500	0.500	—	—	4.000	—	3.000	—	2.500	0.500	2.667	0.471	2.000	—	2.000	—	2.000	—	2.000	—
Decision on stud. admissions	1.500	1.500	—	—	4.000	—	3.000	—	2.500	0.500	2.333	0.943	2.000	1.000	1.500	0.500	0.500	0.500	0.500	0.500
Staff appointments	—	—	—	—	4.000	—	2.500	0.500	3.000	—	3.000	—	3.000	—	2.500	0.500	0.500	0.500	0.500	0.500
Curriculum approval	—	—	—	—	4.000	—	2.000	1.000	3.000	—	3.000	—	3.000	—	3.000	—	0.500	0.500	—	—
Research policy	1.500	1.500	—	—	4.000	—	3.000	—	3.000	—	2.667	0.471	2.500	0.500	2.667	0.471	2.500	0.500	2.000	—
Innovation	2.000	—	—	—	4.000	—	3.000	—	2.000	—	2.500	0.500	2.000	—	2.500	0.500	2.000	—	2.000	—
Extra-curricular activities	—	—	—	—	4.000	—	3.000	—	1.000	—	1.000	—	1.000	—	1.000	—	1.000	—	2.000	1.000

1. 0 = no involvement; 1 = informed; 2 = consulted; 3 = active participation; 4 = final decision or veto.

TABLE VA. (continued)

Areas of decision-making	Central govt.		Regional govt.		Senate or univ. council		Univ. admin.		Faculty		Department		Individual professors		Senior teach. staff		Junior teach. staff		Students	
	Av.[1]	s.d.	Av.	s.d.	Av.	s.d.	Av.	s.d.	Av.	s.d.	Av.	s.d.	Av.	s.d.	Av.	s.d.	Av.	s.d.	Av.	s.d.
4D. *Geographical location: Europe*																				
Major alloc. of funds	1.833	1.803	0.846	1.406	3.294	1.125	2.941	0.872	2.000	1.118	1.875	0.927	0.933	0.854	0.867	0.718	0.533	0.618	0.200	0.400
Planning and development	2.778	1.750	1.308	1.814	3.235	0.807	3.125	0.599	2.312	0.982	1.824	1.150	1.200	1.046	1.071	1.033	1.000	1.000	0.786	0.939
Decision on stud. admissions	0.429	1.050	0.417	0.862	2.312	1.826	3.067	1.340	2.600	1.405	1.133	1.204	0.923	1.269	1.000	1.240	0.800	1.240	1.154	1.231
Staff appointments	1.412	1.817	0.692	1.435	2.471	1.684	3.125	1.317	2.765	1.165	2.059	1.349	1.437	1.413	1.312	1.356	0.800	1.275	0.467	1.204
Curriculum approval	1.312	1.828	0.667	1.732	2.437	1.802	1.933	1.652	2.875	1.053	2.875	0.599	2.000	1.155	2.000	1.033	1.429	1.294	1.143	1.187
Research policy	1.562	1.836	1.000	1.581	2.353	1.607	1.867	1.500	2.429	1.400	2.200	1.166	2.750	0.750	2.800	0.980	1.868	1.408	0.385	0.836
Innovation	1.385	1.689	0.636	1.150	2.067	1.569	2.733	1.289	3.250	0.595	2.727	0.617	2.250	0.924	2.308	0.821	1.667	1.312	1.154	1.167
Extra-curricular activities	0.750	1.479	0.545	0.988	2.846	1.406	2.846	1.350	2.900	1.136	2.182	1.266	1.769	1.049	1.846	1.026	1.385	1.146	1.923	1.071
4E. *Geographical location: North America*																				
Major alloc. of funds	1.000	1.732	1.750	1.785	2.500	1.500	3.600	0.490	1.800	0.748	2.000	—	0.667	0.471	0.667	0.471	0.667	0.471	0.333	0.471
Planning and development	—		2.750	0.829	3.000	0.707	3.600	0.490	1.750	0.433	2.250	0.433	1.000	0.816	1.000	0.816	1.000	0.816	0.667	0.471
Decision on stud. admissions	—		1.250	1.639	3.500	0.866	3.000	1.095	2.500	0.500	1.667	0.471	1.000	0.816	1.000	0.816	1.000	0.816	0.667	0.471
Staff appointments	—		1.000	1.732	1.667	1.700	3.800	0.400	2.750	0.433	2.800	0.400	1.250	0.829	1.250	0.829	1.000	0.816	0.750	0.829
Curriculum approval	—		1.000	1.732	3.500	0.866	3.200	0.748	2.750	0.433	2.750	0.433	1.500	1.118	1.500	1.118	1.500	1.118	1.000	0.632
Research policy	—		1.500	1.658	4.000	—	3.400	0.490	2.750	0.433	2.800	0.400	2.400	0.490	1.500	1.118	1.500	1.118	0.750	0.829
Innovation	—		1.000	1.732	3.500	0.500	3.600	0.490	2.667	0.471	2.500	0.500	1.750	0.829	2.000	0.816	2.000	0.816	1.000	0.816
Extra-curricular activities	—		1.000	1.732	3.250	1.299	3.500	0.500	1.250	0.829	0.333	0.471	1.000	0.707	2.000	0.816	2.000	0.816	3.200	0.400
4F. *Geographical location: Latin and Central America*																				
Major alloc. of funds	1.000	1.455	0.250	0.559	3.529	1.036	3.294	0.456	2.235	0.876	1.882	0.963	0.867	0.884	1.286	0.881	0.500	0.627	0.938	1.088
Planning and development	1.125	1.053	0.333	0.789	3.765	0.546	3.294	0.749	2.471	0.696	2.250	0.829	1.500	0.935	1.800	0.748	1.000	0.632	1.267	1.123
Decision on stud. admissions	0.733	1.062	0.071	0.258	3.687	0.383	3.176	0.923	2.412	1.032	2.059	0.996	1.062	1.197	1.067	1.181	0.600	0.879	0.688	0.464
Staff appointments	0.200	0.542	—		2.882	1.367	3.059	1.056	2.647	0.967	2.471	0.848	0.750	0.901	1.133	0.957	0.467	0.618	0.375	0.599
Curriculum approval	0.938	1.560	—		3.824	0.513	2.562	1.223	2.941	0.539	2.706	0.666	1.312	1.044	1.733	0.998	0.933	0.998	1.312	0.982
Research policy	0.800	0.980	0.357	0.718	3.562	0.864	2.867	1.147	2.625	0.781	2.625	0.696	1.437	1.116	2.600	0.952	1.286	1.030	0.667	0.699
Innovation	0.867	1.087	0.357	0.610	3.812	0.527	3.312	0.768	2.687	0.583	2.625	0.696	1.400	1.143	1.643	1.231	1.154	1.026	1.200	1.046
Extra-curricular activities	0.231	0.421	0.083	0.276	3.786	0.558	3.429	0.623	2.643	0.811	2.308	0.910	1.308	0.991	1.538	1.216	0.833	0.799	1.538	1.151

1. 0 = no involvement; 1 = informed; 2 = consulted; 3 = active participation; 4 = final decision or veto.

TABLE VA. (*continued*)

Areas of decision-making	Central govt.[1]		Regional govt.		Senate or univ. council		Univ. admin.		Faculty		Department		Individual professors		Senior teach. staff		Junior teach. staff		Students	
	Av.[1]	s.d.	Av.	s.d.	Av.	s.d.	Av.	s.d.	Av.	s.d.	Av.	s.d.	Av.	s.d.	Av.	s.d.	Av.	s.d.	Av.	s.d.
5A. Type of control: private																				
Major alloc. of funds	1.200	1.470	0.900	1.221	3.133	1.408	3.062	0.966	1.786	1.143	1.733	0.998	0.533	0.806	0.667	0.943	0.200	0.400	0.267	0.573
Planning and development	1.571	1.635	1.111	1.197	3.571	0.728	2.929	0.961	2.067	0.998	1.786	0.939	0.643	0.811	0.643	0.811	0.429	0.623	0.786	0.939
Decision on stud. admissions	1.000	1.349	—	—	2.800	1.641	2.687	1.210	2.071	1.223	1.629	1.223	0.467	0.712	0.400	0.718	0.333	0.596	0.467	0.618
Staff appointments	0.267	0.998	—	—	2.437	1.580	3.200	0.980	1.929	1.387	2.400	1.083	0.533	0.957	0.333	0.596	0.267	0.442	0.267	0.442
Curriculum approval	0.800	1.600	—	—	3.062	1.391	2.067	1.389	3.000	0.655	2.867	0.884	1.643	1.042	1.571	1.050	1.000	1.000	0.533	0.718
Research policy	0.214	0.773	0.200	0.600	3.200	1.166	3.000	1.069	2.714	0.881	2.857	0.515	1.500	0.961	1.071	0.961	1.071	0.961	0.357	0.479
Innovation	0.714	0.881	0.100	0.300	3.562	0.609	3.200	0.980	2.500	0.906	2.214	1.145	1.500	1.118	1.400	1.143	1.200	1.108	0.733	0.998
Extra-curricular activities	0.154	0.533	—		2.857	1.552	3.385	1.077	1.308	1.323	1.231	1.049	0.692	0.821	0.923	0.997	1.154	1.099	1.692	1.066
5B. Type of control: public																				
Major alloc. of funds	1.492	1.705	0.625	1.201	3.468	0.979	2.984	0.745	2.033	0.983	1.825	0.797	0.907	0.967	1.019	0.933	0.509	0.657	0.404	0.769
Planning and development	2.167	1.614	1.085	1.541	3.443	0.820	3.081	0.725	2.250	0.924	2.102	0.933	1.286	0.995	1.309	1.025	0.873	0.875	0.782	1.039
Decision on stud. admissions	0.873	1.322	0.444	0.956	2.610	1.339	2.814	1.359	2.525	1.212	1.895	1.165	0.944	1.129	0.906	1.051	0.604	0.897	0.528	0.792
Staff appointments	0.966	1.542	0.283	0.993	3.050	1.465	2.900	1.221	2.466	1.118	2.262	0.956	1.276	1.229	1.071	1.147	0.491	0.882	0.250	0.762
Curriculum approval	0.877	1.534	0.267	0.879	3.383	1.266	2.224	1.427	2.932	0.686	2.750	0.649	1.789	1.181	1.860	1.131	1.291	1.201	0.948	1.041
Research policy	1.089	1.503	0.511	1.147	2.983	1.546	2.263	1.505	2.618	1.087	2.586	0.891	2.186	1.097	2.466	1.004	1.509	1.204	0.389	0.731
Innovation	1.160	1.447	0.558	1.085	3.364	1.256	2.839	1.146	2.667	0.856	2.333	0.878	1.580	1.133	1.720	1.132	1.064	1.137	0.820	1.052
Extra-curricular activities	0.510	1.109	0.357	0.921	2.942	1.433	2.923	1.253	2.265	1.352	1.937	1.248	1.380	1.198	1.490	1.227	1.100	1.153	2.056	1.208

1. 0 = no involvement; 1 = informed; 2 = consulted; 3 = active participation; 4 = final decision or veto.

TABLE VI. Trends of change in university structure (1958-68): teaching units

	Percentage of universities where units were added	Percentage of universities where units were dropped	Percentage of universities where units were reorganized
1. Overall sample	92.50	36.25	58.75
2. Existence of a planning system			
Central and university planning	100.00	60.00	100.00
Central planning only	100.00	33.33	33.33
University planning only	100.00	41.17	88.23
Some planning	91.17	35.29	47.05
No planning	85.71	28.57	47.62
3. Level of economic development			
Developing countries	92.85	37.50	55.36
Developed countries	91.66	33.33	66.66
4. Geographical location			
Africa	85.71	35.71	21.43
Asia	95.65	34.78	56.52
Australia and Oceania	100.00	33.33	—
Europe	88.00	33.00	66.00
North America	100.00	60.00	100.00
Latin and Central America	94.11	35.29	82.35
5. University size by number of students			
0-5,000	91.66	36.11	50.00
5,000-10,000	90.00	30.00	70.00
10,000 and over	95.83	41.66	62.50
6. Emphasis on the field of study			
Pure science	100.00	77.77	77.77
Humanities	100.00	57.14	57.14
Social sciences	100.00	25.00	—
Professional training	95.65	34.78	73.91
No special emphasis	24.32	51.35	75.67
7. Emphasis on university function			
Undergraduate teaching	89.47	36.84	61.40
Graduate teaching	100.00	38.89	55.56
Research	100.00	50.00	100.00
Teacher training	100.00	—	—
8. Type of control			
Private	100.00	37.50	62.50
Public	90.62	35.94	57.81
9. Type of admission system			
Open	88.88	33.33	44.44
Selective	91.38	39.65	63.79
Mixed	100.00	23.07	46.15

TABLE VIA. Trends of change in university structure (1958-68): administrative and planning units

	Percentage of universities where responsibilities reorganized	Percentage of universities needing new units	Percentage of universities where existing units out of date
1. Overall sample	75.00	78.75	53.75
2. Existence of planning system			
Central and university planning	100.00	100.00	80.00
Central planning only	100.00	66.66	33.33
University planning only	82.30	70.58	41.17
Some planning	73.53	79.41	50.00
No planning	61.90	80.95	66.66
3. Level of economic development			
Developing countries	67.85	80.35	48.21
Developed countries	91.66	75.00	66.66
4. Geographical location			
Africa	64.28	71.42	35.71
Asia	56.52	86.95	56.52
Australia and Oceania	66.66	33.33	33.33
Europe	83.33	83.33	72.22
North America	100.00	60.00	60.00
Latin and Central America	94.11	82.35	52.94
5. University size by number of students			
0-5,000	72.22	77.70	47.22
5,000-10,000	75.00	80.00	55.00
10,000 and over	79.16	79.16	62.50
6. Type of control			
Private	81.25	75.00	37.65
Public	73.43	79.68	67.18

TABLE VII. Structure of the student body: average number and annual growth rates

		Average number of students						Average annual growth rates of number of students					
		1958/59		1963/64		1968/69		1958/63		1963/68		1958/68	
		No.	Sample	No.	Sample	No.	Sample	%	Sample	%	Sample	%	Sample
1. Overall sample													
Undergraduates		6 818	(49)	7 107	(63)	8 825	(70)	12.85	(46)	13.84	(61)	10.87	(45)
Graduates		2 149	(39)	2 825	(50)	3 024	(59)	15.60	(35)	18.05	(46)	13.80	(33)
TOTAL		9 619	(57)	11 219	(70)	15 207	(78)	14.98	(56)	12.78	(70)	11.82	(56)
2. Existence of a planning system													
Central &	U	9 126	(1)	10 600	(1)	5 718	(2)	3.04	(1)	−0.81	(1)	1.10	(1)
univ.	G	3 386	(4)	5 364	(4)	6 730	(4)	9.42	(4)	5.51	(4)	7.30	(4)
planning	T	7 396	(5)	12 311	(5)	14 714	(5)	12.21	(5)	3.02	(5)	7.46	(5)
Central	U	557	(1)	762	(3)	1 926	(7)	0.88	(1)	29.98	(3)	0.49	(1)
planning	G	246	(3)	288	(1)	161	(2)	3.20	(1)	1.68	(1)	2.44	(1)
only	T	809	(3)	884	(3)	3 546	(3)	2.06	(1)	34.89	(3)	1.34	(1)
Univ.	U	3 669	(12)	4 836	(16)	7 611	(17)	14.15	(11)	15.10	(16)	12.90	(11)
planning	G	5 331	(7)	6 675	(8)	4 737	(14)	10.37	(4)	19.20	(7)	10.10	(4)
only	T	8 376	(13)	11 561	(15)	15 706	(17)	14.62	(12)	13.20	(15)	12.92	(12)
Some	U	10 323	(23)	10 368	(28)	12 228	(31)	10.06	(21)	13.09	(26)	9.35	(20)
planning	G	1 597	(18)	2 339	(25)	2 818	(25)	14.84	(18)	14.56	(22)	11.12	(16)
	T	12 222	(23)	13 178	(30)	18 063	(34)	14.13	(24)	12.17	(30)	11.14	(24)
No	U	3 579	(12)	4 479	(15)	5 415	(17)	18.35	(12)	11.55	(15)	13.21	(12)
planning	G	440	(9)	634	(12)	1 027	(14)	24.55	(8)	29.33	(12)	25.68	(8)
	T	7 734	(14)	8 967	(17)	11 620	(19)	18.66	(14)	12.45	(17)	14.36	(14)
3. Level of economic development													
Developing	U	7 762	(37)	7 775	(49)	10 016	(52)	13.66	(35)	15.09	(48)	11.57	(34)
	G	2 302	(24)	2 799	(34)	2 979	(40)	17.44	(21)	16.91	(31)	12.80	(19)
	T	11 406	(38)	12 300	(49)	17 348	(54)	16.61	(37)	14.72	(49)	13.15	(37)
Developed	U	3 907	(12)	4 768	(14)	5 382	(18)	10.26	(11)	9.24	(13)	8.72	(11)
	G	1 904	(15)	2 879	(16)	3 116	(19)	12.83	(14)	20.42	(15)	15.16	(14)
	T	6 046	(19)	8 695	(21)	10 389	(24)	11.82	(19)	8.26	(21)	9.23	(19)
4. Geographical location													
Africa	U	4 698	(6)	3 769	(12)	4 519	(14)	18.72	(5)	22.98	(12)	15.63	(5)
	G	340	(4)	735	(7)	829	(10)	40.68	(3)	25.12	(7)	27.47	(3)
	T	5 701	(7)	5 881	(11)	6 348	(14)	18.74	(6)	22.15	(11)	15.47	(6)
Asia	U	11 374	(18)	11 807	(21)	14 693	(21)	11.00	(17)	9.63	(20)	8.03	(16)
	G	1 218	(17)	1 488	(20)	2 215	(18)	13.84	(17)	9.95	(17)	10.54	(15)
	T	13 359	(18)	14 809	(21)	22 574	(22)	15.93	(18)	10.24	(21)	10.77	(18)
Australia	U	—	—	2 438	(1)	3 523	(2)	—	—	23.55	(1)	—	—
and	G	—	—	116	(1)	215	(2)	—	—	30.02	(1)	—	—
Oceania	T	720	(1)	2 673	(2)	4 558	(3)	27.47	(1)	18.28	(2)	18.34	(1)

TABLE VII. (*continued*)

		Average number of students						Average annual growth rates of number of students					
		1958/59		1963/64		1968/69		1958/63		1963/68		1958/68	
		No.	Sample	No.	Sample	No.	Sample	%	Sample	%	Sample	%	Sample
Europe[1]	U	5 633	(9)	4 657	(9)	2 220	(13)	13.01	(8)	6.50	(8)	9.65	(8)
	G	3 609	(11)	3 714	(11)	5 671	(13)	7.93	(9)	23.26	(10)	13.62	(9)
	T	5 761	(14)	8 934	(14)	9 582	(17)	13.79	(14)	6.96	(14)	10.26	(14)
N. America	U	2 987	(4)	4 540	(5)	7 354	(5)	13.35	(4)	11.63	(5)	11.82	(4)
	G	554	(4)	957	(4)	1 438	(5)	25.64	(4)	16.45	(4)	20.68	(4)
	T	5 937	(4)	8 140	(5)	12 134	(5)	11.25	(4)	11.05	(5)	10.30	(4)
Latin and	U	4 091	(12)	5 250	(15)	9 438	(15)	12.74	(12)	16.16	(15)	13.10	(12)
Central	G	11 709	(3)	8 954	(7)	6 737	(11)	7.29	(2)	22.44	(7)	4.85	(2)
America[1]	T	12 620	(13)	14 027	(17)	21 377	(17)	13.42	(13)	14.52	(17)	13.25	(13)
5. University size by number of students													
0-5,000	U	952	(18)	1 689	(26)	2 242	(33)	18.34	(17)	17.92	(26)	14.40	(17)
	G	93	(11)	174	(17)	250	(24)	16.52	(9)	31.59	(15)	19.15	(8)
	T	1 016	(19)	1 976	(27)	2 750	(35)	21.34	(18)	17.70	(27)	16.44	(18)
5,000-10,000	U	2 006	(14)	3 108	(18)	4 727	(18)	13.09	(13)	10.27	(18)	10.34	(13)
	G	882	(15)	1 486	(17)	1 867	(19)	20.48	(14)	13.56	(17)	15.60	(14)
	T	3 057	(17)	4 770	(20)	7 107	(20)	16.68	(17)	10.67	(20)	11.82	(17)
10,000 +	U	16 992	(17)	18 309	(19)	24 146	(19)	6.82	(16)	11.39	(17)	7.33	(15)
	G	5 350	(13)	7 063	(16)	8 558	(16)	9.21	(12)	9.00	(14)	7.64	(11)
	T	22 715	(21)	27 676	(23)	41 206	(23)	8.16	(21)	8.84	(23)	7.87	(21)
6. Emphasis on field of study													
Science	U	1 386	(5)	2 838	(7)	3 648	(8)	14.18	(4)	6.59	(7)	8.61	(4)
	G	1 826	(5)	2 174	(8)	2 850	(8)	26.13	(5)	17.61	(8)	16.48	(5)
	T	3 428	(8)	5 807	(9)	7 774	(9)	20.17	(8)	7.09	(9)	12.66	(8)
Humanities	U	1 106	(4)	2 703	(5)	33 667	(5)	19.66	(4)	10.10	(5)	15.94	(4)
	G	249	(2)	329	(4)	682	(4)	36.10	(2)	20.16	(4)	29.28	(2)
	T	1 840	(6)	3 990	(7)	6 096	(7)	19.36	(6)	10.73	(7)	15.75	(6)
Soc. Sciences	U	1 832	(3)	3 717	(3)	4 671	(4)	27.25	(2)	23.09	(3)	21.76	(2)
	G	357	(3)	899	(2)	771	(4)	10.37	(2)	74.41	(2)	35.86	(2)
	T	3 064	(3)	9 906	(2)	9 115	(4)	28.14	(2)	20.32	(2)	24.16	(2)
Professional training	U	2 719	(15)	3 209	(18)	5 488	(20)	14.26	(15)	17.37	(18)	13.11	(15)
	G	337	(10)	1 734	(14)	2 044	(16)	15.10	(8)	16.86	(12)	12.70	(7)
	T	4 179	(17)	5 929	(21)	9 633	(23)	17.41	(17)	15.27	(21)	14.48	(17)
No special emphasis	U	12 556	(22)	11 515	(30)	13 387	(33)	8.92	(21)	13.07	(28)	7.54	(20)
	G	3 568	(19)	4 384	(22)	4 336	(27)	11.19	(18)	12.89	(20)	9.06	(17)
	T	18 680	(23)	18 090	(31)	23 299	(35)	9.10	(23)	12.77	(31)	7.47	(23)

1. In these regions the undergraduate/graduate classification was not standard.

TABLE VII. (*continued*)

		Average number of students			Average annual growth rates of number of students		
		1958/59	1963/64	1968/69	1958/63	1963/68	1958/68
		No. Sample	No. Sample	No. Sample	% Sample	% Sample	% Sample
7. Emphasis on university function							
Undergrad.	U	4 226 (36)	5 291 (47)	6 140 (50)	14.22 (35)	14.12 (46)	12.18 (34)
teaching	G	497 (24)	696 (33)	909 (39)	16.38 (20)	24.32 (29)	16.30 (18)
	T	6 537 (38)	8 283 (50)	11 829 (55)	16.20 (37)	14.21 (50)	13.19 (37)
Graduate	U	15 639 (11)	14 444 (13)	18 476 (16)	10.00 (9)	10.00 (12)	7.87 (9)
teaching	G	5 362 (13)	7 694 (15)	8 676 (16)	16.10 (13)	7.68 (15)	11.75 (13)
	T	17 440 (16)	21 585 (16)	27 620 (18)	14.28 (16)	6.40 (16)	10.02 (16)
Research	U	4 959 (2)	5 591 (2)	6 942 (2)	1.70 (2)	2.37 (2)	2.03 (2)
	G	1 089 (2)	1 417 (2)	2 052 (2)	4.43 (2)	4.99 (2)	4.70 (2)
	T	6 070 (2)	7 214 (2)	9 348 (2)	2.84 (2)	3.11 (2)	2.97 (2)
Teacher	U	— —	84 (1)	612 (2)	— —	70.03 (1)	— —
training	G	— —	— —	5 (2)	— —	— —	— —
	T	8 720 (1)	3 674 (2)	6 562 (3)	5.23 (1)	37.70 (2)	7.65 (1)
8. Type of control							
Private	U	13 903 (13)	14 370 (14)	17 115 (14)	14.63 (13)	10.82 (13)	11.99 (12)
	G	893 (10)	1 007 (11)	1 316 (11)	15.69 (9)	33.99 (10)	18.52 (8)
	T	1 529 (13)	16 606 (14)	24 961 (15)	15.06 (13)	12.01 (14)	12.69 (13)
Public	U	4 260 (36)	5 032 (49)	6 752 (56)	12.15 (33)	14.66 (48)	10.50 (33)
	G	2 582 (29)	3 337 (39)	3 415 (48)	15.56 (26)	13.63 (36)	12.29 (25)
	T	7 950 (44)	9 872 (56)	2 884 (63)	14.96 (43)	12.97 (56)	11.56 (43)
9. Type of admission system							
Open	U	3 468 (4)	2 850 (7)	4 252 (9)	17.80 (4)	23.94 (7)	16.29 (4)
	G	415 (1)	210 (3)	294 (5)	7.50 (1)	18.07 (2)	12.24 (1)
	T	3 955 (4)	3 282 (7)	4 697 (9)	18.18 (4)	22.52 (7)	16.16 (4)
Selective	U	4 791 (36)	6 220 (46)	7 032 (50)	12.34 (35)	12.48 (45)	10.27 (34)
	G	2 188 (30)	2 901 (39)	3 156 (45)	14.43 (28)	18.96 (37)	13.04 (26)
	T	8 359 (41)	10 773 (52)	14 890 (56)	15.70 (41)	12.33 (52)	11.94 (41)
Mixed	U	16 417 (9)	14 161 (10)	20 713 (11)	12.54 (7)	12.79 (9)	10.67 (7)
	G	2 221 (8)	3 429 (8)	3 876 (9)	22.35 (6)	13.27 (7)	17.39 (6)
	T	15 814 (12)	18 376 (11)	23 848 (13)	11.15 (11)	8.70 (11)	9.83 (11)

TABLE VIIA. Structure of the student body: number and growth rate of male and female students

		Average number of male and female students						Average annual growth rate of number of male and female students					
		1958/59		1963/64		1968/69		1958/63		1963/68		1958/68	
		No.	Sample	No.	Sample	No.	Sample	%	Sample	%	Sample	%	Sample
1. Overall sample													
Male		7 963	(47)	8 215	(66)	10 715	(77)	14.76	(46)	12.10	(66)	11.05	(46)
Female		2 430	(46)	3 134	(66)	4 613	(76)	20.16	(43)	17.96	(65)	15.34	(43)
2. Existence of a planning system													
Central & univ. plan.	M	3 906	(5)	5 977	(5)	6 191	(5)	8.27	(5)	0.72	(5)	4.33	(5)
	F	2 778	(5)	4 485	(5)	5 707	(5)	13.34	(5)	4.23	(5)	8.59	(5)
Central plan. only	M	805	(1)	833	(3)	1 947	(3)	1.91	(1)	28.89	(3)	1.29	(1)
	F	4	(1)	38	(3)	158	(3)	22.42	(1)	48.61	(3)	8.45	(1)
Univ. plan. only	M	7 003	(12)	8 236	(16)	11 892	(17)	9.38	(11)	12.64	(16)	9.17	(11)
	F	1 541	(12)	2 184	(16)	3 858	(16)	14.58	(11)	15.69	(15)	14.37	(11)
Some planning	M	11 353	(17)	9 820	(27)	12 508	(34)	18.29	(17)	12.40	(27)	12.59	(17)
	F	3 041	(17)	3 797	(27)	5 514	(34)	23.60	(17)	17.96	(27)	15.16	(15)
No planning	M	6 407	(12)	7 528	(15)	8 936	(18)	18.47	(12)	11.36	(15)	14.25	(12)
	F	2 519	(11)	2 794	(15)	3 992	(18)	23.96	(11)	18.67	(15)	20.29	(11)
3. Level of economic development													
Developing	M	10 170	(30)	9 477	(45)	12 637	(53)	17.90	(29)	14.23	(45)	13.08	(29)
	F	2 830	(29)	3 421	(45)	5 216	(52)	23.73	(26)	21.76	(44)	17.85	(26)
Developed	M	4 068	(17)	5 510	(21)	6 472	(24)	9.40	(17)	7.55	(21)	7.59	(17)
	F	1 748	(17)	2 517	(21)	3 306	(24)	14.72	(17)	10.09	(21)	11.52	(17)
4. Geographical location													
Africa	M	4 208	(7)	4 194	(11)	5 140	(13)	25.76	(6)	21.23	(11)	20.07	(6)
	F	642	(7)	921	(11)	1 384	(13)	25.76	(5)	39.56	(11)	21.35	(5)
Asia	M	13 966	(11)	11 826	(17)	16 008	(21)	16.36	(11)	10.74	(17)	10.12	(11)
	F	4 590	(10)	5 092	(17)	7 369	(21)	32.85	(9)	13.84	(17)	18.90	(9)
Australia & Oceania	M	—	—	729	(2)	1 980	(2)	—	—	17.80	(2)	—	—
	F	—	—	1 944	(2)	3 833	(3)	—	—	19.40	(2)	—	—
Europe	M	4 274	(15)	6 021	(18)	5 947	(18)	11.69	(15)	5.40	(18)	8.43	(15)
	F	1 703	(15)	2 866	(18)	3 279	(18)	11.66	(15)	7.70	(15)	11.99	(15)
N. America	M	4 318	(4)	4 845	(5)	7 946	(5)	8.08	(4)	11.50	(5)	9.17	(4)
	F	1 619	(4)	2 397	(5)	4 187	(5)	13.44	(4)	14.00	(5)	12.97	(4)
Central and Latin America	M	10 979	(10)	11 038	(16)	15 520	(17)	11.28	(10)	13.02	(16)	11.34	(10)
	F	2 935	(10)	3 356	(16)	5 496	(17)	13.90	(10)	19.52	(16)	14.14	(10)
University size by number of students													
-5,000	M	807	(16)	1 434	(26)	2 092	(34)	22.92	(15)	17.24	(26)	16.15	(15)
	F	270	(16)	493	(26)	785	(33)	23.39	(13)	26.39	(25)	18.15	(13)

TABLE VIIA. (*continued*)

		Average number of male and female students			Average annual growth rate of number of male and female students		
		1958/59	1963/64	1968/69	1958/63	1963/68	1958/68
		No. Sample	No. Sample	No. Sample	% Sample	% Sample	% Sample
5,000-10,000	M	2 261 (13)	3 465 (16)	5 160 (19)	17.19 (13)	9.87 (16)	11.95 (13)
	F	488 (12)	1 007 (16)	1 729 (19)	31.32 (12)	14.22 (16)	19.79 (12)
10,000 +	M	18 441 (18)	18 727 (24)	27 331 (24)	6.20 (18)	8.02 (24)	6.15 (18)
	F	5 644 (18)	7 412 (24)	12 159 (24)	10.40 (18)	11.68 (24)	10.36 (18)

6. Emphasis on the field of study

Pure science	M	2 156 (8)	3 539 (9)	4 658 (9)	17.65 (8)	5.81 (9)	10.89 (8)
	F	1 439 (7)	2 198 (9)	3 053 (9)	28.33 (7)	10.66 (9)	16.39 (7)
Humanities	M	1 253 (4)	2 673 (5)	4 503 (6)	36.66 (4)	13.64 (5)	24.63 (4)
	F	421 (4)	860 (5)	1 613 (6)	24.23 (3)	30.98 (5)	20.34 (3)
Soc. sciences	M	1 821 (3)	4 134 (3)	5 889 (4)	30.08 (2)	26.30 (3)	25.01 (2)
	F	1 909 (3)	2 468 (3)	5 063 (3)	21.35 (2)	20.80 (2)	20.99 (2)
Prof. train.	M	3 207 (13)	4 675 (20)	7 241 (23)	14.32 (13)	14.00 (20)	12.54 (13)
	F	487 (13)	1 056 (20)	2 099 (23)	20.97 (12)	18.42 (20)	16.90 (12)
No special emphasis	M	16 045 (19)	13 485 (29)	16 173 (33)	7.62 (19)	10.99 (29)	5.76 (19)
	F	4 630 (19)	5 316 (29)	7 142 (33)	15.88 (19)	17.47 (29)	12.60 (19)

7. Emphasis on university function

Undergrad. teaching	M	5 524 (32)	6 147 (48)	8 467 (54)	16.28 (31)	13.18 (48)	12.37 (31)
	F	1 523 (32)	2 342 (48)	3 674 (54)	20.11 (29)	19.19 (47)	16.71 (29)
Graduate teaching	M	14 603 (13)	16 079 (14)	18 575 (18)	12.97 (13)	6.02 (14)	9.02 (13)
	F	5 094 (12)	6 477 (14)	8 048 (18)	20.99 (12)	8.70 (14)	12.95 (12)
Research	M	805 (1)	6 862 (2)	8 842 (2)	1.91 (1)	3.08 (2)	1.29 (1)
	F	4 (1)	352 (2)	506 (2)	22.42 (1)	1.85 (2)	8.45 (1)
Teacher training	M	6 802 (1)	4 153 (2)	5 274 (3)	3.84 (1)	37.66 (2)	6.33 (1)
	F	1 918 (1)	1 520 (2)	3 163 (2)	9.63 (1)	69.88 (2)	11.40 (1)

8. Type of control

Private	M	12 606 (12)	12 232 (13)	17 809 (14)	20.74 (12)	12.05 (13)	15.25 (12)
	F	3 622 (12)	5 148 (13)	8 505 (14)	21.08 (11)	22.04 (13)	17.36 (11)
Public	M	6 371 (35)	7 230 (53)	9 139 (63)	12.65 (34)	12.11 (53)	9.57 (34)
	F	2 009 (34)	2 639 (53)	3 734 (62)	19.85 (32)	16.94 (52)	14.66 (32)

9. Type of admission system

Open	M	3 981 (2)	3 151 (6)	4 060 (8)	4.10 (2)	17.79 (6)	6.47 (2)
	F	625 (2)	649 (6)	1 645 (7)	11.87 (2)	25.69 (6)	15.23 (2)
Selective	M	6 498 (34)	7 887 (49)	10 167 (57)	16.97 (34)	11.49 (49)	11.90 (34)
	F	2 103 (33)	3 000 (49)	4 358 (57)	22.47 (31)	18.07 (49)	15.91 (31)
Mixed	M	12 123 (11)	12 438 (11)	17 785 (12)	9.36 (10)	11.69 (11)	9.07 (10)
	F	3 738 (11)	5 083 (11)	7 553 (12)	14.68 (10)	12.76 (10)	13.63 (10)

TABLE VIIB. Structure of the student body: average percentage of student drop-out

	1958/59		1963/64		1968/69	
	%	Sample	%	Sample	%	Sample
1. Overall sample						
Undergraduate	17.4	(15)	16.8	(23)	13.0	(34)
Graduate	10.2	(10)	11.9	(15)	8.8	(40)
TOTAL	18.0	(17)	15.1	(26)	14.7	(18)

	1958/59		1963/64		1968/69	
	Undergrad. %	Graduate %	Undergrad. %	Graduate %	Undergrad. %	Graduate %
2. Existence of a planning system						
Cent. & univ. plan	10.5	8.6	19.0	11.3	15.0	11.7
University only	41.3	—	28.3	3.5	21.0	4.0
Some planning	15.6	15.2	11.0	13.3	7.2	12.2
No planning	7.3	—	10.6	19.3	9.5	5.7
3. Level of economic development						
Developing	22.7	15.0	17.0	16.0	12.8	9.3
Developed	6.8	5.4	15.8	5.8	14.0	8.0
4. Geographical location						
Africa	45.0	33.0	29.2	33.0	19.1	18.0
Asia	11.0	14.0	3.8	11.2	3.8	7.8
Australia and Oceania	—	—	—	—	3.0	—
Europe	5.6	4.5	12.8	4.4	12.8	6.3
North America	—	—	—	—	6.0	—
L. & C. America	34.0	—	26.0	—	21.3	—
5. University size by number of students						
0-5,000	21.4	14.0	16.1	21.8	10.4	11.4
5,000-10,000	11.3	10.2	12.2	7.8	12.7	8.3
10,000 and over	15.4	6.3	21.2	5.7	22.1	5.0

153

TABLE VIIC. Structure of the student body: reasons for student drop-out

	1958/59		1963/64		1968/69	
	No. times reason given	Frequency (percentage)	No. times reason given	Frequency (percentage)	No. times reason given	Frequency (percentage)
Overall sample						
Undergraduate students	9 universities		14 universities		18 universities	
Academic reasons	7	33.3	10	33.3	14	38.9
Financial reasons	6	28.6	8	26.7	8	22.2
'Other' reasons	8	38.1	12	40.0	14	38.9
Graduate students	6 universities		6 universities		10 universities	
Academic reasons	4	30.8	4	30.8	7	35.0
Financial reasons	4	30.8	4	30.8	5	25.0
'Other' reasons	5	38.5	5	38.5	8	40.0

TABLE **VIID.** Structure of the student body: socio-economic background of students at nine individual universities

	Percentage in each income group			Ratios over time (percentage)		
	1958	1963	1968	1963/58	1968/63	1968/58
Upper	19.26	21.47	22.08	3.00	1.80	5.40
Middle	57.80	42.94	42.61	2.00	1.74	3.47
Lower	22.92	35.57	35.29	4.18	1.74	7.25
Upper	—	—	8.54	—	—	—
Middle	—	14.29	18.67	—	15.93	—
Lower	—	85.71	72.78	—	10.35	—
Upper	2.04	5.45	9.04	3.51	3.14	11.02
Middle	50.19	35.06	76.61	0.92	4.13	3.80
Lower	47.76	59.47	14.33	1.64	0.46	0.75
Upper	1.85	1.32	18.95	0.24	217.78	51.58
Middle	38.08	97.35	37.91	0.85	5.91	5.03
Lower	60.05	1.32	43.12	0.01	495.44	3.63
Upper	—	10.61	17.37	—	18.16	—
Middle	—	71.23	54.19	—	8.44	—
Lower	—	18.15	28.42	—	17.38	—
Upper	50.62	32.18	31.63	4.09	2.51	10.28
Middle	46.25	50.67	53.48	7.05	2.70	19.02
Lower	3.12	17.13	14.87	35.30	2.22	78.30
Upper	13.96	14.01	8.94	1.20	0.81	0.97
Middle	72.98	73.97	80.09	1.21	1.37	1.66
Lower	13.05	12.01	10.96	1.10	1.16	1.27
Upper	14.69	11.75	11.75	1.88	0.78	1.48
Middle	66.89	72.97	71.64	2.57	0.77	1.98
Lower	18.40	15.27	16.59	1.99	0.85	1.67
Upper	2.29	3.11	7.18	4.77	5.45	26.00
Middle	33.21	28.36	20.88	3.01	1.74	5.23
Lower	64.48	68.52	71.93	3.74	2.48	9.28

TABLE **VIIE.** Structure of the student body: percentage of foreign students in the university, 1968/69

	Percentage		Percentage	Sample
Overall sample	5.54	*3. Geographical location*		
		Africa	10.52	5
		Asia	2.10	4
		Australia & Oceania	8.07	2
		Europe	6.10	11
Level of economic development		North America	10.24	4
Developing countries	4.47	Latin & Cent.		
Developed countries	6.95	America	1.99	10

155

TABLE VIII. Teaching staff: student/staff ratios

	1958	1963	1968	Sample
1. Overall sample	9.9	11.2	10.5	(35)
2. Existence of a planning system				
Central and university planning	8.0	8.0	6.8	(3)
Central planning only	—	—	—	—
University planning	10.9	11.7	12.7	(8)
Some planning	11.2	12.8	11.3	(16)
No planning	6.9	8.7	8.4	(8)
3. Level of economic development				
Developing	10.1	11.0	10.6	(24)
Developed	9.5	11.6	10.4	(11)
4. Geographical location				
Africa	12.2	11.4	10.5	(4)
Asia	10.3	12.5	10.9	(14)
Australia and Oceania	—	—	—	—
Europe	8.7	10.6	9.9	(8)
North America	12.8	15.0	13.3	(3)
Latin and Central America	7.3	8.3	10.2	(6)

ᴬBLE VIIIA. Teaching staff: average number of full-time staff and growth rates

	Full-time staff			Growth rates during		
	1958	1963	1968	1958-63	1963-68	1958-68
	No. Sample	No. Sample	No. Sample	% Sample	% Sample	% Sample
Overall sample	583 (49)	809 (63)	1 152 (78)	13.2 (45)	11.7 (62)	10.9 (47)
Existence of a planning system						
ᵉnt. and univ. an.	959 (5)	1 375 (5)	1 799 (5)	7.9 (5)	6.0 (5)	6.9 (5)
ᵉntral plan. ᵈly	— —	— —	— —	— —	— —	— —
ᵘiversity plan.	953 (10)	812 (15)	1 361 (17)	9.3 (8)	10.6 (15)	7.7 (9)
ᵐe planning	454 (21)	720 (26)	1 046 (33)	13.6 (20)	10.3 (15)	10.9 (20)
ᵒ planning	362 (13)	823 (16)	1 111 (20)	17.4 (12)	14.1 (16)	14.6 (13)
Level of economic development						
ᵉveloping	511 (33)	770 (44)	1 175 (54)	16.0 (29)	11.3 (43)	11.6 (31)
ᵉveloped	904 (16)	1 453 (19)	1 941 (24)	8.1 (16)	12.5 (19)	9.4 (16)
Geographical location						
ʳica	259 (7)	315 (11)	481 (14)	23.6 (5)	18.3 (10)	16.8 (5)
ˢia	479 (18)	708 (21)	983 (22)	13.2 (18)	10.3 (21)	10.4 (18)
ᵘst. & Oceania	227 (1)	361 (2)	500 (3)	12.0 (1)	15.5 (2)	11.6 (1)
ᵘrope	627 (13)	893 (12)	957 (18)	11.3 (12)	10.8 (12)	10.4 (13)
ᵒrth America	598 (3)	644 (5)	1 218 (5)	9.9 (3)	17.0 (5)	12.1 (3)
& C. America	1 137 (7)	1 497 (12)	2 292 (16)	10.2 (6)	6.6 (12)	8.2 (7)
University size by number of students						
ᵌ,000	145 (18)	220 (26)	317 (34)	13.5 (16)	14.0 (25)	11.8 (16)
ᵒ00-10,000	255 (14)	385 (17)	763 (20)	17.0 (14)	11.6 (17)	13.1 (14)
,000 and over	1 317 (17)	1 936 (20)	2 659 (24)	9.3 (15)	8.8 (20)	8.2 (17)
Emphasis on field of study						
ʳe science	424 (7)	460 (9)	598 (8)	12.7 (7)	6.0 (9)	8.1 (7)
ᵘmanities	141 (6)	330 (7)	536 (7)	19.5 (6)	13.1 (7)	16.7 (6)
ᶜial sciences	48 (3)	120 (3)	155 (4)	16.0 (2)	20.2 (3)	15.6 (2)
ᵒfessional ᵘining	472 (11)	560 (15)	1 171 (22)	17.8 (10)	11.6 (15)	13.5 (11)
ᵒ special ᵘphasis	883 (22)	1 233 (29)	1 509 (36)	8.9 (20)	12.3 (28)	8.4 (21)

157

TABLE VIIIA. (*continued*)

| | Full-time staff | | | | | Growth rates during | | | | |
| | 1958 | 1963 | 1968 | 1958-63 | | 1963-68 | | 1958-68 | |
	No. Sample	No. Sample	No. Sample	%	Sample	%	Sample	%	Samp
7. *Emphasis on university function*									
Undergraduate teaching	416 (33)	639 (45)	1 021 (55)	13.1	(29)	12.0	(44)	11.2	(31)
Graduate teaching	889 (14)	1 290 (15)	1 631 (18)	14.8	(14)	7.1	(15)	10.2	(14)
Research	2 296 (1)	2 699 (1)	1 797 (2)	3.3	(1)	5.1	(1)	4.2	(1)
Teacher training	96 (1)	76 (2)	258 (3)	4.7	(1)	42.3	(2)	17.4	(1)
8. *Type of control*									
Private	376 (12)	584 (14)	814 (15)	8.9	(12)	12.8	(14)	10.2	(12)
Public	650 (37)	873 (49)	1 232 (63)	14.8	(33)	11.3	(48)	11.1	(35)
9. *Type of admission system*									
Open	— —	225 (5)	338 (9)	—	—	17.0	(5)	—	—
Selective	636 (38)	939 (46)	1 365 (56)	13.9	(35)	10.4	(45)	10.8	(37)
Mixed	402 (11)	554 (12)	799 (13)	10.7	(10)	14.3	(12)	11.4	(10)

ᴀʙʟᴇ VIIIB.   Teaching staff: average percentage of foreign staff in the universities

	1958		1963		1968	
	%	Sample	%	Sample	%	Sample
. *Overall sample*	15.22	(32)	21.33	(43)	22.69	(58)
. *Existence of planning system*						
ᴄentral & university planning	0.61	(5)	0.88	(5)	1.40	(5)
ᴄentral planning	—	—	66.00	(1)	55.50	(2)
ᵁniversity planning	37.20	(5)	40.57	(8)	34.31	(13)
ᵒme planning	11.85	(13)	11.53	(17)	18.05	(21)
ᴺo planning	16.00	(9)	27.17	(12)	21.94	(17)
. *Level of economic development*						
ᴰeveloping	21.14	(22)	27.03	(31)	27.74	(29)
ᴰeveloped	2.20	(10)	6.58	(12)	12.32	(19)
. *Geographical location*						
ᴬfrica	50.60	(5)	58.56	(9)	60.33	(12)
ᴬsia	14.83	(12)	16.06	(16)	10.21	(19)
ᴬustralia and Oceania	—	—	47.00	(1)	64.51	(2)
ᴱurope	4.00	(11)	4.17	(12)	6.33	(15)
ᴺorth America	—	—	—	—	35.33	(3)
ᴸatin and Central America	3.00	(4)	7.20	(5)	9.71	(7)

TABLE VIIIC. Teaching staff: average proportions of senior/middle/junior-level full-tim
teaching staff

	1958		1963		1968	
	%	Sample	%	Sample	%	Sampl
1. Overall sample						
Senior level	29.43	(30)	24.7	(45)	24.2	(63)
Middle level	32.00	(30)	35.0	(45)	34.9	(63)
Junior level	38.53	(30)	40.1	(45)	40.9	(63)
2. Existence of planning system						
Central and university planning						
Senior level	13.00	(3)	15.25	(4)	17.75	(4)
Middle level	34.00	(3)	33.00	(4)	34.00	(4)
Junior level	53.00	(3)	51.25	(4)	48.25	(4)
Central planning only						
Senior level	—	—	40.00	(1)	24.66	(3)
Middle level	—	—	60.00	(1)	47.00	(3)
Junior level	—	—	—	(1)	28.33	(3)
University planning						
Senior level	71.50	(2)	31.11	(9)	28.57	(14)
Middle level	1.00	(2)	30.77	(9)	33.64	(14)
Junior level	27.50	(2)	38.11	(9)	37.71	(14)
Some planning						
Senior level	22.71	(17)	22.48	(21)	24.56	(30)
Middle level	31.88	(17)	33.96	(21)	33.66	(30)
Junior level	45.41	(17)	43.52	(21)	41.76	(30)
No planning						
Senior level	39.37	(8)	26.00	(10)	20.16	(12)
Middle level	39.25	(8)	39.40	(10)	36.50	(12)
Junior level	21.25	(8)	34.10	(10)	43.41	(12)
3. Level of economic development						
Developing						
Senior level	30.55	(20)	26.00	(31)	22.98	(45)
Middle level	32.75	(20)	36.81	(31)	37.04	(45)
Junior level	36.70	(20)	37.00	(31)	39.96	(45)
Developed						
Senior level	27.20	(10)	21.93	(14)	27.22	(18)
Middle level	30.50	(10)	31.07	(14)	29.39	(18)
Junior level	42.20	(10)	46.86	(14)	43.44	(18)
4. Geographical location						
Africa						
Senior level	41.25	(4)	27.77	(9)	24.70	(12)
Middle level	37.00	(4)	44.00	(9)	42.80	(12)
Junior level	21.75	(4)	27.55	(9)	32.40	(12)
Asia						
Senior level	13.72	(11)	14.14	(14)	16.06	(16)
Middle level	34.90	(11)	40.21	(14)	40.12	(16)
Junior level	51.36	(11)	45.57	(14)	43.75	(16)

TABLE VIIIC. *(continued)*

	1958		1963		1968	
	%	Sample	%	Sample	%	Sample
Australia and Oceania						
Senior level	37.00	(1)	24.50	(2)	20.66	(3)
Middle level	63.00	(1)	59.00	(2)	48.66	(3)
Junior level	—	(1)	16.50	(2)	30.66	(3)
Europe						
Senior level	29.10	(10)	27.63	(11)	27.28	(14)
Middle level	31.00	(10)	28.72	(11)	26.50	(14)
Junior level	38.80	(10)	42.45	(11)	46.35	(14)
North America						
Senior level	16.00	(1)	14.00	(3)	24.00	(4)
Middle level	26.00	(1)	23.66	(3)	25.50	(4)
Junior level	58.00	(1)	62.33	(3)	50.50	(4)
Latin and Central America						
Senior level	71.00	(3)	45.00	(6)	32.85	(14)
Middle level	9.66	(3)	16.83	(6)	30.00	(14)
Junior level	19.33	(3)	38.33	(6)	34.35	(14)
5. Emphasis on university function						
Undergraduate teaching						
Senior level	35.90	(21)	27.47	(32)	25.94	(47)
Middle level	33.19	(21)	36.47	(32)	35.13	(47)
Junior level	28.14	(21)	35.84	(32)	38.43	(47)
Graduate teaching						
Senior level	12.62	(8)	15.00	(11)	16.75	(12)
Middle level	26.87	(8)	28.09	(11)	31.33	(12)
Junior level	60.50	(8)	56.82	(11)	52.00	(12)
Research						
Senior level	—	—	—	—	45.00	(1)
Middle level	—	—	—	—	25.00	(1)
Junior level	—	—	—	—	30.00	(1)
Teacher training						
Senior level	28.00	(1)	34.50	(2)	12.33	(3)
Middle level	48.00	(1)	50.00	(2)	47.33	(3)
Junior level	24.00	(1)	15.50	(2)	40.00	(3)
6. Type of admission system						
Open						
Senior level	77.00	(1)	24.80	(5)	19.71	(7)
Middle level	23.00	(1)	24.20	(5)	29.57	(7)
Junior level	0.00	(1)	50.20	(5)	50.71	(7)
Selective						
Senior level	21.73	(22)	20.70	(30)	22.78	(45)
Middle level	36.77	(22)	39.17	(30)	38.27	(45)
Junior level	41.45	(22)	40.00	(30)	38.93	(45)
Mixed						
Senior level	46.86	(7)	36.80	(10)	32.82	(11)
Middle level	18.29	(7)	28.00	(10)	24.27	(11)
Junior level	34.86	(7)	35.20	(10)	43.00	(11)

TABLE VIIID. Teaching staff: average percentage of staff holding different degrees

	Percentage of staff		
	1958	1963	1968
1. Overall sample			
First degree	25.0	21.8	25.2
Second degree	38.7	42.1	37.7
Higher-than-second degree	33.2	33.0	34.4
Others	3.1	3.0	2.6
(Number in sample)	(35)	(44)	(65)

	Degrees held	Percentage of staff		
		1958	1963	1968
2. Existence of a planning system				
Central & university planning	First degree	13.0	8.4	8.6
	Second degree	54.7	46.7	43.4
	Higher-than-2nd degree	28.8	38.5	42.9
	Others	3.5	6.4	5.2
Central planning only	First degree	—	52.0	34.0
	Second degree	—	48.0	45.3
	Higher-than-2nd degree	—	—	18.0
	Others	—	—	2.7
University planning	First degree	49.0	33.9	32.7
	Second degree	38.7	35.6	33.8
	Higher-than-2nd degree	11.0	26.6	29.6
	Others	1.3	3.8	3.8
Some planning	First degree	26.7	23.6	29.5
	Second degree	36.4	40.2	34.4
	Higher-than-2nd degree	33.0	33.6	33.5
	Others	3.8	2.6	2.5
No planning	First degree	19.4	9.8	16.6
	Second degree	36.5	49.8	42.5
	Higher-than-2nd degree	41.9	38.9	39.5
	Others	2.2	1.5	1.3
3. Level of economic development				
Developing	First degree	28.5	24.3	29.1
	Second degree	38.8	44.6	37.9
	Higher-than-2nd degree	31.5	29.4	31.1
	Others	1.2	1.6	1.8
Developed	First degree	17.4	16.5	15.1
	Second degree	38.4	36.8	37.2
	Higher-than-2nd degree	37.0	40.6	43.1
	Others	7.2	6.1	4.7

TABLE VIIID. (*continued*)

	Degrees held	Percentage of staff		
		1958	1963	1968
. Geographical location				
Africa	First degree	24.0	28.1	27.4
	Second degree	12.0	32.9	30.4
	Higher-than-2nd degree	64.0	35.4	38.8
	Others	—	3.6	3.4
Asia	First degree	17.1	18.0	20.3
	Second degree	52.4	51.4	43.4
	Higher-than-2nd degree	29.3	29.7	35.2
	Others	1.2	0.8	1.1
Australia and Oceania	First degree	18.0	18.0	15.0
	Second degree	24.0	22.0	21.0
	Higher-than-2nd degree	48.0	51.0	56.0
	Others	10.0	9.0	8.0
Europe	First degree	16.7	16.5	14.2
	Second degree	40.5	38.7	44.9
	Higher-than-2nd degree	36.1	38.3	36.5
	Others	6.6	6.4	4.4
North America	First degree	8.0	14.0	7.3
	Second degree	34.0	40.5	27.0
	Higher-than-2nd degree	52.0	45.5	65.0
	Others	6.0	—	0.7
Latin and Central America	First degree	55.3	38.5	52.6
	Second degree	26.7	39.0	28.5
	Higher-than-2nd degree	17.3	21.3	16.6
	Others	0.7	1.2	2.2
. Emphasis on university function				
Undergraduate teaching	First degree	34.4	28.2	33.3
	Second degree	27.3	32.4	29.2
	Higher-than-2nd degree	36.7	37.4	35.5
	Others	1.5	1.9	2.0
Graduate teaching	First degree	11.6	6.1	8.6
	Second degree	58.2	62.2	53.5
	Higher-than-2nd degree	25.0	26.3	33.5
	Others	5.2	5.4	4.4
Research	First degree	—	—	7.5
	Second degree	—	—	61.0
	Higher-than-2nd degree	—	—	31.0
	Others	—	—	0.5
Teacher training	First degree	—	52.0	17.5
	Second degree	30.0	48.0	56.0
	Higher-than-2nd degree	60.0	—	23.0
	Others	10.0	—	3.5

163

TABLE VIIIE. Teaching staff: average teaching load in hours per week for differer levels of teachers, 1968

	Hours per week		
	Senior level	Middle level	Junior level
1. *Overall sample*	8.3	10.4	11.9
(Number in sample)	(58)	(55)	(51)
2. *Existence of planning system*			
Central and university planning	7.0	8.5	11.2
Central planning only	6.7	11.0	10.0
University planning	8.1	9.4	10.1
Some planning	8.7	11.1	13.0
No planning	7.5	10.3	10.6
3. *Level of economic development*			
Developing	8.7	10.8	12.8
Developed	6.9	8.9	8.9
4. *Geographical location*			
Africa	6.8	9.9	11.8
Asia	9.1	12.5	14.8
Australia and Oceania	6.0	10.5	23.5
Europe	5.9	7.6	7.5
North America	8.0	8.0	8.0
Latin and Central America	11.7	11.9	12.5

TABLE IX. Innovation in the teaching work

	1958/59 %	1963/64 %	1968/69 %	1970s %
Overall sample				
New media not used	83.67	60.71	35.21	12.28
New media used principally for traditional methods of instruction	14.28	23.21	16.90	12.28
New media used principally for new methods of instruction	—	3.57	9.85	63.15
New media used partly for traditional methods and partly for new methods of instruction	2.04	12.50	38.02	12.28
(Number in sample)	(49)	(56)	(71)	(57)

TABLE IXA. Innovation in the teaching work: innovation in instructional methods and techniques, 1968/69

	Sample	Instructional television %S	%E	Instructional radio %S	%E	Computer assisted instruction %S	%E	Independent study courses %S	%E	Programmed instruction %S	%E	Team teaching %S	%E	Central service for production of teaching materials %S	%E
1. Overall sample	72	18.0	13.9	8.3	5.6	11.1	19.4	16.7	9.7	9.7	27.8	26.4	12.5	15.3	9.7
2. Existence of planning system															
Central and university	5	40.0	20.0	20.0	—	20.0	20.0	40.0	40.0	40.0	60.0	60.0	20.0	40.0	—
Central only	3	33.0	—	—	—	—	33.3	33.3	33.3	—	66.6	33.3	33.3	66.6	—
University only	14	28.6	14.3	21.4	7.1	21.4	28.6	28.6	—	14.3	21.4	28.6	—	14.3	7.1
Some planning	32	15.6	12.5	—	3.1	9.4	21.9	12.5	6.3	6.3	25.0	21.9	12.5	12.5	15.6
No planning	18	5.6	16.7	11.1	11.1	5.6	5.6	5.6	11.1	5.6	22.2	22.2	16.7	5.6	5.6
3. Level of economic development															
Developing	51	7.8	9.8	3.9	5.8	3.9	11.8	9.8	9.8	5.8	21.6	25.5	7.8	9.8	5.8
Developed	21	42.9	23.8	19.0	4.8	28.6	38.1	33.3	9.5	19.0	42.9	28.6	23.8	28.6	19.0
4. Geographical location															
Africa	11	—	—	9.1	—	—	9.1	—	9.1	—	9.1	9.1	—	9.1	—
Asia	21	—	9.5	—	4.8	—	14.3	14.3	4.8	9.5	9.5	14.3	4.8	4.8	—
Australia and Oceania	3	33.3	—	33.3	—	33.3	—	33.3	—	—	—	—	—	33.3	—
Europe	18	33.3	22.2	11.1	5.6	27.8	33.3	22.2	11.1	16.7	55.6	38.9	33.3	22.2	16.7
North America	4	75.0	25.0	50.0	25.0	25.0	50.0	50.0	25.0	25.0	25.0	25.0	—	25.0	25.0
Central and Latin America	15	20.0	20.0	6.7	6.7	6.7	13.3	13.3	13.3	6.7	40.0	46.7	13.3	20.0	20.0

S = systematice use; E = experimental use.

165

TABLE X. Evaluation of teaching programmes

	Percentage of univ. having evaluation mechanism	Growth rate in no. of courses			Average % of courses changed			
		1958-63	1963-68	1958-68	very little	mode-rately	substan-tially	dras-tically
1. Overall sample	85.0	7.9	9.6	6.9	25.1	25.1	21.2	28.6
(Number in sample)	(80)	(35)	(47)	(40)	(53)	(53)	(53)	(53)
2. Existence of planning system								
Central & university	100.0	4.4	1.6	3.5	17.5	46.2	28.7	7.5
Central plan.	66.7	—	12.8	—	20.0	25.0	30.0	25.0
University plan.	93.3	7.5	11.4	5.5	13.0	16.7	24.3	46.1
Some planning	82.4	7.7	10.4	6.9	29.5	27.9	18.3	24.3
No planning	81.0	10.8	8.4	9.9	36.0	22.0	19.0	23.0
3. Level of economic development								
Developing	83.9	9.3	11.0	8.0	25.6	21.4	19.8	33.1
Developed	87.5	5.5	6.5	4.8	23.9	33.6	24.4	18.1
4. Geographical location								
Africa	78.6	8.2	20.7	8.9	25.7	18.6	18.6	37.1
Asia	81.8	9.6	8.3	8.3	32.4	20.8	17.5	29.3
Aust. & Oceania	100.0	4.1	16.9	5.6	5.0	82.5	10.0	2.5
Europe	83.3	9.5	3.1	6.1	23.2	36.8	25.5	14.5
North America	80.0	6.1	10.9	7.1	25.5	19.6	26.0	29.0
L. & C. America	94.1	4.0	9.2	5.6	20.0	16.7	23.8	39.6
5. University size by number of students								
0-5,000	88.9	10.8	15.1	8.8	28.2	19.0	18.6	34.2
5,000-10,000	80.0	10.0	6.9	8.6	30.0	29.0	25.0	16.2
10,000 and over	83.3	3.9	4.8	4.0	16.3	29.2	21.0	33.4
6. Type of control								
Private	81.3	13.2	9.1	10.6	29.7	14.9	20.5	35.0
Public	85.9	6.6	9.7	6.1	23.8	28.0	21.4	26.7
7. Type of admission system								
Open	66.7	4.0	20.8	8.0	21.4	23.6	13.6	41.4
Selective	87.9	8.2	7.3	7.1	27.6	27.8	24.3	20.3
Mixed	84.6	7.3	11.5	5.9	18.0	15.3	14.4	52.2

TABLE XA. Evaluation of teaching programmes: involvement of different bodies in the evaluation of courses

	1958/59						1963/64						1968/69					
	1	2	3	4	5	6	1	2	3	4	5	6	1	2	3	4	5	6
1. Overall sample	35.41	77.08	95.83	20.45	22.72	28.26	33.92	78.94	100.00	22.64	27.77	32.72	35.48	75.80	98.41	32.75	45.90	37.70
(No. in sample)	(48)	(48)	(48)	(44)	(44)	(46)	(56)	(57)	(56)	(53)	(54)	(55)	(62)	(62)	(63)	(58)	(61)	(61)
2. Existence of planning system																		
Cent. & univ.	100.00	100.00	100.00	40.00	60.00	80.00	100.00	100.00	100.00	40.00	60.00	80.00	100.00	100.00	100.00	40.00	60.00	80.00
(Sample)	(5)	(5)	(5)	(5)	(5)	(5)	(5)	(5)	(5)	(5)	(5)	(5)	(5)	(5)	(5)	(5)	(5)	(5)
Cent. plan.	100.00	100.00	100.00	—	—	100.00	100.00	100.00	100.00	—	—	100.00	100.00	100.00	100.00	50.00	50.00	100.00
(Sample)	(1)	(1)	(1)	(1)	(1)	(1)	(2)	(2)	(2)	(2)	(2)	(2)	(2)	(2)	(2)	(2)	(2)	(2)
Univ. plan.	27.27	81.81	90.90	25.00	50.00	27.27	23.07	92.85	100.00	36.36	50.00	21.42	26.66	92.85	100.00	50.00	80.00	33.33
(Sample)	(11)	(11)	(11)	(8)	(10)	(3)	(13)	(14)	(14)	(11)	(14)	(14)	(15)	(14)	(15)	(12)	(15)	(15)
Some planning	30.00	65.00	95.23	10.52	10.52	26.31	26.08	65.21	100.00	13.04	18.18	34.78	25.00	60.00	100.00	16.66	32.00	37.50
(Sample)	(20)	(20)	(21)	(19)	(19)	(19)	(23)	(23)	(23)	(23)	(22)	(23)	(24)	(25)	(25)	(24)	(25)	(24)
No planning	18.18	81.81	100.00	45.45	—	—	23.07	76.92	100.00	25.00	9.09	9.09	31.25	75.00	93.75	40.00	28.57	20.00
(Sample)	(11)	(11)	(10)	(11)	(9)	(10)	(13)	(13)	(12)	(12)	(11)	(11)	(16)	(16)	(16)	(15)	(14)	(15)
3. Level of economic development																		
Developing	25.80	74.19	96.66	17.24	17.85	17.24	34.21	76.92	100.00	19.44	22.22	22.22	37.20	76.19	97.61	21.05	31.70	35.00
(Sample)	(31)	(31)	(30)	(29)	(28)	(29)	(38)	(39)	(37)	(36)	(36)	(36)	(43)	(42)	(42)	(38)	(41)	(40)
Developed	52.94	82.35	94.44	25.00	31.25	47.05	33.33	83.33	100.00	29.41	38.88	52.63	31.57	75.00	100.00	55.00	75.00	42.85
(Sample)	(17)	(17)	(17)	(16)	(16)	(17)	(18)	(18)	(19)	(17)	(18)	(19)	(19)	(21)	(21)	(20)	(20)	(21)

1. Representative from the Ministry of Education; 2. University administration; 3. Teaching and research staff; 4. Graduate students; 5. Undergraduate students; 6. Business and industry.

TABLE XA. (continued)

	1958/59						1963/64						1968/69					
	1	2	3	4	5	6	1	2	3	4	5	6	1	2	3	4	5	6
4. Geographical location																		
Africa	66.66	100.00	100.00	16.66	—	20.00	75.00	100.00	100.00	12.50	—	42.85	60.00	100.00	100.00	11.11	11.11	60.00
(Sample)	(6)	(6)	(6)	(6)	(5)	(5)	(8)	(8)	(8)	(8)	(7)	(7)	(10)	(10)	(10)	(9)	(9)	(10)
Asia	13.33	60.00	93.33	6.66	—	12.50	22.22	61.11	100.00	5.55	5.55	16.66	31.57	63.15	100.00	10.52	10.52	26.31
(Sample)	(15)	(15)	(15)	(15)	(15)	(16)	(18)	(18)	(18)	(18)	(18)	(18)	(19)	(19)	(19)	(19)	(19)	(19)
Aust. & Oceania	50.00	100.00	100.00	—	—	—	—	50.00	100.00	—	—	—	100.00	100.00	100.00	50.00	50.00	100.00
(Sample)	(2)	(2)	(2)	(1)	(1)	(1)	(2)	(2)	(2)	(2)	(2)	(2)	(2)	(2)	(2)	(2)	(2)	(2)
Europe	66.66	83.33	91.66	25.00	41.66	66.66	53.84	92.30	100.00	25.00	50.00	69.23	46.66	80.00	100.00	42.85	80.55	53.33
(Sample)	(12)	(12)	(12)	(12)	(12)	(12)	(13)	(13)	(13)	(13)	(12)	(13)	(15)	(15)	(15)	(14)	(15)	(15)
North America	25.00	75.00	100.00	—	—	—	—	75.00	100.00	33.33	25.00	—	75.00	75.00	100.00	75.00	75.00	—
(Sample)	(4)	(4)	(4)	(3)	(3)	(4)	(4)	(4)	(4)	(3)	(4)	(4)	(4)	(4)	(4)	(4)	(4)	(4)
L. & C. America	11.11	77.77	100.00	57.14	62.50	25.00	18.18	83.33	100.00	60.00	63.63	18.18	27.27	72.72	91.66	66.66	72.72	30.00
(Sample)	(9)	(9)	(9)	(9)	(8)	(8)	(11)	(12)	(11)	(10)	(11)	(11)	(11)	(11)	(12)	(9)	(11)	(10)

TABLE **XI.** Research in the universities: growth rates of research funds and number of projects

	Growth during the period					
	1958-63		1963-68		1958-68	
	%	Sample	%	Sample	%	Sample
Overall sample						
Research money	19.14	(22)	18.19	(32)	17.64	(22)
Number of projects	13.42	(10)	17.61	(15)	13.71	(10)
Level of economic development						
Developing						
Research money	11.11	(10)	14.41	(18)	13.83	(10)
Number of projects	13.54	(5)	15.16	(7)	17.20	(5)
Developed						
Research money	25.83	(12)	23.04	(14)	20.82	(12)
Number of projects	13.30	(5)	19.75	(8)	10.22	(5)

TABLE XIA. Research in the universities: as a factor of change

	Sample	Yes	No	All research		Basic research		Applied research		Development	
				Inc.	Dec.	Inc.	Dec.	Inc.	Dec.	Inc.	Dec.
1. Overall sample											
Past factor of change	69	81.1	18.9	95.1	4.9	88.5	11.5	94.4	5.6	79.5	20.5
Future factor of change	74	95.0	5.0	100.0	—	98.3	1.7	96.5	3.5	71.4	28.6
2. Existence of planning system											
Past factor of change											
Central & university	5	100.0	—	100.0	—	100.0	—	100.0	—	75.0	25.0
Central only	2	100.0	—	100.0	—	—	—	100.0	—	100.0	—
University only	17	64.7	35.2	92.8	7.1	84.6	15.4	90.9	9.1	71.4	28.6
Some planning	33	78.7	21.3	96.4	3.6	91.3	8.7	92.0	8.0	82.4	17.6
No planning	17	70.6	29.4	92.3	7.7	90.0	10.0	100.0	—	60.0	40.0
Future factor of change											
Central & university	5	100.0	—	100.0	—	100.0	—	100.0	—	60.0	40.0
Central only	2	100.0	—	100.0	—	100.0	—	100.0	—	100.0	—
University only	17	82.4	17.6	100.0	—	90.0	10.0	90.9	9.1	91.7	8.3
Some planning	32	96.9	3.1	100.0	—	100.0	—	96.2	3.8	94.7	5.3
No planning	18	100.0	—	100.0	—	100.0	—	100.0	—	91.7	8.3
3. Level of economic development											
Past factor of change											
Developing countries	51	66.7	33.3	92.7	7.3	82.9	17.1	91.7	8.3	77.8	22.2
Developed countries	23	95.7	4.3	100.0	—	100.0	—	100.0	—	83.3	16.7
Future factor of change											
Developing countries	50	94.0	6.0	100.0	—	97.0	3.0	100.0	—	94.3	5.7
Developed countries	24	100.0	—	100.0	—	100.0	—	88.9	11.1	78.6	21.4

Inc. = increase; Dec. = decrease.

TABLE XIA. (continued)

	Sample	Yes	No	All research		Basic research		Applied research		Development	
				Inc.	Dec.	Inc.	Dec.	Inc.	Dec.	Inc.	Dec.
4. Geographical location											
Past factor of change											
Africa	10	50.0	50.0	75.0	25.0	62.5	37.5	85.7	14.3	71.4	28.6
Asia	22	90.9	9.0	100.0	—	100.0	—	100.0	—	77.8	22.2
Australia and Oceania	3	66.6	33.3	50.0	50.0	50.0	50.0	50.0	50.0	—	100.0
Europe	17	88.3	11.7	100.0	—	100.0	—	100.0	—	88.9	11.1
North America	5	100.0	—	100.0	—	100.0	—	100.0	—	75.0	25.0
Latin and Central America	17	53.0	47.0	100.0	—	83.3	16.7	89.9	9.1	88.9	11.1
Future factor of change											
Africa	9	77.8	22.2	100.0	—	100.0	—	100.0	—	83.3	16.7
Asia	21	100.0	—	100.0	—	100.0	—	100.0	—	92.9	7.1
Australia and Oceania	4	100.0	—	100.0	—	100.0	—	100.0	—	—	—
Europe	18	100.0	—	100.0	—	100.0	—	92.9	7.1	81.8	18.2
North America	5	100.0	—	100.0	—	100.0	—	75.0	25.0	75.0	25.0
Latin and Central America	17	94.1	5.9	100.0	—	91.7	8.3	100.0	—	100.0	—

Inc. = increase; Dec. = decrease.

TABLE XII. Source of university finance: average annual growth rates of total operating expenditure

	1958-63		1963-68		1958-68	
	%	Sample	%	Sample	%	Sample
1. Overall sample	15.65	37	12.71	59	12.56	37
2. Existence of planning system						
Central and university planning	12.35	4	9.67	4	10.95	4
Central planning only	—	—	50.00	1	—	—
University planning only	18.97	6	13.34	13	17.70	6
Some planning	13.24	18	11.65	26	10.00	18
No planning	19.74	9	12.31	15	15.00	9
3. Level of economic development						
Developing countries	14.79	24	10.13	42	11.00	24
Developed countries	17.25	13	19.08	17	15.48	13

TABLE XIIA. Source of university finance

| | Average percentage of total finance from | | | | | | | |
	Government	Private	Industrial	Own funds	Tuition	Foreign aid	Others	Sample
1. Overall sample								
1958	79.40	2.51	0.42	6.47	6.81	0.74	3.56	43
1963	77.70	2.17	0.39	5.71	6.59	4.00	3.37	59
1968	76.66	1.54	1.22	4.93	6.75	4.28	4.12	68
2. Existence of a planning system								
Central & university								
1958	98.80	—	—	0.20	—	—	0.40	5
1963	98.00	—	—	0.20	0.20	—	1.00	5
1968	96.20	—	0.20	0.00	0.20	—	3.00	5
Central planning								
1958	—	—	—	—	—	—	—	—
1963	60.00	12.00	—	—	23.00	5.00	—	1
1968	70.00	—	—	7.00	—	23.00	—	1
University planning								
1958	75.50	1.88	1.37	2.62	12.37	1.88	4.25	8
1963	70.80	1.50	1.30	4.50	13.00	5.80	3.00	10
1968	68.13	1.27	1.27	3.73	10.60	9.53	3.93	15
Some planning								
1958	75.43	4.09	0.29	6.33	8.71	0.52	4.62	21
1963	78.15	2.85	0.11	5.92	6.46	1.46	5.08	26
1968	78.39	2.14	1.89	4.21	7.14	0.93	5.00	28
No planning								
1958	81.33	0.78	0.11	13.67	1.22	0.67	2.22	9
1963	76.12	1.59	0.41	8.06	3.94	7.94	1.88	17
1968	76.05	1.37	0.53	8.10	5.21	5.21	3.47	19
3. Level of economic development								
Developing								
1958	78.21	2.93	0.17	8.90	5.65	1.10	3.03	29
1963	74.40	2.26	0.30	7.49	6.53	5.49	3.49	43
1968	73.00	1.82	1.24	6.47	7.18	5.94	3.84	49
Developed								
1958	81.86	1.64	0.93	1.43	9.21	—	4.64	14
1963	86.56	1.94	0.62	0.94	6.75	—	3.06	16
1968	86.10	0.84	1.16	0.95	5.63	—	4.84	19
4. Geographical location								
Africa								
1958	85.50	6.25	1.25	1.00	5.00	0.25	0.75	4
1963	74.67	1.56	0.22	1.33	6.33	13.00	2.78	9
1968	72.67	0.92	0.33	2.25	3.50	17.33	2.83	12
Asia								
1958	67.62	3.50	0.06	14.81	7.44	0.87	5.69	16
1963	73.38	2.43	0.05	11.62	5.90	1.91	4.67	21
1968	71.40	2.70	1.90	11.50	7.20	1.05	4.25	20
Australia & Oceania								
1958	96.00	—	—	3.00	—	—	1.00	1
1963	93.50	—	—	1.00	5.50	—	—	2
1968	84.33	—	—	0.67	7.00	8.00	—	3

TABLE XIIA. (*continued*)

	Average percentage of total finance from							Sample
	Goverment	Private	Industrial	Own funds	Tuition	Foreign aid	Others	
Europe								
1958	96.40	0.80	0.10	1.00	0.90	—	0.40	10
1963	90.54	2.23	0.46	0.69	1.77	1.61	2.46	13
1968	88.19	1.06	1.25	0.50	3.38	0.25	4.81	16
North America								
1958	35.00	4.67	3.67	2.67	39.66	—	14.33	3
1963	56.00	2.00	1.50	3.00	37.50	—	0.50	2
1968	76.67	2.00	0.33	4.33	16.33	—	0.33	3
Latin & Central America								
1958	91.67	0.56	—	1.78	2.89	1.89	1.22	9
1963	74.58	2.50	0.92	5.33	8.25	4.83	3.58	12
1968	72.79	1.21	1.43	3.93	10.64	2.43	5.93	14
5. *Emphasis on university function*								
Undergraduate teaching								
1958	83.18	1.86	0.21	3.79	7.00	1.14	2.79	28
1963	78.88	1.52	0.43	4.17	6.69	5.31	2.98	42
1968	76.55	1.14	1.61	2.98	8.10	5.24	3.74	49
Graduate teaching								
1958	71.86	3.93	0.79	12.29	6.79	—	4.14	14
1963	75.33	3.40	0.27	10.80	5.60	0.53	3.87	15
1968	76.31	3.00	0.19	11.62	2.88	0.62	5.19	16
Research								
1958	79.00	1.00	1.00	—	2.00	—	17.00	1
1963	81.00	1.00	1.00	—	1.00	—	16.00	1
1968	83.00	1.00	1.00	—	1.00	—	14.00	1
Teacher training								
1958	—	—	—	—	—	—	—	—
1963	60.00	12.00	—	—	23.00	5.00	—	1
1968	79.00	—	—	1.50	7.50	12.00	—	2
6. *Type of admission system*								
Open								
1958	99.00	—	—	—	—	—	1.00	1
1963	60.75	4.50	—	2.50	6.50	25.00	0.50	4
1968	68.00	1.14	1.57	1.57	4.00	14.71	5.57	7
Selective								
1958	79.79	1.30	0.21	7.82	5.73	0.97	4.09	33
1963	78.89	1.31	0.31	6.42	5.91	2.73	4.33	45
1968	78.10	0.96	1.24	5.55	7.33	1.73	4.90	49
Mixed								
1958	75.78	7.22	1.22	2.22	11.56	—	1.89	9
1963	79.10	5.10	0.90	3.80	9.70	1.30	0.20	10
1968	75.83	4.17	0.92	4.33	6.00	8.58	0.08	12

TABLE XIII. Use of indices for university planning: statistical information available for planning purposes

	Percentage of universities with information				Non-response
	Available		Not available		
	Adequate	Inadequate	Desirable	Not needed	
Overall sample					
Acceptances/applications ratio	50.0	21.2	21.2	5.0	2.6
No. of graduates in relation to demand for them	16.3	21.2	58.8	1.3	2.4
Student/teaching staff ratio	76.2	13.8	8.7	—	1.3
Rate of drop-out	43.8	31.3	22.5	1.3	1.1
Proportion of graduate students	66.2	7.5	12.5	2.5	11.4
Proportion of new courses in the curricula per year	41.2	21.2	26.3	10.0	1.3
Books/student ratio	40.0	22.5	28.7	7.5	1.3
Availability of teaching and research equipment	33.8	35.0	27.5	1.3	2.4
Avail. of instructional space	56.3	26.3	16.3	—	1.1
Availability of other space	46.3	31.2	20.0	—	2.5
Unit costs per graduate	43.8	26.2	27.5	—	2.5
Proportion of research of a high professional calibre	22.5	23.7	45.0	2.5	6.3
Weekly utilization rate of instructional space	38.7	17.5	37.5	—	6.3
Distribution of staff time between teaching, research and other activities [1]	26.9	15.4	46.2	11.5	—
4. Existence of a planning system: central and university planning					
Acceptances/applications ratio	80.0	—	20.0	—	—
No. of graduates in relation to demand for them	80.0	20.0	—	—	—
Student/teaching staff ratio	100.0	—	—	—	—
Rate of drop-out	80.0	20.0	—	—	—
Proportion of graduate students	80.0	—	—	20.0	—
Proportion of new courses in the curricula per year	60.0	20.0	20.0	—	—
Books/student ratio	80.0	—	20.0	—	—
Availability of teaching and research equipment	80.0	20.0	—	—	—
Avail. of instructional space	100.0	—	—	—	—
Availability of other space	100.0	—	—	—	—
Unit costs per graduate	80.0	20.0	—	—	—
Proportion of research of a high professional calibre	100.0	—	—	—	—
Weekly utilization rate of instructional space	80.0	20.0	—	—	—
Distribution of staff time between teaching, research and other activities [1]	—	—	—	—	100.0

Based on twenty-six observations. This note is valid for the whole of Table XIII.

175

TABLE XIII. (*continued*)

| | Percentage of universities with information | | | | Non-response |
| | Available | | Not available | | |
	Adequate	Inadequate	Desirable	Not needed	
2B. Existence of a planning system: central planning					
Acceptances/applications ratio	33.3	33.3	33.3	—	—
No. of graduates in relation to demand for them	33.3	33.3	33.3	—	—
Student/teaching staff ratio	100.0	—	—	—	—
Rate of drop-out	100.0	—	—	—	—
Proportion of graduate students	66.7	—	—	—	33.3
Proportion of new courses in the curricula per year	33.3	33.3	—	33.3	—
Books/student ratio	33.3	66.7	—	—	—
Availability of teaching and research equipment	—	100.0	—	—	—
Avail. of instructional space	33.3	66.7	—	—	—
Availability of other space	33.3	66.7	—	—	—
Unit costs per graduate	100.0	—	—	—	—
Proportion of research of a high professional calibre	33.3	33.3	33.3	—	—
Weekly utilization rate of instructional space	66.7	—	—	—	33.3
Distribution of staff time between teaching, research and other activities [1]	—	—	—	—	100.0
2C. Existence of a planning system: university planning					
Acceptances/applications ratio	70.6	17.6	5.9	5.9	—
No. of graduates in relation to demand for them	23.5	35.3	35.3	—	5.9
Student/teaching staff ratio	88.2	5.9	5.9	—	—
Rate of drop-out	76.5	17.6	5.9	—	—
Proportion of graduate students	82.4	—	—	—	17.6
Proportion of new courses in the curricula per year	58.8	11.8	23.5	5.9	—
Books/student ratio	64.7	5.9	17.6	11.8	—
Availability of teaching and research equipment	52.9	17.6	17.6	5.9	5.9
Avail. of instructional space	82.3	11.8	5.9	—	—
Availability of other space	64.7	29.4	5.9	—	—
Unit costs per graduate	47.1	29.4	17.6	—	5.9
Proportion of research of a high professional calibre	23.5	11.8	47.1	5.9	11.8
Weekly utilization rate of instructional space	52.9	17.6	23.5	—	5.9
Distribution of staff time between teaching, research and other activities [1]	33.3	22.2	33.3	11.1	—

TABLE XIII. (*continued*)

	Percentage of universities with information				Non-response
	Available		Not available		
	Adequate	Inadequate	Desirable	Not needed	

2D. Existence of a planning system: some planning

	Adequate	Inadequate	Desirable	Not needed	Non-response
Acceptances/applications ratio	52.9	17.6	20.6	5.9	3.0
No. of graduates in relation to demand for them	5.9	20.6	73.5	—	—
Student/teaching staff ratio	76.5	14.7	8.8	—	—
Rate of drop-out	38.2	29.4	29.4	2.9	—
Proportion of graduate students	70.6	2.9	14.7	2.9	8.9
Proportion of new courses in the curricula per year	41.2	23.5	23.5	11.8	—
Books/student ratio	32.4	26.5	29.4	11.8	—
Availability of teaching and research equipment	32.4	38.2	29.4	—	—
Avail. of instructional space	58.8	20.6	20.6	—	—
Availability of other space	44.1	29.4	23.3	—	3.2
Unit costs per graduate	38.2	29.4	29.4	—	3.0
Proportion of research of a high professional calibre	14.7	26.5	47.1	2.9	8.8
Weekly utilization rate of instructional space	41.2	14.7	38.2	—	5.9
Distribution of staff time between teaching, research and other activities [1]	28.6	14.3	28.6	28.6	—

2E. Existence of a planning system: no planning

	Adequate	Inadequate	Desirable	Not needed	Non-response
Acceptances/applications ratio	23.8	33.3	33.3	4.8	4.8
No. of graduates in relation to demand for them	9.5	9.5	71.4	4.8	4.8
Student/teaching staff ratio	57.1	23.8	14.3	5.0	—
Rate of drop-out	9.5	52.4	33.3	—	4.8
Proportion of graduate students	42.9	23.8	23.8	—	9.5
Proportion of new courses in the curricula per year	23.8	23.8	38.1	9.5	4.8
Books/student ratio	23.8	28.6	42.9	—	4.8
Availability of teaching and research equipment	14.3	38.1	42.9	—	4.8
Avail. of instructional space	23.8	47.6	23.8	—	4.8
Availability of other space	23.8	38.1	33.3	—	4.8
Unit costs per graduate	33.3	23.8	42.9	—	—
Proportion of research of a high professional calibre	14.3	33.3	52.4	—	—
Weekly utilization rate of instructional space	9.5	23.8	61.9	—	4.8
Distribution of staff time between teaching, research and other activities [1]	20.0	10.0	70.0	—	—

TABLE XIII. (*continued*)

	Percentage of universities with information				Non-response
	Available		Not available		
	Adequate	Inadequate	Desirable	Not needed	

3A. Level of economic development: developing

Acceptances/applications ratio	44.6	19.6	26.8	7.1	1.9
No. of graduates in relation to demand for them	12.5	23.3	60.7	—	3.6
Student/teaching staff ratio	69.6	16.1	12.5	—	1.8
Rate of drop-out	35.7	32.1	28.6	1.8	1.8
Proportion of graduate students	60.7	5.4	17.9	1.8	14.2
Proportion of new courses in the curricula per year	35.7	25.0	28.6	8.9	1.8
Books/student ratio	35.7	23.2	32.1	7.1	1.9
Availability of teaching and research equipment	30.4	41.1	26.8	1.8	—
Avail. of instructional space	48.2	28.6	21.4	—	1.8
Availability of other space	42.9	28.6	25.0	—	3.5
Unit costs per graduate	39.3	28.6	32.1	—	—
Proportion of research of a high professional calibre	19.6	30.4	46.4	1.8	1.8
Weekly utilization rate of instructional space	33.9	17.8	42.8	—	5.4
Distribution of staff time between teaching, research and other activities [1]	33.3	—	55.5	11.1	—

3B. Level of economic development: developed

Acceptances/applications ratio	62.5	25.0	8.3	—	4.2
No. of graduates in relation to demand for them	25.0	16.7	54.2	4.2	—
Student/teaching staff ratio	91.7	8.3	—	—	—
Rate of drop-out	62.5	29.2	8.3	—	—
Proportion of graduate students	79.2	12.5	—	4.2	4.2
Proportion of new courses in the curricula per year	54.2	12.5	20.8	12.5	—
Books/student ratio	30.0	20.8	20.8	8.3	20.1
Availability of teaching and research equipment	41.7	20.8	4.2	—	33.3
Avail. of instructional space	75.0	20.8	4.2	—	—
Availability of other space	54.2	37.5	8.3	—	—
Unit costs per graduate	54.2	25.0	16.7	—	4.2
Proportion of research of a high professional calibre	9.2	8.3	50.0	4.2	28.3
Weekly utilization rate of instructional space	50.0	16.7	25.0	—	8.3
Distribution of staff time between teaching, research and other activities [1]	12.5	50.0	25.0	12.5	—

TABLE XIII. (*continued*)

	Percentage of universities with information				Non-response
	Available		Not available		
	Adequate	Inadequate	Desirable	Not needed	

4A. Geographical location: Africa

Acceptances/applications ratio	7.1	28.6	50.0	14.3	—
No. of graduates in relation to demand for them	14.3	28.6	57.1	—	—
Student/teaching staff ratio	85.7	7.1	7.1	—	—
Rate of drop-out	50.0	28.6	21.4	—	—
Proportion of graduate students	71.4	7.1	14.3	—	7.2
Proportion of new courses in the curricula per year	14.3	28.6	28.6	28.6	—
Books/student ratio	21.4	14.3	57.1	7.1	—
Availability of teaching and research equipment	21.4	57.1	21.4	—	—
Avail. of instructional space	21.4	50.0	28.6	—	—
Availability of other space	35.7	35.7	28.6	—	—
Unit costs per graduate	42.9	28.6	28.6	—	—
Proportion of research of a high professional calibre	7.1	42.9	50.0	—	—
Weekly utilization rate of instructional space	35.7	14.3	42.9	—	7.1
Distribution of staff time between teaching, research and other activities [1]	33.3	—	66.7	—	—

4B. Geographical location: Asia

Acceptances/applications ratio	43.5	26.1	26.1	—	4.3
No. of graduates in relation to demand for them	8.7	17.4	69.6	—	4.3
Student/teaching staff ratio	73.9	13.0	8.7	—	4.3
Rate of drop-out	21.7	26.1	43.5	4.3	4.3
Proportion of graduate students	65.2	4.3	13.0	4.3	13.2
Proportion of new courses in the curricula per year	39.1	21.7	30.4	4.3	4.3
Books/student ratio	34.8	30.4	21.7	8.7	4.3
Availability of teaching and research equipment	26.1	43.5	21.7	4.3	4.3
Avail. of instructional space	43.5	26.1	26.1	—	4.3
Availability of other space	26.1	34.8	30.4	—	8.7
Unit costs per graduate	34.8	21.7	39.1	—	4.3
Proportion of research of a high professional calibre	17.4	30.4	47.8	—	4.3
Weekly utilization rate of instructional space	26.1	13.0	56.5	—	4.3
Distribution of staff time between teaching, research and other activities [1]	14.3	—	71.5	14.3	—

179

TABLE XIII. (*continued*)

	Percentage of universities with information				Non-response
	Available		Not available		
	Adequate	Inadequate	Desirable	Not needed	
4C. Geographical location: Australia and Oceania					
Acceptances/applications ratio	33.3	33.3	33.3	—	—
No. of graduates in relation to demand for them	—	33.3	66.7	—	—
Student/teaching staff ratio	66.7	33.3	—	—	—
Rate of drop-out	—	66.7	33.3	—	—
Proportion of graduate students	100.0	—	—	—	—
Proportion of new courses in the curricula per year	66.7	—	—	33.3	—
Books/student ratio	66.7	—	—	33.3	—
Availability of teaching and research equipment	33.3	—	66.7	—	—
Avail. of instructional space	66.7	—	33.3	—	—
Availability of other space	33.3	33.3	33.3	—	—
Unit costs per graduate	33.3	33.3	33.3	—	—
Proportion of research of a high professional calibre	33.3	—	—	33.3	33.3
Weekly utilization rate of instructional space	66.7	—	33.3	—	—
Distribution of staff time between teaching, research and other activities [1]	—	33.3	33.3	33.3	—
4D. Geographical location: Europe					
Acceptances/applications ratio	61.1	16.7	16.7	—	5.5
No. of graduates in relation to demand for them	27.8	16.7	50.0	5.6	—
Student/teaching staff ratio	83.3	16.7	—	—	—
Rate of drop-out	55.6	38.9	5.6	—	—
Proportion of graduate students	66.7	16.7	5.6	5.6	5.5
Proportion of new courses in the curricula per year	50.0	16.7	22.2	11.1	—
Books/student ratio	33.3	27.8	27.8	11.1	—
Availability of teaching and research equipment	38.9	27.8	33.3	—	—
Avail. of instructional space	77.8	22.2	—	—	—
Availability of other space	61.1	33.3	5.6	—	—
Unit costs per graduate	55.6	27.8	16.7	—	—
Proportion of research of a high professional calibre	33.8	11.1	50.0	5.6	—
Weekly utilization rate of instructional space	44.4	16.7	33.3	—	5.6
Distribution of staff time between teaching, research and other activities [1]	33.3	16.7	33.3	16.7	—

TABLE **XIII.** (*continued*)

	Percentage of universities with information				Non-response
	Available		Not available		
	Adequate	Inadequate	Desirable	Not needed	

4E. Geographical location: North America

Acceptances/applications ratio	60.0	40.0	—	—	—
No. of graduates in relation to demand for them	20.0	20.0	60.0	—	—
Student/teaching staff ratio	100.0	—	—	—	—
Rate of drop-out	80.0	20.0	—	—	—
Proportion of graduate students	100.0	—	—	—	—
Proportion of new courses in the curricula per year	60.0	20.0	20.0	—	—
Books/student ratio	80.0	20.0	—	—	—
Availability of teaching and research equipment	60.0	20.0	—	—	—
Avail. of instructional space	80.0	20.0	—	—	—
Availability of other space	60.0	40.0	—	—	—
Unit costs per graduate	40.0	40.0	—	—	20.0
Proportion of research of a high professional calibre	—	20.0	60.0	—	20.0
Weekly utilization rate of instructional space	40.0	40.0	—	—	20.0
Distribution of staff time between teaching, research and other activities [1]	—	100.0	—	—	—

4F. Geographical location: Latin and Central America

Acceptances/applications ratio	82.4	5.9	—	11.8	—
No. of graduates in relation to demand for them	17.6	23.5	52.9	—	6.0
Student/teaching staff ratio	58.8	17.6	23.5	—	—
Rate of drop-out	52.9	29.4	17.6	—	—
Proportion of graduate students	47.1	5.9	23.5	—	23.5
Proportion of new courses in the curricula per year	47.1	23.5	29.4	—	—
Books/student ratio	52.9	17.6	29.4	—	—
Availability of teaching and research equipment	41.2	23.5	35.3	—	—
Avail. of instructional space	70.6	17.6	11.8	—	—
Availability of other space	64.7	17.6	17.6	—	6.0
Unit costs per graduate	47.1	23.5	29.4	—	—
Proportion of research of a high professional calibre	35.3	17.6	35.3	—	11.8
Weekly utilization rate of instructional space	41.2	23.5	29.4	—	5.9
Distribution of staff time between teaching, research and other activities [1]	60.0	—	40.0	—	—

emerging disputes," in which "victims and offenders are essentially similar to each other in a variety of characteristics; and whether one emerges as one sort of homicide statistic rather than another may essentially be a matter of 'chance'" (p. 128).

Pallone and Hennessy focus their explanation of tinderbox criminal violence on the "impulsivity" of "actors with a high taste for risk, which may . . . be construed as the product of neurologic" or "neuropsychological dysfunction." They hypothesize that such offenders "self-select those psychosocial environments that are peopled by like-minded (and likely also neurogenically impulsive) others. Such self-selection in essence constitutes 'rational choice' on the part of such actors that functions so as to create the proximate opportunity for criminal violence" (Pallone and Hennessy 1993, p. 128). They note, also, that lethal weapons are present in a high proportion of tinderbox homicides, and that elevated levels of blood alcohol have been found in a high percentage of both offenders and victims.

The lines between these explanations of violence would seem to be clearly drawn. But are they? Perhaps we should be asking how these explanations complement rather than contradict each other. And, what of the macrosocial level of explanation? Consider reports that much social life in lower SES communities takes place in public, or quasi-public settings—for example, on streets, in parks, and in favored taverns—in contrast to middle- and upper-class communities where most social life takes place in more private settings, in more spacious homes or in private clubs. Consider, also, that the privacy in the latter type of setting provides more opportunities to exclude potential disputants from meeting and offers a larger measure of protection from police intervention. Middle-class persons also have greater opportunities to use third parties, including professionals such as physicians, counselors, and lawyers, in settling altercations when they do arise. These and other relevant macro-level differences have been documented in numerous studies of communities (see e.g., Drake and Clayton 1962; Anderson 1978, 1990; Schwartz 1987; Short and Strodtbeck 1965). In later chapters, I will examine evidence at each level of explanation and assess its significance for controlling violent crime. In the meantime, because the microsocial level of explanation is so little understood, a brief discussion of this level is in order.

Group Process and Gang Delinquency

When my colleagues and I began to study delinquent gangs in Chicago, initial research designs called for detailed observation of gangs in their natural settings as well as more systematic interviews with gang and nongang members from the same communities and study of relationships between both groups and community institutions. We hoped, thus, to test several theories about

TABLE XIII. (*continued*)

	Percentage of universities with information				Non-response
	Available		Not available		
	Adequate	Inadequate	Desirable	Not needed	
5A. University size by number of students: 0-5,000					
Acceptances/applications ratio	50.0	25.0	22.2	2.8	—
No. of graduates in relation to demand for them	16.7	22.2	55.6	2.8	2.7
Student/teaching staff ratio	77.8	13.9	8.3	—	—
Rate of drop-out	44.4	27.8	25.0	2.8	—
Proportion of graduate students	66.7	8.3	8.3	2.8	13.9
Proportion of new courses in the curricula per year	38.9	19.4	25.0	16.7	—
Books/student ratio	36.1	25.0	25.0	13.9	—
Availability of teaching and research equipment	33.3	47.2	16.7	2.8	—
Avail. of instructional space	61.1	30.6	8.3	—	—
Availability of other space	55.5	27.8	16.7	—	—
Unit costs per graduate	50.0	27.8	19.4	—	2.8
Proportion of research of a high professional calibre	22.2	27.8	36.1	5.6	8.3
Weekly utilization rate of instructional space	44.4	16.7	30.6	—	8.3
Distribution of staff time between teaching, research and other activities [1]	21.4	7.1	50.0	21.4	—
5B. University size by number of students: 5,000-10,000					
Acceptances/applications ratio	45.0	25.0	25.0	5.0	—
No. of graduates in relation to demand for them	15.0	15.0	65.0	—	5.0
Student/teaching staff ratio	75.0	15.0	5.0	—	5.0
Rate of drop-out	45.0	20.0	30.0	—	5.0
Proportion of graduate students	75.0	5.0	5.0	—	10.0
Proportion of new courses in the curricula per year	50.0	25.0	15.0	5.0	5.0
Books/student ratio	45.0	25.0	25.0	—	5.0
Availability of teaching and research equipment	40.0	30.0	30.0	—	—
Avail. of instructional space	60.0	20.0	15.0	—	5.0
Availability of other space	40.0	35.0	15.0	—	10.0
Unit costs per graduate	40.0	25.0	35.0	—	—
Proportion of research of a high professional calibre	15.0	25.0	60.0	—	—
Weekly utilization rate of instructional space	45.0	15.0	40.0	—	—
Distribution of staff time between teaching, research and other activities [1]	—	50.0	50.0	—	—

TABLE XIII. (*continued*)

	Percentage of universities with information				Non-response
	Available		Not available		
	Adequate	Inadequate	Desirable	Not needed	
5C. University size by number of students: 10,000 and over					
Acceptances/applications ratio	54.2	12.5	25.0	8.3	—
No. of graduates in relation to demand for them	16.7	25.0	58.3	—	—
Student/teaching staff ratio	75.0	12.5	12.5	—	—
Rate of drop-out	41.7	45.8	12.5	—	—
Proportion of graduate students	58.3	8.3	25.0	4.2	4.2
Proportion of new courses in the curricula per year	37.5	20.8	37.5	4.2	—
Books/student ratio	41.7	16.7	37.5	4.2	—
Availability of teaching and research equipment	29.2	20.8	41.7	—	8.3
Avail. of instructional space	45.8	25.0	29.2	—	—
Availability of other space	37.5	33.3	29.2	—	—
Unit costs per graduate	37.5	25.0	33.3	—	4.2
Proportion of research of a high professional calibre	29.2	16.7	45.8	—	8.3
Weekly utilization rate of instructional space	25.0	20.8	45.8	—	8.3
Distribution of staff time between teaching, research and other activities [1]	50.0	12.5	37.5	—	—
6A. Emphasis on the field of study: pure science					
Acceptances/applications ratio	66.7	11.1	11.1	11.1	—
No. of graduates in relation to demand for them	33.3	11.1	55.6	—	—
Student/teaching staff ratio	88.9	11.1	—	—	—
Rate of drop-out	33.3	44.4	22.2	—	—
Proportion of graduate students	88.9	—	—	—	11.1
Proportion of new courses in the curricula per year	77.8	—	11.1	11.1	—
Books/student ratio	44.4	22.2	22.2	11.1	—
Availability of teaching and research equipment	33.3	44.4	11.1	11.1	—
Avail. of instructional space	55.6	22.2	22.2	—	—
Availability of other space	33.3	33.3	22.2	—	—
Unit costs per graduate	33.3	33.3	33.3	—	—
Proportion of research of a high professional calibre	33.3	22.2	44.4	—	—
Weekly utilization rate of instructional space	22.2	22.2	44.4	—	11.1
Distribution of staff time between teaching, research and other activities [1]	—	33.3	66.7	—	—

TABLE XIII. (*continued*)

	Percentage of universities with information				Non-response
	Available		Not available		
	Adequate	Inadequate	Desirable	Not needed	
6B. Emphasis on the field of study: humanities					
Acceptances/applications ratio	28.6	42.9	14.3	—	14.2
No. of graduates in relation to demand for them	—	14.3	71.4	—	14.3
Student/teaching staff ratio	57.1	14.3	14.3	—	14.3
Rate of drop-out	28.6	28.6	28.6	—	14.2
Proportion of graduate students	71.4	14.3	—	—	14.3
Proportion of new courses in the curricula per year	42.9	—	28.4	14.3	14.4
Books/student ratio	42.9	—	42.9	—	14.2
Availability of teaching and research equipment	42.9	28.6	28.6	—	—
Avail. of instructional space	71.4	14.3	—	—	14.3
Availability of other space	42.9	28.6	14.3	—	14.2
Unit costs per graduate	37.1	14.3	28.6	—	20.0
Proportion of research of a high professional calibre	14.3	28.6	57.1	—	—
Weekly utilization rate of instructional space	28.6	—	57.1	—	14.3
Distribution of staff time between teaching, research and other activities [1]	—	—	100.0	—	—
6C. Emphasis on the field of study: social sciences					
Acceptances/applications ratio	—	75.0	25.0	—	—
No. of graduates in relation to demand for them	—	50.0	50.0	—	—
Student/teaching staff ratio	75.0	25.0	—	—	—
Rate of drop-out	25.0	50.0	25.0	—	—
Proportion of graduate students	75.0	25.0	—	—	—
Proportion of new courses in the curricula per year	75.0	—	—	25.0	—
Books/student ratio	75.0	—	—	25.0	—
Availability of teaching and research equipment	75.0	—	25.0	—	—
Avail. of instructional space	75.0	25.0	—	—	—
Availability of other space	75.0	—	25.0	—	—
Unit costs per graduate	50.0	25.0	25.0	—	—
Proportion of research of a high professional calibre	50.0	—	25.0	25.0	—
Weekly utilization rate of instructional space	50.0	—	50.0	—	—
Distribution of staff time between teaching, research and other activities [1]	25.0	25.0	25.0	25.0	—

184

Table XIII. *(continued)*

	Percentage of universities with information				Non-response
	Available		Not available		
	Adequate	Inadequate	Desirable	Not needed	

5D. Emphasis on the field of study: professional training

Acceptances/applications ratio	65.2	8.7	13.0	8.7	4.4
No. of graduates in relation to demand for them	17.4	13.0	69.6	—	—
Student/teaching staff ratio	78.3	17.4	4.3	—	—
Rate of drop-out	60.9	21.7	13.0	4.3	—
Proportion of graduate students	56.5	8.7	13.0	8.7	13.1
Proportion of new courses in the curricula per year	39.1	39.1	21.7	—	—
Books/student ratio	34.8	26.1	39.1	—	—
Availability of teaching and research equipment	30.4	34.8	34.8	—	—
Avail. of instructional space	69.6	21.7	8.7	—	—
Availability of other space	65.2	26.1	8.7	—	—
Unit costs per graduate	56.5	17.4	21.7	—	4.4
Proportion of research of a high professional calibre	30.4	21.7	43.5	—	4.3
Weekly utilization rate of instructional space	58.3	16.7	20.8	—	4.2
Distribution of staff time between teaching, research and other activities [1]	20.0	—	60.0	20.0	—

5E. Emphasis on the field of study: no special emphasis

Acceptances/applications ratio	45.0	21.6	29.7	2.7	—
No. of graduates in relation to demand for them	16.2	27.0	51.4	2.7	2.7
Student/teaching staff ratio	75.7	10.8	13.5	—	—
Rate of drop-out	40.5	32.4	27.0	—	—
Proportion of graduate students	64.9	5.4	18.9	—	10.8
Proportion of new courses in the curricula per year	29.7	21.6	35.1	13.5	—
Books/student ratio	37.8	27.0	24.3	10.8	—
Availability of teaching and research equipment	29.7	37.8	27.0	—	5.5
Avail. of instructional space	43.2	32.4	24.3	—	—
Availability of other space	35.1	37.8	27.0	—	—
Unit costs per graduate	35.1	32.4	29.7	—	2.8
Proportion of research of a high professional calibre	13.5	27.0	45.9	2.7	10.9
Weekly utilization rate of instructional space	30.5	22.2	41.7	—	5.6
Distribution of staff time between teaching, research and other activities [1]	38.5	15.4	38.5	7.7	—

185

Table XIII. (*continued*)

	Percentage of universities with information				Non-response
	Available		Not available		
	Adequate	Inadequate	Desirable	Not needed	
7A. Emphasis on function: undergraduate teaching					
Acceptances/applications ratio	47.4	24.6	19.3	5.3	3.4
No. of graduates in relation to demand for them	15.8	22.8	57.9	—	3.5
Student/teaching staff ratio	77.2	12.3	8.8	—	1.7
Rate of drop-out	40.4	35.1	21.1	1.8	1.6
Proportion of graduate students	61.4	7.0	14.0	1.8	15.8
Proportion of new courses in the curricula per year	38.6	22.8	26.3	10.5	1.8
Books/student ratio	42.1	17.5	31.6	7.0	1.8
Availability of teaching and research equipment	29.8	38.6	29.8	1.8	—
Avail. of instructional space	59.6	22.8	15.8	—	1.8
Availability of other space	45.6	31.6	21.1	—	1.7
Unit costs per graduate	40.4	31.6	26.3	—	1.7
Proportion of research of a high professional calibre	17.5	29.3	43.8	1.3	8.1
Weekly utilization rate of instructional space	40.3	21.1	33.3	—	11.1
Distribution of staff time between teaching, research and other activities [1]	35.0	20.0	40.0	5.0	5.3
7B. Emphasis on function: graduate teaching					
Acceptances/applications ratio	53.6	16.7	22.2	5.6	1.9
No. of graduates in relation to demand for them	16.7	16.7	61.1	5.6	—
Student/teaching staff ratio	77.8	11.1	11.1	—	—
Rate of drop-out	50.0	16.7	33.3	—	—
Proportion of graduate students	72.2	11.1	11.1	3.6	2.0
Proportion of new courses in the curricula per year	44.4	22.2	27.8	5.6	—
Books/student ratio	44.4	27.8	22.2	5.6	—
Availability of teaching and research equipment	50.0	22.2	22.2	—	5.6
Avail. of instructional space	50.0	27.8	22.2	—	—
Availability of other space	50.0	22.2	22.2	—	5.6
Unit costs per graduate	38.9	16.7	38.9	—	—
Proportion of research of a high professional calibre	38.9	5.6	50.0	—	5.5
Weekly utilization rate of instructional space	33.3	5.6	55.6	—	5.5
Distribution of staff time between teaching, research and other activities [1]	—	—	75.0	25.0	—

TABLE XIII. (*continued*)

| | Percentage of universities with information | | | | Non-response |
| | Available | | Not available | | |
	Adequate	Inadequate	Desirable	Not needed	
C. Emphasis on function: research					
Acceptances/applications ratio	100.0	—	—	—	—
No. of graduates in relation to demand for them	50.0	—	50.0	—	—
Student/teaching staff ratio	100.0	—	—	—	—
Rate of drop-out	100.0	—	—	—	—
Proportion of graduate students	100.0	—	—	—	—
Proportion of new courses in the curricula per year	50.0	—	50.0	—	—
Books/student ratio	—	50.0	50.0	—	—
Availability of teaching and research equipment	—	50.0	—	—	50.0
Avail. of instructional space	50.0	50.0	—	—	—
Availability of other space	50.0	50.0	—	—	—
Unit costs per graduate	100.0	—	—	—	—
Proportion of research of a high professional calibre	50.0	—	50.0	—	—
Weekly utilization rate of instructional space	—	50.0	—	—	50.0
Distribution of staff time between teaching, research and other activities [1]	—	—	—	—	—
D. Emphasis on function: teacher training					
Acceptances/applications ratio	33.3	—	66.7	—	—
No. of graduates in relation to demand for them	—	33.3	66.7	—	—
Student/teaching staff ratio	33.3	66.7	—	—	—
Rate of drop-out	33.3	66.7	—	—	—
Proportion of graduate students	100.0	—	—	—	—
Proportion of new courses in the curricula per year	66.7	—	—	33.3	—
Books/student ratio	—	66.7	—	33.3	—
Availability of teaching and research equipment	33.3	33.3	33.3	—	—
Avail. of instructional space	33.3	66.7	—	—	—
Availability of other space	33.3	66.7	—	—	—
Unit costs per graduate	100.0	—	—	—	—
Proportion of research of a high professional calibre	—	33.3	33.3	33.3	—
Weekly utilization rate of instructional space	66.7	—	33.3	—	—
Distribution of staff time between teaching, research and other activities [1]	—	—	50.0	50.0	—

TABLE XIII. (*continued*)

	Percentage of universities with information				Non-response
	Available		Not available		
	Adequate	Inadequate	Desirable	Not needed	

8A. Type of control: private

Acceptances/applications ratio	50.0	18.8	25.0	—	6.2
No. of graduates in relation to demand for them	6.3	18.8	68.8	—	6.2
Student/teaching staff ratio	62.5	18.8	12.5	—	6.2
Rate of drop-out	43.8	12.5	31.3	6.3	6.2
Proportion of graduate students	62.5	5.3	12.5	—	19.7
Proportion of new courses in the curricula per year	31.3	12.5	43.8	6.3	6.2
Books/student ratio	43.8	12.5	37.5	—	6.2
Availability of teaching and research equipment	25.0	43.8	31.3	—	—
Avail. of instructional space	43.8	25.0	25.0	—	6.2
Availability of other space	31.3	25.0	37.5	—	6.2
Unit costs per graduate	18.8	25.0	50.0	—	6.2
Proportion of research of a high professional calibre	—	37.5	62.5	—	—
Weekly utilization rate of instructional space	18.8	18.8	50.0	—	12.5
Distribution of staff time between teaching, research and other activities [1]	20.0	20.0	60.0	—	—

8B. Type of control: public

Acceptances/applications ratio	50.0	21.9	20.3	6.3	1.5
No. of graduates in relation to demand for them	18.8	21.9	56.3	1.6	1.5
Student/teaching staff ratio	79.7	12.5	7.8	—	—
Rate of drop-out	43.8	35.9	20.3	—	—
Proportion of graduate students	67.2	7.8	12.5	9.1	3.5
Proportion of new courses in the curricula per year	43.8	23.4	21.9	10.9	—
Books/student ratio	39.1	25.0	26.6	9.4	—
Availability of teaching and research equipment	35.9	32.8	26.6	1.6	3.1
Avail. of instructional space	59.4	26.6	14.1	—	—
Availability of other space	50.0	34.4	15.6	—	—
Unit costs per graduate	50.0	28.1	21.9	—	—
Proportion of research of a high professional calibre	28.1	20.3	43.8	3.1	4.7
Weekly utilization rate of instructional space	43.8	17.2	34.4	—	4.7
Distribution of staff time between teaching, research and other activities [1]	28.6	14.3	42.8	14.3	—

TABLE XIIIA. Use of indices for university planning; median values of actual ratios and specified norms applied by universities

	A	B		C		D		E		F		G	
		Actual	Specified	Actual	Specified	Actual	Specified	Actual	Specified	Actual	Specified	Actual	Specified
1. Overall sample	2.0	13.41	9.54	6.0	5.0	5.6	9.5	19.1	10.0	42.0	40.0	1.4	5.0
Number in sample	2	8		2		4		1		3		2	
2. Existence of planning system													
University plan.	2.5	11.53	12.7	6.0	5.0	4.4	9.5	19.1	10.0	41.35	41.0	—	—
Some planning	—	7.0	10.65	—	—	15.9	18.8	—	—	—	—	—	—
No planning	1.5	25.8	10.7	—	—	5.2	5.0	—	—	42.0	40.0	1.4	5.0
3. Level of economic development													
Developing	2.0	19.3	10.7	13.5	15.0	5.6	7.5	—	—	23.85	22.5	—	—
Developed	—	12.2	12.1	6.0	5.0	9.35	13.6	19.1	10.0	77.0	77.0	1.4	5.0

A: Ratio of applications to acceptances for 1968/69 for all disciplines combined.
B: Student/teaching staff ratio defined as in the glossary.
C: Rate of drop-out in percentage for 1968/69.
D: Proportion of graduate students in student body.
E: Proportion of new courses in curricula per year indicated by the average annual growth rate for the last decade.
F: Books available per student.
G: Instructional space per student in square metres.

189

TABLE XIV. Past and future factors of charge in the university: opinions of univesities on past and future problems and their reaction

I. Overall sample

	Past importance				Past reaction				Future importance				Future reaction			
	R	MS	SD	Sample	R	MS	SD	Sample	R	MS	SD	Sample	R	MS	SD	Sample
Increase in applications	4	2.32	1.54	77	3	2.32	1.03	69	6	2.02	1.40	79	7	2.43	1.08	74
Increase in enrolments	1	2.03	1.44	77	5	2.46	1.05	71	7	2.08	1.34	78	11	2.56	1.15	75
Improving quality of incoming students	11	3.46	1.90	76	8	2.66	1.16	53	11	2.65	1.63	77	8	2.45	0.98	67
Increase in applications relative to no. of places available	8	2.92	1.88	74	12-13	2.95	1.04	58	9	2.25	1.52	75	14	2.80	1.14	66
Expanding numbers of teaching and research staff	5	2.60	1.56	76	1	2.22	1.01	71	4	1.96	1.04	77	4	2.24	0.95	76
Improving the quality of teaching and research staff	7	2.89	1.69	75	4	2.44	0.93	64	8	2.23	1.39	75	1-2	2.15	0.86	71
The need to change the curriculum to fit changing needs	6	2.80	1.56	76	7	2.64	1.07	67	3	1.91	0.95	78	3	2.20	0.72	76
The need to change the structure to meet changing needs	9	3.10	1.77	76	6	2.61	1.15	64	5	2.00	1.19	78	5	2.39	1.02	74
The need to increase the volume and sources of financing	2	2.08	1.46	76	11	2.83	1.10	71	1	1.49	0.86	76	15	2.85	1.14	75
The need to expand facilities	3	2.14	1.38	76	10	2.78	1.06	72	2	1.68	0.88	75	12	2.57	1.06	77
The gap between distribution of graduates by field and manpower needs	12	3.84	1.97	70	9	2.69	1.31	43	10	2.57	1.52	70	10	2.54	1.04	65
Changes in the amount and type of research within the university	—	—	—	—	14	2.97	1.11	63	—	—	—	—	9	2.49	0.89	70
Increased participation of students in university governance	10	3.40	1.79	77	2	2.27	1.10	52	14	2.93	1.44	77	1-2	2.15	0.81	67
The need for refresher courses	13	4.45	1.72	75	12-13	2.95	1.29	41	12	2.70	1.40	76	6	2.42	0.99	71
Demand for continuing education for persons in all walks of life	14	4.64	1.60	75	15	3.05	1.11	37	13	2.90	1.49	76	13	2.60	1.02	67

2A. Existence of a planning system: central and university planning

	Sample	Past importance			Past reaction			Future importance			Future reaction		
		R	MS	SD	R	MS	SD	R	MS	SD	R	MS	SD
Increase in applications	5	1	1.60	0.80	1	1.60	0.49	8	3.00	1.55	13	2.25	0.43
Increase in enrolments	5	6	2.00	1.27	3	1.80	0.75	8	3.00	1.67	3	2.00	0.63
Improving quality of incoming students	5	9	2.20	0.98	4	2.00	0.63	2	1.80	0.75	3	2.00	0.63
Increase in applications relative to no. of places available	5	10	2.80	1.83	12	2.25	0.43	11	3.20	1.72	13	2.25	0.43
Expanding numbers of teaching and research staff	5	4	1.80	0.75	8	2.20	0.40	6	2.00	0.89	9	2.20	0.98
Improving the quality of teaching and research staff	5	4	1.80	0.75	4	2.00	0.63	2	1.80	0.75	2	1.80	0.75
The need to change the curriculum to fit changing needs	5	1	1.60	0.80	13	2.40	0.49	6	2.00	0.89	3	2.00	—
The need to change structure of university to meet changing needs	5	1	1.60	1.20	1	1.60	0.80	11	3.20	1.50	13	2.25	0.43
The need to increase the volume and sources of financing	5	6	2.00	0.63	8	2.20	0.40	2	1.80	0.75	9	2.20	0.40
The need to expand facilities	5	6	2.00	0.63	15	2.60	0.80	2	1.80	0.40	3	2.00	—
The gap between distribution of graduates by field and manpower needs	5	13	3.60	1.36	8	2.20	0.98	13	3.40	1.63	3	2.00	0.63
Changes in the amount and type of research within the university	5	—	—	—	8	2.20	0.40	—	—	—	9	2.20	0.40
Increased participation of students in university governance	5	10	2.80	1.72	4	2.00	0.71	14	3.60	1.36	1	1.75	0.43
The need for refresher courses	5	12	3.40	1.50	14	2.50	0.87	1	1.60	0.49	9	2.20	0.40
Demand for continuing education for persons in all walks of life	5	14	4.40	1.62	4	2.00	0.82	8	3.00	1.67	3	2.00	—

191

TABLE XIV. (continued)

2B. Existence of a planning system: central planning only

	Sample	Past importance			Past reaction			Future importance			Future reaction		
		R	MS	SD	R	MS	SD	R	MS	SD	R	MS	SD
Increase in applications	3	10	3.00	2.16	2-3	1.50	0.50	8-9	2.33	1.24	9-11	2.67	0.47
Increase in enrolments	3	6-9	2.67	2.36	2-3	1.50	0.50	10-13	2.67	1.25	12-14	3.00	0.81
Improving quality of incoming students	3	11	3.33	2.05	6-7	2.50	0.50	14	3.33	2.05	7-8	2.50	0.50
Increase in applications relative to no. of places available	3	12-13	3.50	2.50	12-13	3.00	—	1	1.00	—	12-14	3.00	—
Expanding numbers of teaching and research staff	3	6-9	2.67	0.47	1	1.33	0.47	10-13	2.67	1.25	1-3	2.00	—
Improving the quality of teaching and research staff	3	3	2.00	—	8-11	2.67	1.25	6-7	2.00	0.82	1-3	2.00	0.82
The need to change the curriculum to fit changing needs	3	1	1.33	0.47	5	2.33	1.25	6-7	2.00	0.82	1-3	2.00	—
The need to change structure of university to meet changing needs	3	4-5	2.33	0.94	8-11	2.67	0.47	3-5	1.67	0.94	9-11	2.67	0.47
The need to increase the volume and sources of financing	3	6-9	2.67	1.25	14	3.33	0.94	3-5	1.67	0.47	15	3.33	0.47
The need to expand facilities	3	2	1.67	0.47	8-11	2.67	0.94	10-13	2.67	1.25	4-6	2.33	0.47
The gap between distribution of graduates by field and manpower needs	3	6-9	2.67	2.36	12-13	3.00	1.00	10-13	2.67	1.25	4-6	2.33	0.47
Changes in the amount and type of research within the university	3	—	—	—	4	2.00	—	—	—	—	7-8	2.50	0.50
Increased participation of students in university governance	3	4-5	2.33	0.94	8-11	2.67	1.25	3-5	1.67	0.47	12-14	3.00	0.81
The need for refresher courses	3	12-13	3.50	2.50	15	4.00	—	8-9	2.33	1.25	4-6	2.33	0.94
Demand for continuing education for persons in all walks of life	3	14	4.33	1.25	6-7	2.50	0.50	2	1.33	0.47	9-11	2.67	0.47

TABLE XIV. (*continued*)

2C. Existence of a planning system: university planning only

	Sample	Past importance			Past reaction			Future importance			Future reaction		
		R	MS	SD	R	MS	SD	R	MS	SD	R	MS	SD
Increase in applications	17	5	2.35	1.68	1	2.00	0.66	8	2.00	1.49	6	1.94	0.66
Increase in enrolments	17	1	1.71	1.31	7	2.56	0.86	5	1.76	1.16	6	1.94	1.06
Improving quality of incoming students	17	10	3.29	1.87	6	2.50	1.11	9	2.18	1.29	5	1.88	0.69
Increase in applications relative to no. of places available	17	9	3.25	2.04	12	2.82	0.83	10	2.19	1.38	12	2.20	0.91
Expanding numbers of teaching and research staff	17	5	2.35	1.64	4	2.20	0.75	5	1.76	0.94	2	1.76	0.64
Improving the quality of teaching and research staff	17	4	2.12	1.56	2	2.07	0.68	3	1.65	0.96	2	1.76	0.81
The need to change the curriculum to fit changing needs	17	7	2.59	1.37	5	2.40	0.95	7	1.94	1.35	4	1.81	0.73
The need to change structure of university to meet changing needs	17	8	2.88	1.97	9	2.69	1.14	3	1.65	0.84	10	2.18	1.20
The need to increase the volume and sources of financing	17	1	1.71	1.23	11	2.81	1.18	1	1.25	0.43	15	2.87	1.41
The need to expand facilities	17	3	1.94	1.31	7	2.56	1.00	2	1.35	0.76	10	2.18	1.10
The gap between distribution of graduates by field and manpower needs	17	14	4.80	1.76	10	2.80	1.16	12	2.73	1.69	13	2.30	1.07
Changes in the amount and type of research within the university	12	—	—	—	13	3.07	1.22	—	—	—	9	2.13	0.95
Increased participation of students in university governance	15	11	3.89	1.91	3	2.10	1.13	11	2.65	1.41	1	1.71	0.79
The need for refresher courses	15	13	4.59	1.57	14	3.22	1.39	13	2.76	1.80	8	2.00	1.07
Demand for continuing education for persons in all walks of life	15	12	4.17	1.88	15	3.25	1.09	14	2.82	1.46	14	2.33	0.96

TABLE XIV. (*continued*)

2D. Existence of a planning system: some planning

	Sample	Past importance			Past reaction			Future importance			Future reaction		
		R	MS	SD	R	MS	SD	R	MS	SD	R	MS	SD
Increase in applications	34	3	2.39	1.57	3	2.53	1.09	3-4	1.94	1.33	8	2.48	1.16
Increase in enrolments	33	1	2.15	1.54	2	2.47	1.02	6	2.09	1.36	13	2.71	1.08
Improving quality of incoming students	32	10	3.81	1.79	13	2.90	1.23	11	2.69	1.72	11-12	2.67	0.94
Increase in applications relative to no. of places available	33	6	2.91	1.86	15	3.08	1.05	7-8	2.27	1.62	15	2.90	1.12
Expanding numbers of teaching and research staff	33	5	2.54	1.34	1	2.23	1.07	5	2.03	1.07	2	2.28	0.80
Improving the quality of teaching and research staff	32	9	3.31	1.57	5-6	2.59	0.91	9	2.44	1.43	1	2.27	0.81
The need to change the curriculum to fit changing needs	33	7	3.09	1.49	8	2.71	0.99	3-4	1.94	0.69	3	2.31	0.68
The need to change structure of university to meet changing needs	33	8	3.28	1.42	5-6	2.59	1.10	7-8	2.27	1.26	5	2.44	0.97
The need to increase the volume and sources of financing	32	2	2.28	1.60	11	2.86	1.07	1	1.47	0.79	14	2.87	1.02
The need to expand facilities	33	4	2.41	1.52	10	2.80	1.05	2	1.82	0.94	11-12	2.67	1.03
The gap between distribution of graduates by field and manpower needs	29	11	4.00	1.89	7	2.67	1.29	10	2.48	1.52	9	2.52	1.03
Changes in the amount and type of research within the university	26	—	—	—	12	2.88	1.05	—	—	—	6-7	2.45	0.80
Increased participation of students in university governance	33	12	4.06	1.56	4	2.56	1.10	13	3.03	1.38	4	2.43	1.72
The need for refresher courses	32	13	4.75	1.54	9	2.75	1.20	12	2.94	1.20	6-7	2.45	0.84
Demand for continuing education for persons in all walks of life	32	14	4.93	1.41	14	3.07	1.03	14	3.16	1.52	10	2.61	1.08

TABLE XIV. (*continued*)

2E. Existence of a planning system: no planning

	Sample	Past importance			Past reaction			Future importance			Future reaction		
		R	MS	SD	R	MS	SD	R	MS	SD	R	MS	SD
Increase in applications	20	4	2.26	1.29	3	2.50	1.12	5-6	1.90	1.34	7-8	2.78	1.23
Increase in enrolments	20	1-3	2.00	1.12	5	2.67	1.20	7	2.00	1.22	13-14	2.95	1.19
Improving quality of incoming students	20	10	3.37	2.08	6	2.69	1.20	14	3.10	1.61	6	2.76	1.11
Increase in applications relative to no. of places available	20	5	2.63	1.63	11-12	3.00	1.19	8	2.10	1.34	15	3.29	1.22
Expanding numbers of teaching and research staff	20	8	3.17	1.64	2	2.41	1.19	5-6	1.90	0.99	5	2.63	1.26
Improving the quality of teaching and research staff	18	9	3.33	1.86	4	2.64	1.04	10	2.56	1.64	3-4	2.50	0.86
The need to change the curriculum to fit changing needs	20	6	3.05	1.76	8	2.87	1.32	4	1.80	0.93	2	2.40	0.80
The need to change structure of university to meet changing needs	20	11	3.53	2.04	10	2.93	1.28	2-3	1.60	0.92	3-4	2.50	1.07
The need to increase the volume and sources of financing	20	1-3	2.00	1.49	9	2.89	1.15	2-3	1.60	1.20	9-10	2.89	1.21
The need to expand facilities	20	1-3	2.00	1.38	11-12	3.00	1.15	1	1.55	0.74	13-14	2.95	1.10
The gap between distribution of graduates by field and manpower needs	19	7	3.10	1.92	7	2.80	1.47	9	2.33	1.27	11-12	2.94	1.06
Changes in the amount and type of research within the university	17	—	—	—	15	3.37	1.11	—	—	—	11-12	2.94	0.94
Increased participation of students in university governance	20	12	4.15	1.93	1	1.83	0.90	13	3.05	1.50	1	1.94	0.75
The need for refresher courses	19	13	4.21	1.91	13	3.09	1.38	11	2.58	1.31	7-8	2.78	1.13
Demand for continuing education for persons in all walks of life	19	14	4.68	1.52	14	3.30	1.19	12	2.79	1.32	9-10	2.89	1.05

TABLE XIV. (*continued*)

3A. Level of economic development: developing

	Sample	Past importance			Past reaction			Future importance			Future reaction		
		R	MS	SD	R	MS	SD	R	MS	SD	R	MS	SD
Increase in applications	55	4	2.37	1.55	3	2.48	0.98	6	1.91	1.27	10	2.53	1.06
Increase in enrolments	54	1	2.02	1.46	5	2.56	0.90	7	1.96	1.22	13	2.61	1.06
Improving quality of incoming students	53	10	3.38	1.91	9	2.84	1.22	11	2.58	1.56	7	2.40	0.98
Increase in applications relative to no. of places available	52	7	2.77	1.77	13	3.07	0.97	9	2.19	1.51	14-15	2.83	1.12
Expanding numbers of teaching and research staff	54	5	2.70	1.62	1	2.20	1.04	3	1.83	0.97	3	2.19	0.93
Improving the quality of teaching and research staff	54	8	2.83	1.62	4	2.49	0.94	8	2.07	1.27	2	2.08	0.78
The need to change the curriculum to fit changing needs	55	6	2.74	1.58	7	2.69	1.08	4	1.87	1.01	1	2.06	0.66
The need to change structure of university to meet changing needs	55	9	3.30	1.76	6	2.68	1.20	5	1.89	1.11	6	2.31	1.00
The need to increase the volume and sources of financing	54	2	2.07	1.54	11	3.00	1.15	1	1.48	0.94	14-15	2.83	1.14
The need to expand facilities	55	3	2.17	1.42	10	2.92	1.01	2	1.69	0.87	12	2.60	1.07
The gap between distribution of graduates by field and manpower needs	50	11	3.61	2.05	8	2.81	1.36	10	2.48	1.56	8-9	2.47	1.00
Changes in the amount and type of research within the university	47	—	—	—	15	3.32	1.06	—	—	—	8-9	2.47	0.85
Increased participation of students in university governance	53	12	4.34	1.66	2	2.34	1.00	12	2.85	1.38	4	2.21	0.82
The need for refresher courses	54	13	4.67	1.70	14	3.15	1.32	13	2.94	1.48	5	2.23	0.87
Demand for continuing education for persons in all walks of life	53	14	4.83	1.48	12	3.04	1.04	14	3.06	1.47	11	2.55	1.05

TABLE XIV. (*continued*)

3B. Level of economic development: developed

	Sample	Past importance			Past reaction			Future importance			Future reaction		
		R	MS	SD	R	MS	SD	R	MS	SD	R	MS	SD
Increase in applications	24	4	2.22	1.50	1	1.95	1.04	7	2.29	1.64	2	2.19	1.10
Increase in enrolments	24	1	2.04	1.40	4	2.24	1.31	8	2.33	1.55	5	2.43	1.31
Improving quality of incoming students	24	11	3.65	1.88	3	2.20	0.83	12	2.79	1.75	9	2.55	0.97
Increase in applications relative to no. of places available	23	10	3.27	2.07	13-14	2.60	1.14	9	2.39	1.55	13	2.74	1.21
Expanding numbers of teaching and research staff	24	5	2.36	1.40	5-6	2.29	0.93	5	2.25	1.13	3	2.35	0.96
Improving the quality of teaching and research staff	21	9	3.05	1.84	5-6	2.29	0.89	11	2.62	1.59	4	2.37	1.04
The need to change the curriculum to fit changing needs	23	8	2.95	1.49	12	2.53	1.04	3	2.00	0.78	7-8	2.52	0.77
The need to change structure of university to meet changing needs	20	6	2.64	1.69	11	2.45	1.02	6	2.26	1.33	10	2.60	1.07
The need to increase the volume and sources of financing	22	2-3	2.09	1.24	9-10	2.43	0.85	1	1.50	0.64	15	2.91	1.12
The need to expand facilities	23	2-3	2.09	1.28	9-10	2.43	1.10	2	1.65	0.91	6	2.50	1.03
The gap between distribution of graduates by field and manpower needs	20	14	4.38	1.65	8	2.38	1.15	13	2.80	1.36	11-12	2.70	1.10
Changes in the amount and type of research within the university	23	—	—	—	7	2.35	0.91	—	—	—	7-8	2.52	0.97
Increased participation of students in university governance	24	7	2.92	1.68	2	2.15	1.24	14	3.12	1.54	1	2.00	0.77
The need for refresher courses	23	12	3.90	1.66	13-14	2.60	1.14	4	2.13	0.95	14	2.83	1.09
Demand for continuing education for persons in all walks of life	23	13	4.18	1.77	15	3.08	1.26	10	2.56	1.47	11-12	2.70	0.95

TABLE XIV. (*continued*)

4A. Geographical location: Africa

	Sample	Past importance			Past reaction			Future importance			Future reaction		
		R	MS	SD	R	MS	SD	R	MS	SD	R	MS	SD
Increase in applications	13	4-5	2.58	1.44	1	2.00	1.13	5	2.07	1.14	11-12	2.85	0.94
Increase in enrolments	13	3	2.08	1.19	2	2.08	1.12	6	2.15	1.10	13	3.17	0.90
Improving quality of incoming students	12	10-11	3.83	1.72	8-11	2.75	1.20	10-11	3.00	1.58	7	2.60	0.49
Increase in applications relative to no. of places available	11	9	3.64	2.01	14	3.57	1.05	10-11	3.00	1.95	15	3.87	0.78
Expanding numbers of teaching and research staff	12	6	2.67	1.18	5-6	2.42	1.26	4	2.00	0.71	2-3	2.42	0.76
Improving the quality of teaching and research staff	13	7	3.08	1.75	4	2.22	0.92	8	2.61	1.27	2-3	2.42	0.86
The need to change the curriculum to fit changing needs	13	4-5	2.58	1.25	11	2.91	1.08	7	2.23	1.05	1	2.15	0.53
The need to change structure of university to meet changing needs	13	8	3.58	1.55	7	2.67	0.67	3	1.92	0.99	8	2.61	0.92
The need to increase the volume and sources of financing	13	2	2.00	1.29	8-11	2.75	1.09	1	1.61	0.74	11-12	2.85	0.66
The need to expand facilities	13	1	1.92	1.12	5-6	2.42	1.04	2	1.77	0.80	4	2.46	0.50
The gap between distribution of graduates by field and manpower needs	12	10-11	3.73	2.05	3	2.14	0.99	13-14	3.42	1.85	6	2.56	0.83
Changes in the amount and type of research within the university	8	—	—	—	13	3.50	0.95	—	—	—	10	2.75	0.43
Increased participation of students in university governance	12	12	4.33	1.55	8-11	2.75	1.20	9	2.75	1.01	9	2.73	0.62
The need for refresher courses	12	13	4.83	1.40	14	3.57	1.29	13-14	3.42	1.38	5	2.54	0.73
Demand for continuing education for persons in all walks of life	12	14	5.17	0.99	12	3.33	0.74	12	3.08	1.44	14	3.18	0.57

TABLE XIV. (*continued*)

4B. Geographical location: Asia

	Sample	Past importance			Past reaction			Future importance			Future reaction		
		R	MS	SD	R	MS	SD	R	MS	SD	R	MS	SD
Increase in applications	23	5	2.52	1.64	5	2.70	0.78	5	2.13	1.39	6	2.64	1.23
Increase in enrolments	23	1	2.00	1.25	6	2.73	0.81	7	2.18	1.30	9	2.73	1.05
Improving quality of incoming students	23	10	3.13	1.82	9	3.12	1.08	11	2.59	1.26	8	2.71	1.08
Increase in applications relative to no. of places available	23	4	2.43	1.61	10	3.14	0.88	5	2.13	1.15	13	2.96	1.08
Expanding numbers of teaching and research staff	23	6	2.83	1.40	1	2.09	0.93	4	2.09	1.12	4	2.50	1.08
Improving the quality of teaching and research staff	23	9	3.04	1.37	4	2.68	1.02	7	2.18	1.11	2	2.32	0.76
The need to change the curriculum to fit changing needs	23	7	2.91	1.50	3	2.67	1.08	2	1.87	0.80	1	2.24	0.62
The need to change structure of university to meet changing needs	23	11	3.60	1.66	8	3.00	1.21	10	2.22	1.25	7	2.68	0.87
The need to increase the volume and sources of financing	23	2	2.04	1.36	11	3.18	1.19	1	1.73	1.21	15	3.19	1.10
The need to expand facilities	23	2	2.04	1.08	14	3.30	0.99	3	1.91	1.02	14	3.09	1.14
The gap between distribution of graduates by field and manpower needs	23	8	2.95	1.96	7	2.93	1.39	9	2.20	1.29	11	2.79	1.06
Changes in the amount and type of research within the university	23	—	—	—	13	3.21	0.95	—	—	—	10	2.78	0.95
Increased participation of students in university governance	23	14	5.04	1.27	2	2.40	0.80	13	3.18	1.67	3	2.44	0.60
The need for refresher courses	23	12	4.39	1.88	15	3.36	1.07	12	2.86	1.39	4	2.50	0.80
Demand for continuing education for persons in all walks of life	23	13	4.65	1.76	12	3.20	1.16	14	3.26	1.54	12	2.80	1.03

TABLE XIV. (continued)

4C. Geographical location: Australia and Oceania

	Sample	Past importance			Past reaction			Future importance			Future reaction		
		R	MS	SD	R	MS	SD	R	MS	SD	R	MS	SD
Increase in applications	3	2	3.33	1.88	5	1.50	0.50	4	2.00	0.82	6	2.20	0.82
Increase in enrolments	3	12	4.66	1.25	7	2.00	1.00	9	2.67	1.70	4	2.00	1.41
Improving quality of incoming students	3	8	4.33	2.36	13	3.00	—	8	2.66	0.47	9	3.00	0.82
Increase in applications relative to no. of places available	3	1	3.00	2.16	5	1.50	0.50	3	1.67	0.94	8	2.67	1.25
Expanding numbers of teaching and research staff	3	2	3.33	2.06	12	2.50	1.50	13	4.33	0.47	3	1.67	0.47
Improving the quality of teaching and research staff	3	6	3.67	1.70	15	3.50	0.50	10	3.67	0.94	4	2.00	0.82
The need to change the curriculum to fit changing needs	2	13	5.00	1.00	1	1.00	—	11	4.00	2.00	9	3.00	—
The need to change structure of university to meet changing needs	2	9	4.50	1.50	7	2.00	—	4	2.00	1.00	13	4.00	1.00
The need to increase the volume and sources of financing	2	4	3.50	2.50	7	2.00	—	1	1.00	—	14	4.50	0.50
The need to expand facilities	2	4	3.50	2.50	1	1.00	—	1	1.00	—	14	4.50	0.50
The gap between distribution of graduates by field and manpower needs	3	14	5.33	0.47	7	2.00	1.00	13	4.33	0.94	9	3.00	0.82
Changes in the amount and type of research within the university	3	—	—	—	14	3.33	1.89	—	—	—	9	3.00	—
Increased participation of students in university governance	3	7	4.00	1.63	1	1.00	—	11	4.00	0.82	1	1.33	0.47
The need for refresher courses	2	9	4.50	1.50	7	2.00	—	4	2.00	—	7	2.50	0.50
Demand for continuing education for persons in all walks of life	2	9	4.50	1.50	1	1.00	—	4	2.00	—	2	1.50	0.50

TABLE XIV. (continued)

4D. Geographical location: Europe

	Sample	Past importance			Past reaction			Future importance			Future reaction		
		R	MS	SD	R	MS	SD	R	MS	SD	R	MS	SD
Increase in applications	18	3-4	2.29	1.64	1	2.00	1.21	6	2.28	1.73	3-4	2.40	1.20
Increase in enrolments	18	1	2.00	1.41	11	2.40	1.40	5	2.22	1.47	9	2.58	1.33
Improving quality of incoming students	18	10	3.41	1.82	3	2.17	0.69	10	2.78	1.78	10	2.60	0.95
Increase in applications relative to no. of places available	18	6	2.87	1.93	14	2.75	1.23	8	2.35	1.57	15	2.92	1.14
Expanding numbers of teaching and research staff	17	5	2.62	1.65	5	2.27	0.77	3	2.00	0.94	5-6	2.41	0.91
Improving the quality of teaching and research staff	18	11	3.47	2.03	2	2.10	0.54	12	2.93	1.81	7	2.42	0.95
The need to change the curriculum to fit changing needs	15	8-9	2.94	1.76	13	2.57	1.05	4	2.06	0.78	8	2.56	0.76
The need to change structure of university to meet changing needs	18	8-9	2.94	1.76	7-8	2.33	1.01	7	2.33	1.37	12	2.67	0.87
The need to increase the volume and sources of financing	18	2	2.18	1.25	10	2.37	0.78	1	1.50	0.69	11	2.61	1.06
The need to expand facilities	18	3-4	2.29	1.36	12	2.50	1.00	2	1.67	0.82	5-6	2.41	0.91
The gap between distribution of graduates by field and manpower needs	16	12	4.19	1.71	6	2.30	1.27	11	2.80	1.22	3-4	2.40	1.08
Changes in the amount and type of research within the university	17	—	—	—	9	2.35	1.02	—	—	—	2	2.35	0.65
Increased participation of students in university governance	18	7	2.89	1.72	7-8	2.33	1.19	13-14	2.94	1.51	1	2.00	0.79
The need for refresher courses	18	13	4.56	1.73	4	2.25	1.09	9	2.56	1.34	13	2.76	1.06
Demand for continuing education for persons in all walks of life	18	14	5.06	1.43	15	2.83	1.07	13-14	2.94	1.68	14	2.79	0.77

TABLE XIV. (*continued*)

4E. Geographical location: North America

	Sample	Past importance			Past reaction			Future importance			Future reaction		
		R	MS	SD	R	MS	SD	R	MS	SD	R	MS	SD
Increase in applications	5	5-6	1.60	0.80	2-4	1.80	0.40	7-8	2.00	1.26	1	1.60	0.49
Increase in enrolments	5	3-4	1.40	0.49	2-4	1.80	0.40	5-6	1.80	1.17	3-4	1.80	0.75
Improving quality of incoming students	5	12	3.60	2.06	1	1.67	0.47	13-14	2.60	1.74	5-8	2.00	0.71
Increase in applications relative to no. of places available	5	13	4.20	2.23	5-10	2.00	—	9-12	2.20	0.98	5-8	2.00	0.89
Expanding numbers of teaching and research staff	5	5-6	1.60	0.49	5-10	2.00	0.63	9-12	2.20	0.75	3-4	1.80	0.75
Improving the quality of teaching and research staff	5	7	2.00	1.09	2-4	1.80	0.75	3-4	1.60	0.80	5-8	2.00	0.89
The need to change the curriculum to fit changing needs	5	10	2.80	1.17	12	2.50	0.50	3-4	1.60	0.80	10-11	2.40	0.80
The need to change structure of university to meet changing needs	5	3-4	1.40	0.49	13-14	3.00	0.89	1	1.40	0.80	5-8	2.00	0.89
The need to increase the volume and sources of financing	5	1-2	1.20	0.40	5-10	2.00	0.89	2	1.50	0.50	15	3.25	1.29
The need to expand facilities	5	1-2	1.20	0.40	5-10	2.00	1.09	5-6	1.80	1.17	9	2.20	0.98
The gap between distribution of graduates by field and manpower needs	4	14	5.00	1.73	5-10	2.00	—	7-8	2.00	1.22	14	3.00	1.22
Changes in the amount and type of research within the university	5	—	—	—	11	2.20	0.75	—	—	—	10-11	2.40	1.02
Increased participation of students in university governance	5	8-9	2.60	1.74	5-10	2.00	1.22	13-14	2.60	1.36	2	1.75	0.83
The need for refresher courses	5	11	3.20	0.98	13-14	3.00	1.09	9-12	2.20	1.17	12-13	2.60	1.20
Demand for continuing education for persons in all walks of life	5	8-9	2.60	1.36	15	3.75	1.09	9-12	2.20	1.17	12-13	2.60	1.02

TABLE XIV. *(continued)*

4F. Geographical location: Latin and Central America

	Sample	Past importance			Past reaction			Future importance			Future reaction		
		R	MS	SD	R	MS	SD	R	MS	SD	R	MS	SD
Increase in applications	17	2	1.94	1.26	5-6	2.62	0.93	6-7	1.59	1.24	13-14	2.19	0.73
Increase in enrolments	17	1	1.76	1.59	9	2.73	0.77	8	1.71	1.27	13-14	2.19	0.95
Improving quality of incoming students	17	11	3.47	1.97	7-8	2.67	1.43	11-12	2.35	1.91	4	1.79	0.86
Increase in applications relative to no. of places available	16	9	2.75	1.56	11	2.86	0.83	9	1.94	1.64	12	2.14	0.83
Expanding numbers of teaching and research staff	17	5-7	2.41	1.85	3	2.33	1.07	2	1.23	0.42	7	1.82	0.86
Improving the quality of teaching and research staff	17	3-4	2.18	1.46	4	2.50	0.87	3	1.29	0.75	2-3	1.65	0.68
The need to change the curriculum to fit changing needs	17	5-7	2.41	1.50	5-6	2.62	1.11	5	1.41	0.49	2-3	1.65	0.59
The need to change structure of university to meet changing needs	17	8	2.59	1.78	2	2.27	1.34	6-7	1.59	0.91	1	1.53	0.78
The need to increase the volume and sources of financing	17	3-4	2.18	1.72	13	3.20	0.98	1	1.12	0.47	15	2.41	1.24
The need to expand facilities	17	5-7	2.41	1.68	12	2.93	0.68	4	1.35	0.59	9-10	2.00	0.91
The gap between distribution of graduates by field and manpower needs	16	12	4.12	1.90	14	3.33	1.15	10	2.00	1.32	11	2.13	0.88
Changes in the amount and type of research within the university	15	—	—	—	15	3.38	0.84	—	—	—	9-10	2.00	0.63
Increased participation of students in university governance	17	10	3.44	1.62	1	2.08	0.92	14	2.65	1.23	5	1.80	0.83
The need for refresher courses	17	14	4.53	1.72	7-8	2.67	1.41	11-12	2.35	1.37	6	1.81	0.95
Demand for continuing education for persons in all walks of life	16	13	4.44	1.41	10	2.80	0.98	13	2.56	1.17	8	1.87	1.02

TABLE XIV. (*continued*)

5A. University size by number of students: 0-5,000

	Sample	Past importance			Past reaction			Future importance			Future reaction		
		R	MS	SD	R	MS	SD	R	MS	SD	R	MS	SD
Increase in applications	35	5	2.82	1.87	3	2.31	0.99	7	2.29	1.57	7	2.25	0.90
Increase in enrolments	34	3	2.30	1.70	6	2.45	1.04	5	2.15	1.35	11	2.37	0.99
Improving quality of incoming students	33	10	3.62	1.87	9	2.52	0.96	11-12	2.88	1.72	4-5	2.12	0.87
Increase in applications relative to no. of places available	31	7	3.10	1.86	15	3.09	0.97	8	2.39	1.66	15	2.85	1.17
Expanding numbers of teaching and research staff	33	4	2.39	1.45	2	2.26	1.16	3	1.88	0.95	2	2.06	0.83
Improving the quality of teaching and research staff	32	6	3.06	1.84	4	2.32	0.97	9	2.44	1.50	3	2.07	0.96
The need to change the curriculum to fit changing needs	35	8	3.18	1.66	7	2.48	1.20	4	2.03	1.05	4-5	2.12	0.73
The need to change structure of university to meet changing needs	35	9	3.61	1.65	5	2.36	0.93	6	2.26	1.25	8-9	2.30	1.06
The need to increase the volume and sources of financing	34	1	1.97	1.45	12	2.84	1.11	1	1.38	0.64	14	2.79	1.18
The need to expand facilities	35	2	2.12	1.34	11	2.71	1.02	2	1.60	0.87	12	2.44	1.09
The gap between distribution of graduates by field and manpower needs	31	11	4.13	1.93	10	2.59	1.24	10	2.71	1.57	10	2.32	0.97
Changes in the amount and type of research within the university	28	—	—	—	14	3.00	1.13	—	—	—	1	1.47	0.89
Increased participation of students in university governance	34	12	4.30	1.67	1	2.00	0.77	13	3.06	1.60	6	2.14	0.82
The need for refresher courses	34	14	5.16	1.25	8	2.50	0.96	14	3.12	1.47	8-9	2.30	1.07
Demand for continuing education for persons in all walks of life	34	13	4.82	1.40	13	2.87	0.93	11-12	2.88	1.43	13	2.48	1.04

TABLE XIV. (continued)

5B. *University size by number of students: 5,000-10,000*

	Sample	Past importance			Past reaction			Future importance			Future reaction		
		R	MS	SD	R	MS	SD	R	MS	SD	R	MS	SD
Increase in applications	20	2-3	1.95	1.12	2	2.30	1.19	7-8	2.30	1.45	4	2.26	1.25
Increase in enrolments	20	1	1.80	0.98	3	2.35	1.12	9	2.35	1.31	2-3	2.20	0.98
Improving quality of incoming students	20	10	2.80	1.78	5	2.56	1.17	10	2.40	1.39	10-11	2.67	1.00
Increase in applications relative to no. of places available	20	9	2.75	1.81	12	2.94	1.14	7-8	2.30	1.14	8	2.63	1.09
Expanding numbers of teaching and research staff	20	7	2.55	1.40	1	2.05	0.80	6	2.15	1.11	5-6	2.35	0.96
Improving the quality of teaching and research staff	20	8	2.65	1.06	7-8	2.75	0.77	2	1.80	0.87	2-3	2.20	0.68
The need to change the curriculum to fit changing needs	20	5	2.25	1.13	6	2.70	1.00	4-5	2.05	0.97	5-6	2.35	0.65
The need to change structure of university to meet changing needs	20	6	2.45	1.53	7-8	2.75	1.26	3	2.00	1.34	10-11	2.67	0.82
The need to increase the volume and sources of financing	20	4	2.15	1.59	9	2.83	1.12	1	1.55	1.16	14	3.05	0.99
The need to expand facilities	20	2-3	1.95	1.16	10	2.85	1.15	4-5	2.05	0.97	12	2.70	1.00
The gap between distribution of graduates by field and manpower needs	19	11	3.16	1.98	4	2.50	1.45	12	2.79	1.57	9	2.65	1.03
Changes in the amount and type of research within the university	18	—	—	—	13	3.17	1.07	—	—	—	13	2.94	0.78
Increased participation of students in university governance	20	12	3.60	1.80	11	2.86	1.12	13	3.25	1.30	1	2.18	0.86
The need for refresher courses	20	13	3.75	1.76	14	3.27	1.18	11	2.58	1.09	7	2.58	0.75
Demand for continuing education for persons in all walks of life	20	14	4.95	1.60	15	3.86	0.99	14	3.55	1.56	15	3.12	0.60

TABLE XIV. (*continued*)

5C. *University size by number of students: 10,000 and over*

	Sample	Past importance			Past reaction			Future importance			Future reaction		
		R	MS	SD	R	MS	SD	R	MS	SD	R	MS	SD
Increase in applications	24	2	1.94	1.10	4	2.35	0.91	1	1.42	0.76	13	2.83	1.05
Increase in enrolments	24	1	1.83	1.31	5	2.59	0.98	6	1.75	1.27	15	3.13	1.26
Improving quality of incoming students	24	11	3.79	1.91	13	2.94	1.34	14	2.54	1.63	10	2.71	0.98
Increase in applications relative to no. of places available	24	6	2.83	1.93	7-8	2.79	1.00	8	2.04	1.59	14	2.90	1.13
Expanding numbers of teaching and research staff	24	8-9	2.96	1.78	3	2.33	0.91	7	1.92	1.08	5-6	2.37	1.07
Improving the quality of teaching and research staff	23	7	2.87	1.87	2	2.26	0.96	11	2.30	1.52	3	2.24	0.87
The need to change the curriculum to fit changing needs	23	5	2.74	1.56	9	2.80	0.93	4-5	1.61	0.64	2	2.17	0.76
The need to change structure of university to meet changing needs	23	8-9	2.96	1.90	7-8	2.79	1.24	4-5	1.61	0.76	7-8	2.45	1.12
The need to increase the volume and sources of financing	22	3	2.17	1.34	11	2.82	1.07	3	1.59	0.83	12	2.77	1.16
The need to expand facilities	23	4	2.22	1.59	10	2.81	1.01	2	1.48	0.71	9	2.65	1.05
The gap between distribution of graduates by field and manpower needs	21	12	4.05	1.86	14-15	3.00	1.19	9	2.15	1.28	11	2.75	1.09
Changes in the amount and type of research within the university	24	—	—	—	6	2.78	1.10	—	—	—	5-6	2.37	0.86
Increased participation of students in university governance	24	10	3.58	1.85	1	2.11	1.20	13	2.48	1.17	1	2.14	0.77
The need for refresher courses	23	13-14	4.09	1.89	14-15	3.00	1.51	10	2.17	1.31	7-8	2.45	1.03
Demand for continuing education for persons in all walks of life	23	13-14	4.09	1.73	12	2.86	1.19	12	2.36	1.26	4	2.35	1.11

6A. Type of control: private

	Sample	Past importance			Past reaction			Future importance			Future reaction		
		R	MS	SD	R	MS	SD	R	MS	SD	R	MS	SD
Increase in applications	16	5	2.44	1.87	4	2.31	0.91	6-7	2.12	1.80	7	2.36	1.23
Increase in enrolments	16	3	1.81	1.38	5	2.33	1.07	3	1.75	1.09	10	2.44	1.12
Improving quality of incoming students	15	9	3.40	1.92	6	2.40	1.02	10-11	2.47	1.82	8	2.38	1.21
Increase in applications relative to no. of places available	16	10	3.50	1.94	11-12	3.00	0.85	6-7	2.12	1.36	13	2.87	1.20
Expanding numbers of teaching and research staff	16	4	2.00	1.17	1-2	2.00	0.93	4-5	1.87	1.05	4	2.19	0.88
Improving the quality of teaching and research staff	16	8	3.25	1.85	7	2.46	1.01	12	2.50	1.58	6	2.33	0.79
The need to change the curriculum to fit changing needs	16	7	2.81	1.59	9	2.54	1.15	2	1.56	0.79	2	2.12	0.78
The need to change structure of university to meet changing needs	16	6	2.69	1.65	3	2.29	1.03	8	2.19	1.38	3	2.13	0.88
The need to increase the volume and sources of financing	16	1	1.56	0.70	13-14	3.06	1.09	1	1.40	0.71	15	3.47	1.09
The need to expand facilities	16	2	1.69	0.92	13-14	3.06	1.25	4-5	1.87	0.93	14	3.19	1.24
The gap between distribution of graduates by field and manpower needs	15	11	4.20	2.01	15	3.43	1.05	10-11	2.47	1.63	12	2.77	1.05
Changes in the amount and type of research within the university	14	—	—	—	10	2.91	1.16	—	—	—	9	2.43	1.05
Increased participation of students in university governance	16	12	4.56	1.77	1-2	2.00	0.76	9	2.33	1.49	1	1.83	0.77
The need for refresher courses	16	14	5.12	1.27	8	2.50	1.26	14	3.06	1.34	5	2.29	1.03
Demand for continuing education for persons in all walks of life	16	13	4.69	1.72	11-12	3.00	1.15	13	2.81	1.33	11	2.53	1.15

TABLE XIV. (continued)

6B. Type of control: public

	Sample	Past importance			Past reaction			Future importance			Future reaction		
		R	MS	SD	R	MS	SD	R	MS	SD	R	MS	SD
Increase in applications	63	8	2.95	1.44	3	2.32	1.05	5-6	2.00	1.28	6	2.45	1.04
Increase in enrolments	62	1	2.08	1.45	5	2.50	1.03	8	2.16	1.38	12	2.59	1.15
Improving quality of incoming students	62	10	3.47	1.90	10	2.72	1.19	11	2.69	1.57	7-9	2.46	0.92
Increase in applications relative to no. of places available	59	4	2.76	1.83	12	2.94	1.08	12	2.89	1.56	15	2.78	1.13
Expanding numbers of teaching and research staff	61	5	2.77	1.62	1	2.29	1.02	4	1.98	1.03	4	2.25	0.96
Improving the quality of teaching and research staff	59	6-7	2.80	1.62	4	2.43	0.91	7	2.13	1.32	1	2.11	0.88
The need to change the curriculum to fit changing needs	60	6-7	2.80	1.55	7	2.67	1.05	5-6	2.00	0.97	2-3	2.22	0.71
The need to change structure of university to meet changing needs	62	9	3.22	1.78	8-9	2.70	1.17	3	1.95	1.13	7-9	2.46	1.05
The need to increase the volume and sources of financing	61	2	2.22	1.57	11	2.76	1.09	1	1.51	0.90	14	2.70	1.10
The need to expand facilities	62	3	2.27	1.46	8-9	2.70	0.98	2	1.63	0.87	5	2.41	0.95
The gap between distribution of graduates by field and manpower needs	55	12	3.74	1.95	6	2.55	1.31	9-10	2.60	1.48	10	2.48	1.03
Changes in the amount and type of research within the university	56	—	—	—	13	2.98	1.10	—	—	—	11	2.50	0.84
Increased participation of students in university governance	62	11	3.72	1.76	2	2.31	1.13	14	3.08	1.38	2-3	2.22	0.81
The need for refresher courses	60	13	4.27	1.78	14	3.03	1.28	9-10	2.60	1.39	7-9	2.46	0.97
Demand for continuing education for persons in all walks of life	60	14	4.63	1.56	15	3.06	1.10	13	2.93	1.53	13	2.61	0.98

Table XIVA.   Obstacles to change encountered by universities

	Order of importance of	
	Past obstacles	Future obstacles
1. Overall sample		
Obstacles already listed under previous question		
Increase in number of students	8	6-7
Low quality of incoming students	12-14	16-17
Insufficient numbers of qualified staff	2	2-3
Need to improve quality of teaching	21	18-20
Need to change curriculum	9	16-17
Need to change the university structure	12-14	18-20
Insufficient financial support	1	1
Need to expand facilities	4	2-3
Need to lessen gap between university work and the socio-economic needs of the country	11	6-7
Need for change in amount and type of research	19-20	12-13
Demand for continuing education	22	21
Obstacles put forward by universities themselves		
Tradition/resistance to change	3	4
Insufficient university autonomy	16	10-11
Present distribution of university decision-making powers	15	18-20
Lack of clearly formulated university goals	10	14-15
Lack of university planning	5-6	10-11
Lack of university statistics	17-18	22
Administrative problems (lack of qualified staff and methods)	7	8
Lack of central planning	17-18	14-15
Lack of student vocation	19-20	12-13
Student unrest	12-14	9
Politics and other external influences	5-6	5

209

TABLE XIVA. (*continued*)

	Developing		Developed	
	Order of importance of		Order of importance of	
	Past obstacles	Future obstacles	Past obstacles	Future obstacles
2. Level of economic development				
Obstacles already listed under previous question				
Increase in number of students	10-11	6	5	5
Low quality of incoming students	12-14	15-19	8-13	12-17
Insufficient numbers of qualified staff	2-3	2	2	6-7
Need to improve quality of teaching	20-21	15-19	8-13	—
Need to change curriculum	8-9	20	8-13	8-11
Need to change the university structure	16	15-19	6-7	—
Insufficient financial support	1	1	1	1
Need to expand facilities	6	4-5	3-4	2
Need to lessen gap between university work and the socio-economic needs of the country	8-9	7	—	4
Need for change in amount and type of research	20-21	13-14	8-13	8-11
Demand for continuing education	22	21-22	—	12-17
Obstacles put forward by universities themselves				
Tradition/resistance to change	2-3	4-5	3-4	3
Insufficient university autonomy	15	10-11	14-18	12-17
Present distribution of university decision-making powers	12-14	15-19	—	—
Lack of clearly formulated university goals	12-14	13-14	8-13	12-17
Lack of university planning	5	10-11	14-18	12-17
Lack of university statistics	17-19	21-22	14-18	—
Administrative problems (lack of qualified staff and methods)	7	8-9	8-13	6-7
Lack of central planning	17-19	15-19	14-18	8-11
Lack of student vocation	17-19	12	—	12-17
Student unrest	10-11	8-9	14-18	—
Politics and other external influences	4	3	6-7	8-11

TABLE XV. University functions and their priorities

	Percentage of univ- ersities	Ranking	Mean score	Standard deviation	Sample
1. Overall sample					
A. Teaching undergraduate students	97	1	1.54	1.22	79
B. Preparing graduate students	92	2	2.35	1.69	77
C. Training teachers for second-level education	81	8	2.95	1.93	79
D. Training teachers for higher education	61	11	3.74	2.03	71
E. Extension work	70	13	4.10	1.52	76
F. Refresher courses	70	14	4.33	1.49	75
G. Preparation of instructional materials for second-level education	39	16	4.96	1.56	75
H. Preparation of instructional materials for higher education	60	15	4.37	1.74	75
I. Preparation of instructional materials for a complete system of education	17	17	5.48	1.13	58
J. Theoretical research	95	3	2.40	1.45	79
K. Applied research	91	4	2.64	1.51	77
L. Development	70	12	3.76	1.82	60
M. Physical planning	88	5	2.86	1.73	73
N. Financial planning	87	7	2.90	1.75	75
O. Working with government	90	8	2.87	1.63	78
P. Working with industry	82	9	3.57	1.61	76
Q. Working with the local community	79	10	3.64	1.63	73

TABLE XV. (*continued*)

	Central and univ. planning					Central planning					University planning					Some planning					No planning				
	%	R	MS	SD	S	%	R	MS	SD	S	%	R	MS	SD	S	%	R	MS	SD	S	%	R	MS	SD	S
2. Existence of a planning system																									
A.	80	3	2.00	2.00	5	100	1	1.00	—	3	100	1	1.41	0.97	17	97	1	1.67	1.32	33	100	1	1.40	0.97	20
B.	100	1	1.00	—	5	67	13-15	3.67	2.05	3	76	6	2.71	1.96	17	97	2	2.06	1.46	32	100	4	2.68	1.62	19
C.	100	5	2.20	1.60	5	67	7-9	2.67	2.36	3	82	8	2.82	1.88	17	73	8	3.29	2.00	31	90	5	2.76	1.74	21
D.	100	7	2.40	1.74	5	100	5-6	2.33	0.94	3	53	13	3.88	2.11	17	50	12	4.04	2.03	27	67	9	3.74	1.91	19
E.	100	14	3.60	0.80	5	100	10-11	3.00	1.63	3	82	11	3.53	1.61	17	64	13	4.26	1.31	30	55	15	4.62	1.56	21
F.	100	10	2.80	1.17	5	67	16	4.50	1.50	2	76	14	4.18	1.50	17	66	14	4.58	1.31	31	61	12	4.44	1.57	18
G.	60	16	4.20	1.60	5	67	7-9	2.67	2.36	3	35	16	4.82	1.65	17	37	16	5.27	1.15	30	33	16	5.17	1.46	18
H.	100	3	2.00	1.27	5	100	4	2.00	1.41	3	58	15	4.35	1.64	17	41	15	4.93	1.56	28	71	14	4.55	1.40	20
I.	60	16	4.20	1.60	5	33	17	5.00	1.41	3	21	17	5.22	1.42	14	8	17	5.78	0.72	23	8	17	5.85	0.36	13
J.	100	2	1.40	0.49	5	67	13-15	3.67	2.05	3	94	4	2.47	1.37	17	94	3	2.34	1.49	32	100	2	2.37	1.33	21
K.	80	8	2.60	1.74	5	100	2	1.67	0.47	3	82	9	2.88	1.75	17	90	4	2.78	1.54	32	100	2	2.37	1.13	19
L.	80	15	3.80	1.72	5	100	2	1.50	0.50	3	64	12	3.81	2.04	14	68	11	3.83	1.67	24	76	10	3.88	1.81	17
M.	80	11	3.00	2.10	5	50	12	3.50	2.50	2	100	2	2.00	1.06	16	85	7	2.97	1.69	31	88	7	3.32	1.78	19
N.	80	11	3.00	2.10	5	67	7-9	2.67	2.36	3	100	3	2.15	1.17	13	88	6	2.90	1.58	30	78	8	3.42	1.93	19
O.	100	5	2.20	0.98	5	67	13-15	3.67	2.05	3	94	5	2.59	1.46	17	87	5	2.87	1.71	30	90	6	3.15	1.59	20
P.	100	8	2.60	1.02	5	100	5-6	2.33	0.94	3	76	10	3.29	1.81	17	77	9	3.64	1.66	31	85	11	4.16	1.22	19
Q.	100	13	3.20	0.98	5	67	10-11	3.00	2.16	3	87	7	2.80	1.64	16	80	10	3.67	1.56	30	70	13	4.45	1.36	20

%=percentage of universities performing a function; R=ranking; MS=mean score; SD=standard deviation; S=sample.

TABLE XV. (*continued*)

	Developing					Developed				
	%	R	MS	SD	S	%	R	MS	SD	S
3. Level of economic decelopment										
A. Teaching undergraduate students	100	1	1.36	0.94	55	92	3	1.96	1.63	23
B. Preparing graduate students	89	2	2.67	1.82	54	100	2	1.59	0.98	22
C. Training teachers for second-level education	85	4	2.76	1.82	54	71	9	3.39	2.10	23
D. Training teachers for higher education	52	12	4.06	1.95	49	78	6	3.00	2.00	22
E. Extension work	66	13	4.09	1.53	54	48	14-15	4.14	1.49	22
F. Refresher courses	63	15	4.52	1.43	50	83	11	3.91	1.53	23
G. Preparation of instructional materials for second-level education	43	16	4.76	1.67	50	29	14	5.39	1.17	23
H. Preparation of instructional materials for higher education	58	14	4.47	1.64	51	65	14.15	4.14	1.94	22
I. Preparation of instructional materials for a complete system of education	15	17	5.49	1.13	39	27	17	5.47	1.14	19
J. Theoretical research	93	7	2.80	1.47	55	100	1	1.43	0.82	23
K. Applied research	91	3	2.72	1.51	54	91	4	2.45	1.50	22
L. Development	68	11	3.63	1.83	41	74	13	4.06	1.75	18
M. Physical planning	92	6	2.79	1.64	52	77	7	3.05	1.91	21
N. Financial planning	86	8	2.90	1.72	48	87	5	2.91	1.81	22
O. Working with government	89	5	2.77	1.70	53	92	8	3.09	1.41	22
P. Working with industry	73	10	3.61	1.74	52	100	10	3.48	1.25	23
Q. Working with the local community	78	9	3.47	1.73	51	82	12	4.04	1.30	22

TABLE XV. (continued)

4. Geographical location

	Africa					Asia					Australia & Oceania					Europe					North America					L. & C. America			
	%	R	MS	SD	S	%	R	MS	SD	S	%	R	MS	SD	S	S	%	R	MS	SD	S	%	R	MS	SD	S	R	MS	SD
A.	100	1	1.07	0.26	14	100	1	1.56	1.13	23	100	1	1.00	—	3	18	100	3	1.94	1.81	5	100	1-2	1.60	0.49	16	1	1.50	1.06
B.	92	7	3.15	1.56	13	91	2	2.34	1.71	23	67	6	3.50	2.50	3	17	100	2	1.53	1.04	5	87	3	1.80	0.75	16	7	2.62	1.93
C.	100	2	2.21	1.21	14	67	8	3.48	2.15	21	67	6	3.50	2.50	3	18	80	8	3.28	2.02	5	94	7	2.80	1.94	17	6	2.53	1.61
D.	73	8	3.45	1.83	11	40	14	4.85	1.12	20	67	11	4.50	1.50	3	17	60	5	2.76	1.89	5	56	13-14	4.00	1.90	16	12	3.37	2.15
E.	86	9-10	3.57	1.50	14	52	13	4.71	1.28	21	100	10	4.00	2.00	3	18	100	15	4.65	1.28	5	76	8-9	3.20	1.47	17	13	3.53	1.46
F.	64	16	4.91	1.08	11	55	12	4.45	1.66	20	33	15	6.00	—	3	18	100	13	4.11	1.56	5	71	10	3.40	1.36	17	15	4.23	1.31
G.	42	15	4.50	1.98	12	25	16	5.25	1.45	20	100	13	5.00	1.00	3	17	40	17	5.35	1.18	5	59	16	5.20	1.17	17	16	4.35	1.57
H.	62	14	4.31	1.81	13	40	15	5.24	0.97	21	67	14	5.50	0.50	3	17	40	11	3.71	1.93	5	75	15	5.00	1.56	15	14	3.60	1.74
I.	11	17	5.67	0.94	9	16	17	5.78	0.42	17	33	15	6.00	—	3	13	—	16	5.23	1.31	5	33	17	6.00	—	11	17	4.82	1.70
J.	93	9-10	3.57	1.45	14	95	4	2.52	1.47	23	100	2	2.00	1.00	3	18	100	1	1.50	0.99	5	88	1-2	1.60	0.80	16	5	2.50	1.32
K.	93	5	2.86	1.30	14	90	3	2.41	1.34	22	67	11	4.50	1.50	3	17	100	4	2.47	1.68	5	94	4	2.20	0.75	16	8	2.87	1.65
L.	61	12	3.77	1.89	13	72	10	3.89	1.59	19	33	15	6.00	—	3	14	75	12	3.86	1.85	4	75	12	3.75	1.92	8	10	3.00	1.87
M.	92	3	2.50	1.61	12	90	6	3.14	1.58	21	67	6	3.50	2.50	3	17	100	9	3.35	2.00	4	94	5-6	2.25	0.83	17	4	2.35	1.49
N.	85	6	2.92	1.80	12	67	7	3.29	1.70	21	67	6	3.50	2.50	3	18	100	7	3.17	1.99	4	94	5-6	2.25	0.83	13	2	2.00	1.04
O.	100	4	2.61	1.33	13	100	5	2.77	1.70	22	67	3	2.50	1.50	3	17	100	6	3.06	1.73	5	81	8-9	3.20	0.98	16	9	2.94	1.75
P.	85	11	3.69	1.59	13	100	9	3.85	1.77	20	100	4	3.00	2.00	3	18	100	10	3.39	1.38	5	71	13-14	4.00	0.89	17	11	3.29	1.67
Q.	72	13	3.91	1.62	11	68	11	4.10	1.62	22	100	4	3.00	2.00	3	17	100	14	4.23	1.44	5	100	11	3.60	0.80	16	3	2.31	1.16

TABLE XV. (*continued*)

	0 — 5,000					5,000 — 10,000					10,000 +				
	%	R	MS	SD	s	%	R	MS	SD	s	%	R	MS	SD	s
5. University size by number of students															
A. Teaching undergraduate students	100	1	1.14	0.67	36	100	1	1.55	1.12	20	91	3	2.18	1.64	22
B. Preparing graduate students	85	7	2.91	1.86	33	95	2	2.00	1.52	20	100	1-2	1.87	1.30	23
C. Training teachers for second-level education	75	8	3.23	1.96	35	79	6	3.00	1.95	19	92	6	2.48	1.77	23
D. Training teachers for higher education	41	13	4.53	1.85	32	75	10-11	3.94	1.63	17	78	5	2.41	1.87	22
E. Extension work	67	12	4.14	1.51	36	81	15	4.29	1.36	17	67	14	3.91	1.61	23
F. Refresher courses	61	15	4.82	1.22	33	94	14	4.17	1.12	18	62	13	3.73	1.84	22
G. Preparation of instructional materials for second-level education	38	16	4.91	1.58	34	50	16	4.82	1.69	17	30	17	5.14	1.39	22
H. Preparation of instructional materials for higher education	50	14	4.71	1.62	34	76	12-13	4.06	1.63	17	62	15	4.09	1.90	22
I. Preparation of instructional materials for a complete system of education	11	17	5.64	0.85	28	8	17	5.85	0.36	13	33	16	4.94	1.63	17
J. Theoretical research	94	4	2.71	1.54	35	95	3	2.45	1.43	20	95	1-2	1.87	1.15	23
K. Applied research	86	6	2.83	1.63	35	89	4	2.68	1.45	19	100	4	2.32	1.29	22
L. Development	61	11	3.81	1.84	26	71	10-11	3.94	1.59	17	82	10	3.50	1.97	16
M. Physical planning	91	2	2.39	1.59	33	88	7	3.53	1.59	15	82	7-8	3.00	1.85	21
N. Financial planning	91	3	2.40	1.58	30	89	8	3.55	1.60	20	78	7-8	3.00	1.90	20
O. Working with government	91	5	2.75	1.70	32	100	5	2.80	1.29	20	79	9	3.09	1.77	23
P. Working with industry	76	10	3.50	1.87	34	94	9	3.72	1.28	18	79	11	3.56	1.41	23
Q. Working with the local community	79	9	3.42	1.71	33	82	12-13	4.06	1.43	18	78	12	3.64	1.61	22

TABLE XV. (continued)

6. Emphasis on the field of study

	Science					Humanities					Social sciences					Professional training					No special emphasis				
	%	R	MS	SD	s	%	R	MS	SD	s	%	R	MS	SD	s	%	R	MS	SD	s	%	R	MS	SD	s
A.	100	1-2	1.56	1.07	9	100	1	1.14	0.35	7	100	1	1.00	—	4	95	1	1.52	1.31	23	97	1	1.67	1.33	35
B.	89	1-2	1.56	1.26	9	100	2	1.43	0.73	7	75	8	3.50	1.80	4	91	2	2.04	1.55	22	94	5	2.82	1.77	34
C.	62	7	3.25	2.22	8	71	6	2.86	2.10	7	100	2-3	1.75	0.83	4	70	12	3.65	1.99	23	92	2	2.57	1.68	35
D.	75	10-13	3.50	1.94	8	67	10	3.67	1.79	6	—	15-17	6.00	—	4	65	11	3.40	1.93	20	61	9	3.76	2.12	33
E.	89	14	3.67	1.25	9	86	8	3.57	1.50	7	50	11	4.50	1.12	4	73	14	4.32	1.33	22	62	12-13	4.15	1.68	34
F.	89	15	4.00	1.15	9	100	11-12	3.71	1.03	6	50	12	5.00	1.22	4	73	15	4.41	1.19	22	59	14	4.42	1.79	31
G.	62	16	4.50	1.32	8	33	16	5.17	1.46	6	—	15-17	6.00	—	4	43	16	4.70	1.57	23	35	16	5.09	1.63	32
H.	87	8-9	3.37	1.32	8	57	13-14	4.29	1.91	7	25	14	5.75	0.43	4	62	13	4.09	1.74	21	57	15	4.64	1.72	33
I.	43	17	5.00	0.76	7	—	17	6.00	—	6	—	15-17	6.00	—	4	16	17	5.41	1.29	17	17	17	5.46	1.26	24
J.	100	3	2.00	1.05	9	100	3	1.86	0.83	7	100	5-6	2.75	1.09	4	91	3	2.32	1.46	22	94	4	2.61	1.60	36
K.	78	5	2.78	1.75	9	80	7	3.20	1.47	5	50	9	3.75	2.28	4	95	9	2.36	1.26	22	97	3	2.58	1.40	36
L.	62	10-13	3.50	1.94	8	80	9	3.60	1.74	5	25	13	5.25	1.30	4	87	9	2.87	1.41	15	68	12-13	4.15	1.80	27
M.	89	6	3.00	1.33	9	75	5	2.80	1.72	5	75	5-6	2.75	2.05	4	91	7	2.65	1.78	23	88	6	3.00	1.73	32
N.	79	8-9	3.37	1.58	8	80	4	2.67	1.70	6	100	2-3	1.75	0.83	4	96	5	2.37	1.63	19	82	8	3.27	1.80	33
O.	100	4	2.56	1.07	9	71	11-12	3.71	1.75	7	100	4	2.25	1.30	4	91	6	2.43	1.59	21	89	7	3.12	1.66	34
P.	87	10-13	3.50	1.22	8	67	15	4.83	1.07	6	75	10	4.25	1.92	4	87	8	2.70	1.46	23	80	10	3.88	1.53	34
Q.	87	10-13	3.50	1.32	8	71	13-14	4.29	1.66	7	75	7	3.25	1.92	4	86	10	3.18	1.47	22	75	11	3.91	1.66	32

TABLE XV. (*continued*)

7. Emphasis on university function

	Undergraduate teaching					Graduate teaching					Research					Teacher training				
	%	R	MS	SD	s	%	R	MS	SD	s	%	R	MS	SD	s	%	R	MS	SD	s
A.	100	1	1.09	0.29	55	89	5	2.78	1.87	18	100	3-6	2.00	1.00	2	100	2	2.00	1.47	3
B.	91	3-4	2.70	1.73	54	100	1	1.06	0.23	17	100	3-6	2.00	1.00	2	67	8-9	3.67	2.05	3
C.	84	7	2.89	1.80	55	71	7	3.18	2.20	17	50	13-14	5.50	0.50	2	100	1	1.00	—	3
D.	54	12-13	3.94	2.03	50	75	11	3.37	1.93	16	100	3-6	2.00	1.00	2	67	6	3.33	2.05	3
E.	73	12-13	3.94	1.53	55	69	14-15	4.31	1.40	16	50	13-14	5.50	0.50	2	67	16	5.00	1.41	2
F.	68	15	4.56	1.36	52	76	12	3.65	1.57	17	50	10-11	4.50	1.50	2	67	10-11	4.00	2.00	3
G.	40	16	4.86	1.59	52	41	17	5.25	1.20	16	—	15-17	6.00	—	2	33	12-14	4.33	2.36	3
H.	57	14	4.38	1.71	52	69	14-15	4.31	1.79	16	100	8	3.00	2.00	2	33	17	5.33	0.94	3
I.	7	17	5.71	0.74	41	43	16	4.85	1.70	13	—	15-17	6.00	—	2	50	15	4.50	1.50	2
J.	93	2	2.65	1.53	55	100	2	1.56	0.76	18	100	1	1.00	—	2	100	8-9	3.67	0.47	3
K.	31	5	2.72	1.50	53	94	3	2.33	1.41	18	100	2	1.50	0.50	2	67	10-11	4.00	1.63	3
L.	70	9	3.58	1.81	43	67	13	4.17	1.63	12	100	12	5.00	—	1	67	12-14	4.33	2.36	2
M.	91	3-4	2.70	1.64	53	87	8	3.19	1.74	16	100	9	4.00	2.00	2	50	7	3.50	2.50	2
N.	89	6	2.78	1.65	50	88	6	3.13	1.82	15	100	3-6	2.00	1.00	2	33	12-14	4.33	2.36	2
O.	87	8	2.96	1.68	53	100	4	2.35	1.28	17	50	10-11	4.50	1.50	2	100	4-5	3.00	1.41	3
P.	74	11	3.75	1.68	53	100	9-10	3.35	1.28	17	100	7	2.50	1.50	2	100	3	2.33	0.94	3
Q.	78	10	3.69	1.66	51	94	9-10	3.35	1.23	17	—	15-17	6.00	—	2	67	4-5	3.00	2.16	3

Table XV. (*continued*)

	Private					Public				
	%	R	MS	SD	S	%	R	MS	SD	S
8. Type of control										
A. Teaching undergraduate students	100	1	1.19	0.53	16	97	1	1.63	1.32	62
B. Preparing graduate students	87	5-6	2.56	1.87		93	2	2.30	1.64	60
C. Training teachers for second-level education	75	8	3.13	2.06	15	82	5	2.90	1.89	62
D. Training teachers for higher education	40	14	4.44	1.97	16	66	9	3.53	2.00	55
E. Extension work	60	12	4.31	1.49		72	13	4.05	1.52	60
F. Refresher courses	53	13	4.33	1.95	15	73	15	4.33	1.34	58
G. Preparation of instructional materials for second-level education	27	16	5.13	1.50		42	16	4.91	1.57	58
H. Preparation of instructional materials for higher education	37	15	5.06	1.20	16	66	14	4.17	1.82	57
I. Preparation of instructional materials for a complete system of education	7	17	5.71	0.59	14	20	17	5.41	1.25	44
J. Theoretical research	100	3	2.19	1.24	16	94	3	2.45	1.50	62
K. Applied research	93	2	2.13	1.09	15	90	4	2.77	1.57	61
L. Development	80	9	3.53	1.59	15	67	12	3.84	1.88	44
M. Physical planning	93	4	2.44	1.50	16	86	8	2.98	1.74	57
N. Financial planning	86	7	2.80	1.64	15	87	6	2.93	1.77	55
O. Working with government	94	5-6	2.56	1.50	16	89	7	2.95	1.65	59
P. Working with industry	73	11	3.67	1.85	15	84	10	3.55	1.54	60
Q. Working with the local community	67	10	3.62	1.76	16	83	11	3.65	1.59	57

TABLE XV. (*continued*)

	Open					Selective					Mixed				
	%	R	MS	SD	s	%	R	MS	SD	s	%	R	MS	SD	s
9. Type of admission system															
A. Teaching undergraduate students	100	1	1.00	—	9	98	1	1.46	1.12	56	92	6	3.31	1.67	13
B. Preparing graduate students	75	11-12	4.00	1.73	8	95	2	2.22	1.58	55	92	1	1.92	1.54	13
C. Training teachers for second-level education	85	3-4	2.00	1.63	9	80	8	3.16	1.89	55	77	3	2.69	2.01	13
D. Training teachers for higher education	37	10	3.75	2.28	8	66	12	3.72	1.93	50	54	8	3.77	2.22	13
E. Extension work	67	11-12	4.00	1.89	9	70	13	4.00	1.49	54	69	14	4.61	1.21	13
F. Refresher courses	37	16	5.12	0.78	8	74	15	4.23	1.51	52	69	11	4.23	1.58	13
G. Preparation of instructional materials for second-level education	25	15	4.62	1.93	8	49	16	4.77	1.57	53	—	17	6.00	—	12
H. Preparation of instructional materials for higher education	44	13-14	4.12	2.09	8	68	14	4.19	1.73	52	38	15	5.23	1.19	13
I. Preparation of instructional materials for a complete system of education	—	17	6.00	—	4	20	17	5.42	1.20	45	11	16	5.89	0.31	9
J. Theoretical research	89	7	2.89	1.37	9	96	3	2.30	1.41	56	92	2	2.46	1.60	13
K. Applied research	89	8-9	3.00	1.70	9	93	4	2.36	1.33	56	82	9	3.82	1.58	11
L. Development	50	13-14	4.12	1.76	8	76	9	3.50	1.80	40	64	13	4.45	1.67	11
M. Physical planning	100	2	1.78	1.31	9	87	6	3.00	1.75	53	80	5	3.09	1.62	11
N. Financial planning	89	3-4	2.00	1.41	8	87	7	3.02	1.73	51	80	4	3.00	1.86	11
O. Working with government	89	5	2.12	1.45	8	91	5	2.85	1.62	55	85	7	3.42	1.56	12
P. Working with industry	56	6	2.87	1.96	8	85	10	3.56	1.56	55	83	10	4.08	1.38	12
Q. Working with the local community	89	8-9	3.00	1.66	8	79	11	3.61	1.60	54	73	12	4.27	1.54	11

TABLE XVA. University functions and their priorities : priority listing of functions which universities would like to develop

	Teaching undergraduate students	Preparing graduate students	Training teachers	Continuing education	Preparing instruct. materials	Research	Physical planning	Working with outside organizations
1. Overall sample	3	2	4	5	7	1	6	8
2. Existence of a planning system								
Central and university	4	1	5	3	6	2	7	8
Central planning	1-2	6	1-2	4	5	3	7	8
University planning	4	1	3	5	7	2	6	8
Some planning	1	2	4	5	6	3	7	8
No planning	3	2	4	6	8	1	5	7
3. Level of economic development								
Developing	2	3	4	5	7	1	6	8
Developed	3	1	5	4	8	2	7	6
4. Geographical location								
Africa	1	4	3	5	8	2	6	7
Asia	3	1	4	6	7	2	5	8
Australia and Oceania	1	2-3	5-6	4	5-6	2-3	8	7
Europe	3	2	5	4	7	1	6	8
North America	1-2	1-2	4-5	4-5	8	3	7	6
Latin and Central America	4	3	2	5	6	1	8	7
5. University size by number of students								
0-5,000	1	3	4	5	7	2	6	8
5,000-10,000	2	1	4	5	7	3	6	8
10,000 and over	3	2	4	5	6	1	7	8

TABLE XVB. Reasons for non-development of selected priority functions

	Percentage of universities giving each reason						
	Shortage of funds	Shortage of space	Shortage of professional personnel	Shortage of physical facilities	Administrative difficulties	Other	Sample
1. Overall sample	86.3	52.1	67.1	52.1	24.6	23.3	73
2. Existence of a planning system							
Central and university	50.0	75.0	75.0	100.0	25.0	50.0	4
Central planning	100.0	100.0	50.0	—	—	—	2
University planning	86.7	33.3	73.3	53.3	6.7	26.7	15
Some planning	87.5	65.6	62.5	53.1	21.9	15.6	32
No planning	90.0	35.0	70.0	45.0	45.0	30.0	20
3. Level of economic development							
Developing	90.6	52.8	69.8	56.6	28.3	22.6	53
Developed	75.0	50.0	60.0	40.0	15.0	25.0	20
4. Geographical location							
Africa	91.7	66.7	83.3	50.0	16.7	16.7	12
Asia	86.4	63.6	54.5	63.6	31.8	13.6	22
Australia and Oceania	100.0	—	50.0	—	—	100.0	2
Europe	75.0	56.3	62.5	43.8	31.2	37.5	16
North America	75.0	—	50.0	25.0	—	—	4
Latin and Central America	94.1	41.2	82.3	58.8	23.5	23.5	17
5. University size by number of students							
0-5,000	88.2	52.9	67.6	47.1	26.5	23.5	34
5,000-10,000	87.5	50.0	75.0	50.0	31.2	25.0	16
10,000 and over	82.6	52.2	60.9	60.9	17.4	21.7	23

Appendixes

APPENDIX I. METHODS OF ANALYSIS OF THE QUESTIONNAIRE

Although receipt of sufficient information by means of the questionnaire was important for our research, suitable methods of analysis to draw the correct conclusions were equally important.

Therefore it was considered necessary to discuss these methods with experts; the advice of statisticians, educationalists and computer specialists was sought. It was rather difficult to devise a scheme of work because the heterogeneous nature of the questionnaire demanded a combination of quantitative data, a simple yes or no and the opinions of heads of universities. However, it was necessary to bear in mind that the responses would have to be analysed in such a way as to enable maximum objective conclusions to be drawn from them.

One of our basic methodological assumptions was that the university should be considered as a sub-system of higher education, which is part of the socio-economic structure of each country. Although it is a sub-system of society as a whole, the university is, itself, a very complex system, consisting of many inter-related and interacting elements. Thus, it was of interest to measure the inter-dependence and interaction of these elements not only by analysing information relating directly to specific aspects of university activity, but also by comparing them and establishing connexions and correlations, as well as average indices, variations, rates of growth and so on. Some attempts were made to give a qualitative interpretation of quantitative data as well.

In other words, we tried to consider each university as a working unit and endeavoured to compare the most important tendencies in the total sample and in the different sub-groups of universities. Although we are well aware that information from individual universities in different parts of the world is hardly comparable, the questionnaire and glossary of terms were designed to generalize the maximum amount of information within each grouping.

It will be seen that our results are presented only by these different groups, since one of the conditions laid down for participation in the study was that confidentiality of information from the individual universities would be respected. In this regard it is important to mention the main concern of our investigation, which is not so much absolute figures as the basic tendencies of the development of universities.

Throughout the text it can be seen that we have made use of diagrams and charts to demonstrate the most interesting phenomena and trends. These are based on detailed tables which can be found elsewhere in this book.

A. Classifications

As stated in Chapter II, in addition to analysis of the overall sample, the following eight classifications were used, divided into sub-classes:

1. Existence of planning system

The division of universities into sub-classes for this classification was those following:
(*i*) a combination of central government and their own university plans;
(*ii*) a central plan only;
(*iii*) their own university plan;
(*iv*) some kind of planning;
(*v*) no plan.

In order to identify universities belonging to the various sub-classes, for (*i*), the type of planning system of the country was taken into account, as well as information furnished in the questionnaire which indicated the existence of university plans. Questions relating to the existence of the need for planning units were contained in the questionnaire, in addition to demands as to whether they were using factual information or established norms for planning purposes, and the role of different bodies in decision-making.

In sub-class (*ii*) are those universities under central government planning, but whose responses to the questionnaire indicated that no planning existed at university level. For sub-class (*iii*) the existence of a planning mechanism and use of indices for planning were taken into account and for sub-class (*iv*) the use of indices only was considered to warrant the university's inclusion in this group. In sub-class (*v*) are those universities which do not have any planning unit or other mechanism, did not use indices for planning purposes and whose government did not have a national plan.

This classification was considered as one of the most important because it takes into account the socio-economic structures of different countries.

2. Level of economic development, supplemented by GNP per capita (in US$)

Universities belonging to countries which have a GNP *per capita* of $1,000 or less were classified as belonging to developing countries; those above this amount were considered as developed.

This classification was supplemented by a more detailed grouping into eight sub-classes of GNP *per capita* (US$): $0-100; $100-200; $200-300; $300-400; $400-500; $500-1,000; $1,000-2,000; $2,000 and above.

This detailed sub-classification created a problem in that some of the sub-classes included only a few universities, and our sample contained no university belonging to a country with a GNP *per capita* in the range $400-500, so that, finally, very little use was made of these groups of information.

3. *Geographical location*

Here there are six sub-classes: Africa; Asia; Australia and Oceania; Europe; North America; Latin and Central America.

4. *University size by number of students*

Here we considered the total number of students attending the university at the time of completion of the questionnaire and divided the universities into three sub-classes: up to 5,000 students; 5,000-10,000 students; 10,000 and over.

5. *Emphasis on field of study*

The universities were divided on the basis of information furnished by them in respect of the principal disciplines taught at different levels and the number of students in different fields. Five sub-classes were formed: emphasis on pure science; emphasis on the humanities; emphasis on social sciences; emphasis on professional training, including agriculture, law, medicine, engineering; no emphasis on any particular field of study.

6. *Emphasis on university function*

This classification was made on the basis of information given by universities as to whether different functions were performed and the relative importance assigned to them. The four most important university functions were: undergraduate teaching; graduate teaching; research; teacher training.

7. *Type of control*

The classification of universities into public or state universities and private universities was determined by the response of the universities themselves to our questionnaire.

8. *Type of admission system*

This classification was also determined by responses to the questionnaire. It was found that there were three types: open system of admission; selective system; mixed system.

The mixed system includes those universities which had an open system for some disciplines and a selective system for others.

B. Computation of state of replies

In this case, the number of universities responding to a specific question was expressed as a percentage of the total number of universities in the overall sample. If there was more than one part to a question, the responses for all the parts were added and then expressed as a percentage of the product of the number of parts and the number of universities in the sample. It should be noted here that some summarization of responses had to be made when analysing the questionnaire and computing the state of replies.

With regard to questions concerning the principal disciplines taught, the subjects under each discipline were not separately considered. For example, if any one of the subjects from astronomy to zoology was taught at a particular level, it was considered that pure science was taught at that university at that level.

C. Computation of growth rate

Our main concern was to establish the dynamics of each single university, but units of measurement of various characteristics vary (particularly for financial information). However, a calculation of growth rates reduces, to a great extent, difficulties of interpretation and definition of the terms used to express different characteristics and, therefore, we have taken this as a comparable index of behaviour of various university characteristics.

Three specific years were considered in analysing the evolution of different characteristics: 1958/59, 1963/64 and 1968/69. Where data were available for these three points of time, the average annual growth was computed for each university. These individual growth rates were then averaged for each sub-class of university to gain an idea of the evolution of each particular characteristic in each particular sub-class. In our analysis of the questionnaire, much emphasis has been laid on these growth rates to pinpoint inconsistencies, or consistencies, in the expansion of different components of university activity during the last decade and the effects the heads of universities think these will have on the operations of the university in the next decade.

In our analysis of growth rates, some universities could not furnish statistics relating to a particular characteristic for all three points of time (this might be due to the date of establishment of the university or because it had no record of information from the early period, etc.) and, therefore, the number of replies correspondingly varies. However, since our analysis is concerned mainly with revealing basic trends in university development, comparisons of average rates of growth for different periods from different numbers of universities were considered as valid. However, we calculated the growth rates for a small control group of universities who had been able to complete all the questions; the results do not differ greatly from the figures in the tables calculated from a varied response rate.

D. Analysis of opinions

A significant part of the analysis is based on opinions and judgements expressed by the heads of universities. Their opinions were sought on the following: the degree of autonomy enjoyed by the university; the priority given to different functions of a university; past and future factors of change; the degree of availability of different types of information; the degree of involvement of different kinds of persons in university decision-making.

Usually single figures (percentages and averages, for example, or rank ordering of variables) were used to measure them. It is a fair assumption that the average is a reasonable estimate of what rank a particular variable has. It may not unquestionably represent reality, but it is more probable that a large number of observers will come closer to the truth than that a large number will err.

1. Degree of autonomy

This was measured on a four-point scale: complete autonomy in an area of decision was assigned a weight of 3; partial autonomy 2; slight autonomy 1; and no autonomy 0.

Priority of functions and objectives was given a five-point scale: top priority being assigned a weight of 5 and low priority a weight of 1.

2. Past and future factors of change

These were measured on a six-point scale ranging from very serious (1) to not at all serious (5); where the factor was not considered as a problem, it was designated 6. Reactions to factors of change were also measured in the same way: if well managed, it was assigned a weight of 1 and if badly, a weight of 5. Future factors of change were analysed in the same way.

Weighted arithmetic means for all universities were computed for each of the variables and a standard deviation of the scores for each variable was calculated to check on divergence. If the standard deviation was too high, opinions varied too much and reasons were looked for.

3. Degree of availability of different types of information

There could only be one response to four possible alternatives: the information was adequately available; inadequately available; not available but desirable; or not available and not needed. Each box ticked was given a score of 1 and the percentage of universities having a particular type of information adequately available, and so on, was obtained by counting up the score and expressing the number as a percentage of the total number of universities responding.

4. *Degree of involvement of different kinds of persons in university decision-making*

The scores for the degree of involvement were given by the universities themselves according to our instructions for completing the question. Authority for a final decision or veto power was assigned a score of 4; active participation in decision-making a score of 3; consulted about decisions 2; informed about decisions 1; and no involvement 0.

In some cases, analyses of interdependence between different factors of change and reactions to change, between different agents of decision-making and different areas of decision-making, were made by computation of intercorrelation coefficients between scores.

Introduction

This questionnaire is one of the earlier steps in an overall study entitled 'Planning the development of universities'. Enormous changes have occurred in universities throughout the world in recent decades, and universities will face equally large changes in the coming years. The purpose of the study is to determine how universities might more effectively cope with the changes that are occurring now and with the pressures to change that will be occurring over the next few years, both inside and outside the university.

Although not all planning decisions can be made according to a prescribed outline, we want to develop : (1) a system of principles for working out adequate planning mechanisms which can be used by university managers for developing universities in the changing environment; and (2) a system of indices, both quantitative and qualitative, which will guide university planners in decision-making and give them some measure of the extent to which they are achieving their own objectives, and perhaps, of the validity of the objectives themselves as well.

In this portion of the study we are seeking detailed information from a carefully selected sample of approximately 100 universities. Some of these universities will already have faced major changes in recent years, while for others these changes have not yet occurred. From the answers to the questionnaire, we want to analyse: (1) each university in the particular context in which it operates; (2) changes that have occurred in the last decade; (3) the university's mechanisms for dealing with the problems of change; and (4) changes that are anticipated in the next ten years.

We also feel that the questionnaire will pave the way for some broad conclusions about the types of changes university managers should try to bring about in the future and give them some guidance about the types of planning decisions to make in order best to bring about these changes. Our later research will concentrate on developing these conclusions by studying some selected universities in depth.

Although we are well aware of the fact that some information about individual universities is hardly comparable, we have designed this questionnaire, and the glossary, in such a way as to be able to generalize the maximum amount of information within designated university groups.

Individual universities in different countries do reveal some common problems which they are facing in the process of planning; they must all undergo a process of adaptation to progress—scientific, technological, and social.

Because our sample has been so carefully selected, it is exceedingly important that each university to which we send the questionnaire should co-operate. It is not possible to compensate each university fully for the time involved in providing the information requested; we are, however, offering when necessary a small sum to cover in part the clerical costs involved. In addition, a copy of the results of the full study will be sent to all universities participating in the study. Needless to say, the results will be shown only in grouped form, so that data concerning any one university cannot be identified.

General recommendations for completing the questionnaire

There is a great deal we hope to learn about the universities from this questionnaire and it is therefore fairly long. Since it is translated into three languages and distributed to universities in a number of different countries, we have tried to be as explicit as possible in stating the questions. In order to avoid misunderstandings over certain terms, we have also prepared a glossary, which is to be found at the end of the questionnaire. This will enable respondents to know what we understand by certain terms and, as far as possible, to answer in a way which will provide comparable data from different countries.

Briefly, the general recommendations for completing the questionnaire are as follows:

1. Read each item carefully before answering.
2. If possible, answer in English, French or Spanish as these are the three languages into which the questionnaire is translated. This will prevent the meaning of answers being lost or changed in translation.
3. Refer to the glossary of terms (Appendix III) before filling in an item. Each term appearing in the glossary is given in italic (e.g. *applied research*). If the meaning of a term is different at your university and the data given is based on your understanding of that term, give your definition of it in the questionnaire. This will avoid confusion.
4. Reply to each item as completely as possible and do not hesitate to give supplementary explanations where they appear necessary.
5. Use separate sheets of paper if more space is needed and mark these sheets carefully with the page, section and item number to which they refer.
6. In cases where data are in no way available, please write 'not available' or 'not applicable' as the case may be.
7. In cases where data are not available within the university, but may found through another agency, indicate the name and address of the agency involved.

8. Data are requested for the beginning and end of the last decade 1958/59 and 1968/69. We would also like to have data for the five-year interval 1963/64. If and where possible please give *annual* data. This additional information may be given on separate sheets of paper. Mark these sheets with the page, section and item number to which they refer.

Documentation

When you return the questionnaire, please send us all the documentation concerning your university. This would include the University Calendar or Handbook, reports of special committees, Annual reports and any other publication which offers information relevant to the university.

Name of the university ....

Address ....

....

Name(s) of respondent(s) with position and number of years' service in the university ....

....

Date of commencing work on the questionnaire ....

Date of completion ....

I. Background information

1. In what year was your university founded? ....

2. Which of the following types of institution is your university?
   - A. State (Public) university ☐
   - B. Private university ☐
     - (i) Religious affiliation ☐
       (specify) ....
     - (ii) No religious affiliation ☐
   - C. Other ☐
     (specify) ....

3. How many *full-time students* are enrolled at the university at the present time?
   Undergraduate students ....
   Graduate students ....

4. How many *part-time students* are enrolled at the university at the present time?
   Undergraduate students ....
   Graduate students ....

5. What are the principal *disciplines* taught? Check the following and add any which are taught and are not included in the list.

	First degree level	Second and higher degree level
A. PURE SCIENCES	☐	☐
Astronomy	☐	☐
Bacteriology	☐	☐
Biochemistry	☐	☐
Biology	☐	☐
Botany	☐	☐
Chemistry	☐	☐

	First degree level	Second and higher degree level		First degree level	Second and higher degree level
Entomology	☐	☐	Animal husbandry	☐	☐
Geology	☐	☐	Crop husbandry	☐	☐
Geophysics	☐	☐	Dairy farming	☐	☐
Mathematics	☐	☐	Fisheries	☐	☐
Meteorology	☐	☐	Food technology	☐	☐
Mineralogy	☐	☐	Forestry	☐	☐
Physics	☐	☐	Horticulture	☐	☐
Zoology	☐	☐	Soil and water sciences	☐	☐
....	☐	☐	Veterinary medicine	☐	☐
....	☐	☐	....	☐	☐
			....	☐	☐
B. ARCHITECTURE	☐	☐			
C. TECHNOLOGY:	☐	☐			
Applied sciences	☐	☐	**F. HUMANITIES**	☐	☐
Construction	☐	☐	Archeology	☐	☐
Geodesy	☐	☐	History	☐	☐
Metallurgy	☐	☐	Languages	☐	☐
Mining	☐	☐	Library science	☐	☐
Surveying	☐	☐	Literature	☐	☐
Technology	☐	☐	Philosophy	☐	☐
Textile engineering	☐	☐	Psychology	☐	☐
....	☐	☐	Theology	☐	☐
....	☐	☐	....	☐	☐
			....	☐	☐
D. MEDICAL SCIENCES			**G. FINE ARTS**	☐	☐
Anatomy	☐	☐	Drawing	☐	☐
Dentistry	☐	☐	Music	☐	☐
Medicine	☐	☐	Painting	☐	☐
Midwifery	☐	☐	Sculpture	☐	☐
Nursing	☐	☐	Speech and dramatic art	☐	☐
Optometry	☐	☐	....	☐	☐
Osteopathy	☐	☐	....	☐	☐
Pharmacy	☐	☐			
Physiotherapy	☐	☐	**H. EDUCATION:**	☐	☐
Public health	☐	☐	Education	☐	☐
Surgery	☐	☐	Pedagogy	☐	☐
....	☐	☐	Physical education	☐	☐
....	☐	☐			
E. AGRICULTURE	☐	☐	**I. LAW**	☐	☐
Agricultural econ.	☐	☐			

	First degree level	Second and higher degree level		First degree level	Second and higher degree level
J. SOCIAL SCIENCES			International rel.	☐	☐
			Journalism	☐	☐
Banking	☐	☐	Political science	☐	☐
Commerce	☐	☐	Public admin.	☐	☐
Diplomacy	☐	☐	Social welfare	☐	☐
Economics	☐	☐	Sociology	☐	☐
Ethnology	☐	☐	Statistics	☐	☐
Geography	☐	☐	....	☐	☐
Home economics	☐	☐	....	☐	☐

6. What are the organizational structures which correspond to these disciplines? e.g. *faculties, colleges, schools, departments* or other *units*. Please describe.

....

....

7. Estimate the degree of autonomy of your university in the following table.

Area of decision	Degree of autonomy			
	Complete	Partial	Slight	None
Finance	☐	☐	☐	☐
Curriculum	☐	☐	☐	☐
Selection of students	☐	☐	☐	☐
Staff recruitment	☐	☐	☐	☐
Academic objectives	☐	☐	☐	☐
Research policy	☐	☐	☐	☐
General objectives	☐	☐	☐	☐

8. To what extent is the Minister of Education or delegated representatives from the Ministry involved in the following kinds of decisions? To what extent are the administrative officers of the university involved? [1]

Area of decision	Minister of Education or representatives		Administrative officers of the university	
	Not involved	Involved in decision-making capacity	Not involved	Involved in decision-making capacity
Finance	☐	☐	☐	☐
Curriculum	☐	☐	☐	☐
Selection of students	☐	☐	☐	☐
Staff recruitment	☐	☐	☐	☐
Academic objectives	☐	☐	☐	☐
Research policy	☐	☐	☐	☐
General objectives	☐	☐	☐	☐

1. Administrative officers include the head of the university.

II. Basic data on university operations

This section is concerned with selected factual information on the operation of your university, using 1958/59 as a base year. We would like the same data ten years later—1968/69—in order to study changes that have occurred over time. If the data are not available for those years, please provide the information for the nearest years possible (INDICATE THE YEARS ON WHICH THE DATA ARE BASED). If your university is newly established, please use 1963/64 as the base year. If the precise data are not available, but you can provide estimates, place an 'E' beside your answer to indicate that it is an estimate. If the data for some items are not available and you cannot provide estimates, please write 'not available' in the answer space. (Part of the purpose of this study is to determine what information *is* available.)

1 A. Which of the following programmes of classes are current in your university?

Regular programme of	In 1958/59		In 1963/64		In 1968/69	
	Yes	No	Yes	No	Yes	No
Full-time day classes	☐	☐	☐	☐	☐	☐
Evening classes	☐	☐	☐	☐	☐	☐
Correspondence classes	☐	☐	☐	☐	☐	☐
Part-time day classes	☐	☐	☐	☐	☐	☐
Summer classes	☐	☐	☐	☐	☐	☐

B. How many weeks in the year is the university fully functional: for instruction ....; for research ....

2. What was the total number of students enrolled in each of the following types of instruction offered by your university?

| | Regular programme of classes | | | | | | | | | | | |
| | In 1958/59 | | | | In 1963/64 | | | | In 1968/69 | | | |
	Full time	Evening classes	Correspondence classes	Part-time day classes	Full time	Evening classes	Correspondence classes	Part-time day classes	Full time	Evening classes	Correspondence classes	Part-time day classes
Undergraduate students												
Graduate students												
Second degree												
Higher than second												
Total												
Total undergraduate and graduate students[1]												
All other students												
Total students												

1. If not available separately.

3. What is the date of enrolment quoted? (e.g. the beginning or the end of the academic year) ....

237

4. What information is available on the composition of the student body?

	In 1958/59				In 1963/64				In 1968/69			
	Under-graduate students	Graduate students	All other students	Total students	Under-graduate students	Graduate students	All other students	Total students	Under-graduate students	Graduate students	All other students	Total students
A. Number of students from various *economic origins:*												
i) Upper income group												
ii) Middle income group												
iii) Lower income group												
B. Number of students by occupation of parent. Number of students whose father's occupation was:												
i) Professional												
ii) Owner, manager												
iii) White-collar employee												
iv) Blue-collar skilled worker												
v) Blue-collar, unskilled worker												
vi) Farm worker or labourer												
vii) Other (specify)												
C. Number of students from various geographic locations:												
i) From city in which university is located												
ii) From district or province in which university is located												
iii) Students from elsewhere in your country												
iv) Foreign students												

Question 4. *(continued)*

	In 1958/59				In 1963/64				In 1968/69			
	Under-graduate students	Graduate students	All other students	Total students	Under-graduate students	Graduate students	All other students	Total students	Under-graduate students	Graduate students	All other students	Total students
D. Number of students by source of support:												
i) Students supported privately through their employment												
ii) Students supported privately through own or families' wealth												
iii) Students supported by private sources other than family or self												
iv) Students supported by government sources												
v) Students supported by other sources (Please describe sources)												
E. Number of students by sex:												
i) Number of male students												
ii) Number of female students												

5. Indicate the number of *applications* for places and the ratio of *applications* to *acceptances* in the following disciplines (If there were 1,000 applications and 100 students were accepted, the ratio would be 10:1):

	In 1958/59				In 1963/64				In 1968/69			
	Under-graduate students	Graduate students	All other students	Total students	Under-graduate students	Graduate students	All other students	Total students	Under-graduate students	Graduate students	All other students	Total students

A. Number of *applications:*

   i) Pure science
  ii) Architecture
 iii) Technology
 iv) Medical sciences
   v) Agriculture
 vi) Humanities
vii) Fine arts
viii) Education
 ix) Law
   x) Social sciences

B. Ratio of *applications* to *acceptances.*[1]

   i) Pure science
  ii) Architecture
 iii) Technology
 iv) Medical sciences
   v) Agriculture
 vi) Humanities
vii) Fine arts
viii) Education
 ix) Law
   x) Social sciences

1. Please read our definition in the glossary before answering this question.

240

6. Is your admissions system *open* or *selective?*

Open ☐   Selective ☐

A. If the system varies from discipline to discipline, check for each discipline

	Open	Selective
i) Pure science	☐	☐
ii) Architecture	☐	☐
iii) Technology	☐	☐
iv) Medical sciences	☐	☐
v) Agriculture	☐	☐
vi) Humanities	☐	☐
vii) Fine arts	☐	☐
viii) Education	☐	☐
ix) Law	☐	☐
x) Social sciences	☐	☐

B. If the system is *open,* what are the basic qualifications?

i) Completed *second-level education* ☐

ii) Diploma (awarded after an examination) of *second-level education* ☐

iii) Satisfactory record of *second-level education* ☐

iv) Technical or vocational diploma ☐

v) Others

....

....

C. If the system is *selective* what criteria are used for selection? If checking more than one box, give order of priority.

i) National criteria ☐

ii) Regional criteria ☐

iii) Criteria of the university ☐

iv) Number of places available ☐

v) Manpower needs ☐

D. What are the means used to implement the above criteria? If checking more than one box, give order of priority.

i) Entrance examination ☐

ii) Interview ☐

iii) Academic record ☐

iv) Place of residence ☐

v) Others

....

....

Questions 7 and 8, see page 242.

9. How many degrees were granted and at what level?

	In 1958/59	In 1963/64	In 1968/69
A. *First degree*	....	....	....
B. *Second degree*	....	....	....
C. *Higher-than-second degree*	....	....	....
D. Other *special degrees or certificates* (describe)			
	....	....	....
	....	....	....

10. What percentage of the teaching staff are foreign citizens?

.... | .... | ....

11. What is the total number of academic staff in the university?

Full time	....	....	....
Part time	....	....	....

7. What was the percentage of *student drop-out* in relation to total enrolment?

	In 1958/59				In 1963/64				In 1968/69			
	Under-graduate students	Graduate students	All other students	Total students	Under-graduate students	Graduate students	All other students	Total students	Under-graduate students	Graduate students	All other students	Total students
Percentage of *drop-out*												
Please give a brief description of your method for calculating *drop-out*												

8. What was the total number of students who dropped out?

Number of students who dropped out	
Reasons given:	
A. Number dropped out for academic reasons	
B. Number dropped out for financial reasons	
c. Number dropped out for other reasons	

How many of this total were engaged?	In 1958/59	In 1963/64	In 1968/69
A. Primarily as *teaching staff*	....	....	....
B. Primarily as *research staff*	....	....	....
C. Primarily administrative work	....	....	....
D. Combination of administration and teaching or research	....	....	....
E. Other (describe)			
....	....	....	....
....	....	....	....

F. Does the academic staff have pedagogical training?   Yes ☐   No ☐

12. What academic degrees are held by *teaching and research staff?*

A. Percentage of those whose highest academic degree is a *first degree*	....	....	....
B. Percentage of those whose highest academic degree is a *second degree*	....	....	....
C. Percentage of those whose highest academic degree is a *higher-than-second degree*	....	....	....
D. Others	....	....	....

13. We need to know the number of *teaching and research staff* members at various academic levels. List the teaching and research staff posts in your university from highest to lowest. Indicate the usual teaching load for each category and the number of personnel in each category.

		Average salary for each level [1]	Teaching & research staff posts (from highest to lowest)	Usual teaching load in hours per week	Number of personnel in each category		
					1958/59	1963/64	1968/69
A. Senior level	*i)*	....	....	....	....	....	....
	ii)	....	....	....	....	....	....
	iii)	....	....	....	....	....	....
B. Middle level	*iv)*	....	....	....	....	....	....
	v)	....	....	....	....	....	....
	vi)	....	....	....	....	....	....
C. Junior level	*vii)*	....	....	....	....	....	....
	viii)	....	....	....	....	....	....
	ix)	....	....	....	....	....	....

1. If data are not available, please give salary scale.

14. Number of publications written by the *teaching and research staff* of the university during the year :

	In 1958/59	In 1963/64	In 1968/69
A. *Textbooks*	....	....	....
B. *Other books*	....	....	....
C. *Monographs*	....	....	....
D. *Articles*	....	....	....
E. *Research reports*	....	....	....

15. Financial aspects: What percentage of the total income to the university during the year came from each of the following? If necessary, estimate the answers and put 'E' beside them to indicate they are an estimate.

	In 1958/59	In 1963/64	In 1968/69
A. Government sources	.... %	.... %	.... %
B. Private sources (e.g. gifts)	.... %	.... %	.... %
C. Industrial sources	.... %	.... %	.... %
D. Income from the university's own funds or property	.... %	.... %	.... %
E. Tuition	.... %	.... %	.... %
F. Foreign aid	.... %	.... %	.... %
G. Other sources (specify)	.... %	.... %	.... %
....	.... %	.... %	.... %
	100 %	100 %	100 %

16. What was the total *operating expenditure* for the university? (PLEASE GIVE ANSWERS IN THE CURRENCY OF YOUR COUNTRY AND INDICATE THE UNIT OF CURRENCY USED IN ANSWERS.) [1]

	In 1958/59	In 1963/64	In 1968/69
A. Total *operating expenditure*	....	....	....
B. *Materials and services*	....	....	....
C. *Student scholarship and support*	....	....	....
D. Operating expenditure for instructional salaries	....	....	....
E. Operating expenditure for administrative salaries	....	....	....
F. *Overheads*	....	....	....
G. Others (specify)	....	....	....

17. What were the total *capital expenditures* made—that is, money actually disbursed during the year? (GIVE ANSWERS IN THE CURRENCY OF YOUR COUNTRY AND INDICATE THE UNIT OF CURRENCY USED IN ANSWERS.)

	In 1958/59	In 1963/64	In 1968/69
A. Total *capital expenditures*	....	....	....
B. *Capital expenditures* for new buildings other than living and eating facilities	....	....	....
C. *Capital expenditures* for new buildings for living and eating facilities	....	....	....
D. *Capital expenditures* for re-modelling or renewing old buildings	....	....	....
E. *Capital expenditures* for equipment	....	....	....
F. Others (specify)	....	....	....

1. Would you please send us copies of your annual budgets for the relevant years?

18. From what source or sources were the salaries of the *teaching and research staff* paid?

	Teaching staff			Research staff		
	1958/59	1963/64	1968/69	1958/59	1963/64	1968/69
A. Partly by the university	☐	☐	☐	☐	☐	☐
B. Entirely by the university	☐	☐	☐	☐	☐	☐
C. Partly by the government	☐	☐	☐	☐	☐	☐
D. Entirely by the government	☐	☐	☐	☐	☐	☐
E. Partly from other sources (specify)	☐	☐	☐	☐	☐	☐
F. Entirely from other sources (specify)	☐	☐	☐	☐	☐	☐

19. Give the approximate index of total *useable instructional space* (lecture halls, classrooms, libraries, laboratories, etc.), using 1958/59 as a base of 100. For example, if you had 50,000 square metres in 1958/59 and 60,000 square metres in 1968/69, the index for 1968/69 would be

$$\frac{60,000}{50,000} \text{ or } 120$$

	1958/59	1963/64	1968/69
	....	....	....
Please give for any one of these years the TOTAL amount of instuctional space available (in square metres)	....	....	....

20. The volume of *research* conducted during the year.

A. What new money was available for research in the course of each academic year : (ANSWER IN THE TERMS OF THE CURRENCY OF YOUR COUNTRY AND INDICATE THE UNIT OF CURRENCY USED IN ANSWERS.)

	In 1958/59	In 1963/64	In 1968/69
i) *All research*	....	....	....
ii) *Basic or theoretical research*	....	....	....
iii) *Applied research*	....	....	....
iv) *Development*	....	....	....

	In 1958/59	In 1963/64	In 1968/69
B. How many separate research projects within your institution received research grants during the year?			
i) All research	....	....	....
ii) Basic or theoretical research	....	....	....
iii) Applied research	....	....	....
iv) Development	....	....	....
C. How many *graduate students* were engaged in research?	....	....	....
21. What percentage of the university budget is allocated to the library?	....	....	....
22. What is the total number of items in your library?	....	....	....
Please indicate the following:			
A. The total number of *library items* available (books, monographs, periodicals, etc.)	....	....	....
B. The total number of *library titles* available (books, monographs, periodicals, etc.)	....	....	....
C. Total *number of textbooks* available	....	....	....
D. Number of *textbook titles* available	....	....	....
E. The total number of *library items* acquired during the year (books, monographs, periodicals, etc.)	....	....	....
F. The total number of *library titles* acquired during the year (books, monographs, periodicals, etc.)	....	....	....

III. University functions and objectives

1. Indicate whether the following functions are performed at the university by checking ☐ Yes ☐ No.

   In the second column indicate the relative importance of each function on the five-point scale from 'Top priority' to 'Low priority'.

Top priority				Low priority
1	2	3	4	5
☐	☐	☐	☐	☐

   For example, if the university is principally an undergraduate institution and thus has little research activity, for undergraduate teaching you would check 1. For research in this same case you would check 5.

	Is function performed		Relative importance of function				
	Yes	No	Top priority 1	2	3	4	Low priority 5
A. Teaching *undergraduate* students	☐	☐	☐	☐	☐	☐	☐
B. Preparing *graduate* students	☐	☐	☐	☐	☐	☐	☐
C. Training of teachers:							
i) for *second-level* education	☐	☐	☐	☐	☐	☐	☐
ii) for *higher* education	☐	☐	☐	☐	☐	☐	☐
D. *Continuing education:*							
i) *extension work*	☐	☐	☐	☐	☐	☐	☐
ii) *refresher courses*	☐	☐	☐	☐	☐	☐	☐
E. Preparation of instructional materials:							
i) for *second-level* education	☐	☐	☐	☐	☐	☐	☐
ii) for *higher* education	☐	☐	☐	☐	☐	☐	☐
iii) for a complete system of education	☐	☐	☐	☐	☐	☐	☐
F. Research:							
i) *theoretical research*	☐	☐	☐	☐	☐	☐	☐
ii) *applied research*	☐	☐	☐	☐	☐	☐	☐
iii) *development*	☐	☐	☐	☐	☐	☐	☐
G. Physical planning for the universities	☐	☐	☐	☐	☐	☐	☐
H. Financial planning in the universities	☐	☐	☐	☐	☐	☐	☐
I. Working with outside organizations:							
i) *government*	☐	☐	☐	☐	☐	☐	☐
ii) *industry*	☐	☐	☐	☐	☐	☐	☐
iii) *local community*	☐	☐	☐	☐	☐	☐	☐
J. Others	☐	☐	☐	☐	☐	☐	☐

2. If a choice had to be made of areas to develop, which function would you most
like to see developed? Give a rank order by numbers from 1-9.
For example, if research were your first choice you would put 1 opposite research.

A. Teaching *undergraduate* students ....
B. Preparing *graduate students* ....
C. Training teachers ....
D. *Continuing education* ....
E. Preparation of instructional materials ....
(Continued)

F. Research ....   G. Physical planning ....
- *i) Basic or theoretical research*   (...........)
- H. Working with outside organizations ....
- *ii) Applied research*   (...........)   I. Others ....
- *iii) Development*   (...........)

3. Why have the three functions, which you checked 1, 2, 3, in question 2 above, not been expanded at the university? Check the following reasons and give explanations where possible.

Explanation

Shortage of funds ☐ ....

Shortage of space ☐ ....

Shortage of professional personnel ☐ ....

Shortage of physical facilities ☐ ....

Administrative difficulties ☐ ....

Other .... ☐ ....

.... ☐ ....

IV. Academic programmes and teaching materials

Academic programmes

	Number of courses offered:		
	In 1958/59	In 1963/64	In 1968/69
1. Please enter the total number of *courses* offered in the curriculum	....	....	....
2. Please enter the total number of *courses* offered in 1968/69 which were NOT offered in 1958/59			....
3. Please enter the total number of *courses* offered in 1958/59 that were NOT offered in 1968/69	....		

248

4. Do you have any sort of continuous
   evaluation of the existing *courses*
   and of the need for new ones.
   Yes ☐ No ☐
   Please give a brief explanation of
   your answers

....

....

5. If the answer to question 4 is yes, which of the following kinds of person were
   involved in the evaluation? Describe in what way.

	In 1958/59		In 1963/64		In 1968/69	
	Involved	Not involved	Involved	Not involved	Involved	Not involved
Representatives from the Ministry of Education						
In what way?	☐	☐	☐	☐	☐	☐
University administration						
In what way?	☐	☐	☐	☐	☐	☐
Teaching and research staff						
In what way?	☐	☐	☐	☐	☐	☐
Graduate students						
In what way?	☐	☐	☐	☐	☐	☐
Undergraduate students						
In what way?	☐	☐	☐	☐	☐	☐
Business and industry						
In what way?	☐	☐	☐	☐	☐	☐

Others (specify)

6. The extent to which there have been CHANGES OF CONTENTS in *courses* offered
   ten years ago and still offered today.
   What is your estimate of how much the actual content of *courses* offered in
   1958/59, and still offered in 1968/69, has changed?
   (Answers must total 100 %)
   ....% of all *courses* have changed very little.
   ....% of all *courses* have changed moderately (up to 25 % new content).
   ....% of all *courses* have changed substantially (between 25 % and 50 %
   new content).
   ....% of all *courses* have changed drastically (50 % or more new content).

7. What are the tendencies in composition of *courses* over the years?

A. For a typical student in the following fields of study, what percentage of his *courses* out of the total would be *requirements* (obligatory). Give percentage for all disciplines.

	Requirements (obligatory)		
	1958/59	1963/64	1968/69
i) Pure science	%	%	%
ii) Architecture	%	%	%
iii) Technology	%	%	%
iv) Medical sciences	%	%	%
v) Agriculture	%	%	%
vi) Humanities	%	%	%
vii) Fine arts	%	%	%
viii) Education	%	%	%
ix) Law	%	%	%
x) Social sciences	%	%	%

B. Of the *requirements* above what percentage would be in fields other than the major fields of study? Give percentage for all disciplines.

	Requirements in fields other than the major		
	1958/59	1963/64	1968/69
i) Pure science	%	%	%
ii) Architecture	%	%	%
iii) Technology	%	%	%
iv) Medical sciences	%	%	%
v) Agriculture	%	%	%
vi) Humanities	%	%	%
vii) Fine arts	%	%	%
viii) Education	%	%	%
ix) Law	%	%	%
x) Social sciences	%	%	%

EXAMPLE : A STUDENT GRADUATING IN ECONOMICS.
The starred courses are obligatory. In all, the student must take eight courses out of the following ten.

* 1. Economics   * 6. Economics
  2. Economics   * 7. Economics
* 3. Sociology   8. Sociology
* 4. Statistics   * 9. Political science
  5. Mathematics   10. History

In this case A: $\dfrac{5}{8} =$ 62.5 per cent.

Sociology and statistics being outside the main area of study:

$$B: \dfrac{2}{5} = 40 \text{ per cent.}$$

8. Degrees offered at your university
A. Number of years normally required to complete a *first degree*.
B. Percentage of all students taking final examination who graduate in these *disciplines*.

	1958/59		1963/64		1968/69	
	A	B	A	B	A	B
i) Pure science						
ii) Architecture						
iii) Technology						
iv) Medical sciences						
v) Agriculture						
vi) Humanities						
vii) Fine arts						
viii) Education						
ix) Law						
x) Social sciences						

9. List by name all types of *second and higher degrees* offered and the length of time (in years) after the first degree normally required to obtain them.

	Type of second or higher degree offered	Number of years required to obtain it	Offered in: 1958/59	1963/64	1968/69
A. Pure science					
B. Architecture					
C. Technology					
D. Medical sciences					
E. Agriculture					
F. Humanities					
G. Fine arts					
H. Education					
I. Law					
J. Social sciences					

251

Academic structures between 1958/59 and 1968/69

1. Have any new *faculties, departments* or other *units* been ADDED between 1958/59 and 1968/69?
   Yes ☐   No ☐

2. If yes, give the name of the *faculty* or *department,* and give a brief description of it, and the reason it was added:

   Names of *units* added   Description

   i) ....

   ii) ....

   iii) ....

   ...   ...

   xv) ....

3. Have any *faculties, departments* or *units* been DROPPED in the last ten years?
   Yes ☐   No ☐

4. If yes, give the name of such *units* and give a brief description of them and the reasons they were dropped.

   Names of *units* dropped   Description

   i) ....

   ii) ....

   iii) ....

   ...   ...

   x) ....

5. Have any *faculties, departments* or *units* been significantly REORGANIZED or COMBINED.
   Yes ☐   No ☐

6. If yes, please give the names of those which have been reorganized or combined and give a brief description of them, and the reasons for reorganization.

   Names of *faculties, departments* or   Description
   units reorganized or combined

   i) ....

   ii) ....

   iii) ....

   ...   ...

   x) ....

252

Teaching materials and methodology : major innovations in instructional methods

Indicate which of the items listed below are major innovations in your university since 1958/59 and which are now in SYSTEMATIC OR EXPERIMENTAL USE. Please briefly describe how each *innovation* is used.

	Description of how innovation is used	Experi-mental stage	System-atized stage
A. Instructional television		☐	☐
B. Instructional radio		☐	☐
C. Computer-assisted instruction (in other than computer studies)		☐	☐
D. Independent study courses		☐	☐
E. Programmed instruction		☐	☐
F. *Team teaching*		☐	☐
G. Central service for production of teaching materials		☐	☐
H. Other (specify)		☐	☐
		☐	☐

Uses of new media

New media may be used simply to transmit traditional methods of teaching (e.g. a televised lecture). Television may be used in a completely new way to present programmed instruction. Which of the following comes closest to describing the way *new media* have been used at your university? Please check expectations for 1970s.

	1958/59	1963/64	1968/69	1970s
1. *New media* not used	☐	☐	☐	☐
2. *New media* used mostly for traditional methods of instruction	☐	☐	☐	☐
3. *New media* used mostly for new methods of instruction	☐	☐	☐	☐
4. *New media* used partly for traditional methods and partly for new methods of instruction	☐	☐	☐	☐

Size of classes

How many classes do you have of the following class sizes?

Number of students	Undergraduate students				Graduate students
	1st year	2nd year	3rd year	4th year	
More than fifty	....	....	....	....	....
Between twenty and fifty	....	....	....	....	....
Between ten and twenty	....	....	....	....	....
Less than ten	....	....	....	....	....

V. Governance and management of the university

Organization and distribution of responsibilities

1. Has there been any significant reorganization since 1958/59 of major responsibilities for planning, evaluation and decision-making in your institution (e.g., new planning office, internal *institutional research bureau*, new faculty planning bodies or legislative bodies, new ways of involving students in decision-making processes)?

   Yes ☐   No ☐

2. If yes, list these changes and describe each, giving the date the reorganization took place.

Name	Description and date of reorganization
A.	....
B.	....
C.	....
...	...
J.	....

3. In what ways, if any, has student participation in the following areas of university governance changed?

   A. Academic policy   ....

   B. Administrative policy ....

   C. Social policy   ....

4. In what ways, if any, has participation of the *senior teaching and research staff* in the governance of the university changed?

....

....

5. In what ways, if any, has the participation of *junior teaching and research staff* in the governance of the university changed?

....

....

Changes and innovations in management tools and methods

1. Have there been any important *innovations* and changes in your university since 1958/59 in management tools and methods? Check the following table and add other *innovations* not included, giving dates of introduction.

Innovation		Date of introduction
A. Establishment of new *information system*	☐	....
B. Introduction of *programme planning*	☐	....
C. Introduction of *programme budgeting*	☐	....
D. Use of computers for record-keeping	☐	....
E. Use of computers for analysis	☐	....
F. Use of *analytical models*	☐	....
G. Others	☐	....
....	☐	....

2. Indicate *any* major change within the last ten years which was the result of a stimulus from one of the following. Give explanations where possible.

	Major change	Explanation
A. Government	....	....
		....
		....
	....	....
B. Industry	...	...
C. University administration	...	...
D. Other universities and research organizations	...	...
E. *Teaching and research staff* (other than *junior teaching staff*)	...	...
F. *Junior teaching staff*	...	...
G. Students	...	...
H. Former graduates	...	...
I. Other	...	...

255

VI. Decision-making and planning mechanisms

1. Check the table below to show the relative weight (measured from 1-5) of the decision-making bodies (horizontal axis) in the different areas of decision (vertical axis). The figures have the following meanings: 1. no involvement; 2. informed about decision; 3. consulted about decision; 4. active participation in decision-making; 5. authority for final decision or veto power.

Decision-making body	Central government	Regional government	Senate or university council	University administration	Faculty	Department	Individual professors	Senior teaching and research staff	Junior teaching and research staff	Students
Major allocation of funds within the university										
Planning and development										
Decision on student admissions										
Staff appointments										
Curriculum approval										
Research policy										
Innovation										
Extra-curricular activities										

2. How far ahead are the following types of decisions made, with regard to planning?
Check the table below.

Types of decision	Length of time in the future					
	1 year	2 years	3 years	4 years	5 years	6 years +
Major financial decisions						
Minor financial decisions						
Major curriculum decisions						
Minor curriculum decisions						
Research policy decisions						
Staff planning decisions						

Above what amount of money is a financial decision considered to be a major
one? ....

3. Do you think new methods or organizational *units* for planning are needed at
your university?
Yes ☐   No ☐

4. If yes, what kind of new methods or *units* do you think are needed?
....
....

5. Do you think any of the existing methods or *units* are out of date?
Yes ☐   No ☐

6. If yes, which method or *unit* do you think should be changed and how?

Method or unit	How should it be changed?
A.	
B.	
C.	
...	...
J.	

257

7. Is the statistical information listed below available for planning purposes or not? If it is available, is it adequate in its present form? If it is not available, please indicate whether it would be desirable for planning purposes.

	Available		Not available	
Types of information	Ade- quate	Inade- quate	Desi- rable	Not needed
A. Ratio of *acceptances* to *applications*	☐	☐	☐	☐
B. Number of *graduates* in relation to demand for them, by field of specialization	☐	☐	☐	☐
C. *Student/teaching staff ratio*	☐	☐	☐	☐
D. Rate of drop-out—*student wastage*	☐	☐	☐	☐
E. Proportion of *graduate students* in student body	☐	☐	☐	☐
F. Proportion of new *courses* in the curricula per year	☐	☐	☐	☐
G. Ratio of books available per student	☐	☐	☐	☐
H. Availability of teaching and research equipment	☐	☐	☐	☐
I. Availability of *instructional space*	☐	☐	☐	☐
J. Availability of other space	☐	☐	☐	☐
K. *Unit costs* per graduating student	☐	☐	☐	☐
L. Proportion of research that is of a high professional calibre	☐	☐	☐	☐
M. Number of hours per week instructional space is fully utilized	☐	☐	☐	☐
N. Distribution of staff time among teaching, research and other activities	☐	☐	☐	☐

	Yes	No
8. For planning purposes A. is factual information used;	☐	☐
B. are established norms applied.	☐	☐

If normative figures are used please quote below: Norms used

A. Ratio of *acceptances* to *applications* ....
B. Number of *graduates* in relation to demand for them, by field of specialization ....
C. *Student/teaching staff ratio* ....
D. Rate of drop-out—*student wastage* ....
E. Proportion of *graduate students* in student body ....
F. Proportion of new *courses* in the curricula per year ....
G. Ratio of books available per student ....
H. Availability of teaching and research equipment ....
I. Availability of *instructional space* ....
J. Availability of other space ....
K. *Unit costs* per graduating student ....
L. Proportion of research that is of a high professional calibre ....
M. Number of hours per week instructional space is fully utilized ....
N. Distribution of staff time among teaching, research and other activities ....

VII. Assessments of past and future changes

1. In the list below, indicate for each item whether it was a factor of change in your university in the last ten years.
2. For each factor in which change took place, indicate how serious the change was to the overall successful operation of the university. Place a check across from each item in the five-point scale to indicate how important each item was.
3. Indicate on the five-point scale to what extent it was possible for your university to cope with each change over the last ten years.
4. Indicate on the five-point scale how well you expect the university to react in the NEXT ten years.

A. Increase in applications

Past	Future
A factor of change in the past ten years?	A factor of change in the next ten years?
Yes ☐ No ☐	Yes ☐ No ☐
How serious was the change?	How serious will the change be?

Very serious				Not serious	Very serious				Not serious
1	2	3	4	5	1	2	3	4	5
☐	☐	☐	☐	☐	☐	☐	☐	☐	☐

How well was the university able to cope?	How well will the university be able to cope?

Very well				Badly	Very well				Badly
1	2	3	4	5	1	2	3	4	5
☐	☐	☐	☐	☐	☐	☐	☐	☐	☐

[THE SAME QUESTIONS WERE ASKED IN THE SAME WAY FOR THE FOLLOWING ITEMS, WITH THE EXCEPTION OF ITEM L.]

B. Increase in enrolments
C. Improvement in the quality of incoming students
D. Increase in *applications* relative to the number of places available
E. Expanding the numbers of *teaching and research staff*
F. Improvement in the quality of *teaching and research staff*
G. The need to change the curriculum to fit changing conditions
H. The need to change the structures of the university to meet changing needs
I. The need to increase the volume and sources of financing
J. The need to expand facilities
K. The gap between the distribution of *graduates* by field and *manpower needs*
M. Increased participation of students in university governance
N. The need for *refresher courses*
O. The demand for *continuing education* for people in all walks of life
P. Other (specify) ....

....

259

L. Changes in the amount (in terms of cost) and type of research within the university

Past			Future		

A factor of change in the past ten years?

Yes ☐　　No ☐

	Increase	Decrease
Basic or theoretical research	☐	☐
Applied research	☐	☐
Development research	☐	☐

How well was the university able to cope?

Very well				Badly
1	2	3	4	5
☐	☐	☐	☐	☐

A factor of change in the next ten year?

Yes ☐　　No ☐

	Increase	Decrease
Basic or theoretical research	☐	☐
Applied research	☐	☐
Development research	☐	☐

How well will the university be able to cope?

Very well				Badly
1	2	3	4	5
☐	☐	☐	☐	☐

5. Please indicate below, on the same list of factors of change, to what extent you think these changes are desirable for the future. Place a check across from each item in the five-point scale to indicate how desirable or not is the change.

	Factor will occur or continue to occur		How desirable is the factor?	
	Yes	No	Very desirable	Not desirable
A. Increase in *applications*	☐	☐	: ...... : ...... : ...... : ...... : ...... :
B. Increase in enrolments	☐	☐	: ...... : ...... : ...... : ...... : ...... :
C. Improving the quality of incoming students	☐	☐	: ...... : ...... : ...... : ...... : ...... :
D. Increase in *applications* relative to number of students that can be accepted	☐	☐	: ...... : ...... : ...... : ...... : ...... :
E. Attracting *teaching and research staff* in increasing numbers	☐	☐	: ...... : ...... : ...... : ...... : ...... :
F. Improving the quality of *teaching and research staff*	☐	☐	: ...... : ...... : ...... : ...... : ...... :
G. Changes in curriculum to keep pace with changing conditions	☐	☐	: ...... : ...... : ...... : ...... : ...... :
H. Changes in *structural organization* of university to meet changing needs	☐	☐	: ...... : ...... : ...... : ...... : ...... :
I. Increasing the volume and sources of financing	☐	☐	: ...... : ...... : ...... : ...... : ...... :
J. Expansion of facilities	☐	☐	: ...... : ...... : ...... : ...... : ...... :

	Factor will occur or continue to occur		How desirable is the factor?	
	Yes	No	Very desirable	Not desirable
K. Diminishing the gap between distribution of *graduates* by field and needs of society	☐	☐	: ...... : ...... : ...... : ...... : ...... :
L. Changes in the amount and type of *research* within the university	☐	☐	: ...... : ...... : ...... : ...... : ...... :
M. Increase of participation by students in governance of university	☐	☐	: ...... : ...... : ...... : ...... : ...... :
N. Increased demand for *refresher courses* —that is, courses designed to bring the person out of school up to date	☐	☐	: ...... : ...... : ...... : ...... : ...... :
O. Increased demand for *continuing education* for persons in all walks of life	☐	☐	: ...... : ...... : ...... : ...... : ...... :
P. Other (specify)	☐	☐	: ...... : ...... : ...... : ...... : ...... :

6. What, in your estimation, have been the most important obstacles to needed or desirable changes at your university in the LAST ten years? For example, there are obstacles inside and outside the university, there are financial obstacles, there are psychological factors among students and among instructional and research staff. These are examples only. Do not restrict yourself to these.

A. ....
B. ....
C. ....
...
J. ....

7. What do you estimate will be the most important obstacles to needed or desirable changes at your university in the NEXT ten years?

A. ....
B. ....
C. ....
...
J. ....

8. To what extent does your university see itself as a factor in political and social change within your country?

A. ....
B. ....
C. ....
D. ....

The following glossary explains in more detail many of the terms used in the questionnaire. In the questionnaire, each term which is given in this glossary is printed in italic, e.g. *applied research*. Each time you come upon a term in italic in the questionnaire, please refer to this glossary to be certain that you use and interpret the term in the same way as we have. We do not mean to imply that the only correct meaning of the various terms is the one given in the glossary. The primary purpose of the glossary is to obtain comparable data from the various universities participating in the study. In cases where you do not have data on the basis we have defined here, but where you have similar data, please give us the data you have but take care to EXPLAIN the basis of your data.

In the definition of a term, any words or phrases enclosed in quotes are also defined in the glossary.

Acceptances: See 'Applications'.

All other students: Includes all special students of one kind or another who are not working towards a degree. These students may be enrolled in special classes or even in day classes, but the classes have the purpose of training a person more specifically for his job or of updating his training and do not lead to a degree. The important feature is that these students are *not* working towards a degree.

Analytical model: A diagrammatic or mathematical description of a certain number of factors and functions pertaining to the university. This representation is used for a rational study of university operations.

Applications and acceptances: The two terms we would like used. 'Applications' is the number of persons who file the initial form requesting entrance. If this information is not available then perhaps the number who took entrance examinations following the initial application or who were interviewed following the initial application is available. Similarly, we would like information on 'acceptances', that is, the number who passed all requirements for entrance. However, not all who are accepted actually enter, so data on those actually entering may be all that are available. Remember, we prefer data on 'applications' and 'acceptances'. If data are not available on these bases, then please provide data on any other bases available, but do not fail to define the bases you use.

Applied research: Investigations that are directed to the discovery of new scientific knowledge and that have specific and sometimes commercial objectives and applications with respect to products or processes.

Article: A short publication in a journal or periodical of recognized standing.

Basic research: Research undertaken in pursuit of new knowledge, with no apparent immediate practical application.

Blue collar, skilled worker: A worker skilled in a specific trade and in the employ of another person, for example, carpenters or bricklayers.

Blue collar, unskilled worker: A worker unskilled in any specific trade and employed by someone else, often simply called a labourer. 'Farm workers and labourers' are not included here.

Capital expenditures: Monies spent on physical facilities and equipment which will be in use for a period of not less than one year. Not included here are 'operating expenditures' such as salaries.

Colleges: Organizational structures similar to 'faculties' which, nevertheless, group together a smaller number of 'departments' or 'disciplines'.

Continuing education: Education provided by the university for those no longer in formal education. The courses offered do *not* lead to a degree.

Correspondence classes: Classes which are not attended in person and which, like evening classes, lead to a degree. These should be included in 'regular programme of courses' for the purpose of this questionnaire.

Course: A subject or subject area studied within a programme. A certain number of subjects or courses go to make up the programme for a degree.

Degree of autonomy: The distribution of responsibility in the different decision-making areas among universities, governments and other bodies.

Departments: Usually the smallest organizational units within the university, grouping together a varying number of 'disciplines' in the same field of study.

Development: Technical activities which are not of a routine nature but are concerned with translating research findings or other scientific knowledge into products or processes.

Disciplines: Areas of study, which cover related subject-matter.

Drop-out: Those students who were officially enrolled in the university and who left the university without finishing their degree.

Economic origins: This term will be used in a very simple sense. It is intended to distinguish between the socio-economic groups in society from which an individual comes. Those in the top 30 per cent, 'higher income group' can easily afford not only the necessities of life, but most of the luxuries. Those in the 'middle income group', 40 per cent, can afford the necessities of life, and some of the luxuries. Those in the 'lower income group', 30 per cent, can afford few, if any, of the luxuries of life and may have difficulties in acquiring the necessities. If this definition is not applicable, please apply the standards of your country and explain your definitions.

Evening classes: Classes conducted in the evening for part-time students and which lead to a degree. These classes should be included in 'regular programme of courses' for the purpose of this questionnaire.

Extension work: Courses offered by the university to all possible branches of the community. These courses are designed to bring people up to date in their own field, but do *not* lead to a degree. Such courses may be conducted outside the university.

Faculties: Frequently the traditional organizational structure within a university, which groups together a certain number of 'departments' for administrative, learning and research purposes.

Farm workers or labourers: Persons who work on farms in the employ of another person.

Financial planning: The term is used here in its broadest sense. It includes planning of capital outlay and of operational costs (salaries, maintenance of buildings and equipment, etc.).

First degree: The first qualification awarded by the university, after a period of not less than three years and which indicates that the first stage of higher education has been completed.

Full-time day classes: Normal classes conducted during the day for full-time students.

Full-time student : (See also 'undergraduate student'.) As a general guide we mean a person working toward a 'first degree' and who is carrying at least the normal number or load of courses that will lead to the degree sought in the normal length of time. Most universities have a definition of full-time, sometimes in terms of hours per week spent in classes or number of classes attended per week, etc.

Graduate student: Students in the university who have a 'first degree' and who are working toward a 'second or higher degree'.

Graduates: Those persons who have a university degree, but who have left the university and are no longer in formal education.

Higher education: Education above the 'second level' which offers at least a 'first degree', that is, a degree corresponding to a bachelor's degree under the British and American systems.

Higher-than-second degree: See 'second or higher degree'.

Information system: An organized collection of data and information concerning the university, put together in a systematic way. Such a system is designed to facilitate decision-making processes.

Innovation: An innovation means something new. But it can mean either something new in a general sense all over the world, or something new within your university. You may use it either way. Even if a particular technique has been used elsewhere for some time, if it is new to your university it would still be considered an innovation for the purposes of this study.

Institutional research bureau: A unit which evaluates university activities, makes recommendations concerning them, and conducts research on university operations.

Instructional materials: This term, unless specified further in the question, is used in a broad sense. It includes conventional items such as course outlines, 'textbooks', etc., and also newer items such as programmed instruction, etc.

Junior teaching and research staff: Staff members of the university engaged in teaching or research or both, who occupy academic positions below the middle rate in your scale of appointments.

Library items: The total number of items, including multiple copies of the same publication.

Library titles: The total number of *unduplicated items;* thus, under this heading, two copies of the same book count only as one.

Manpower needs: In this context, the needs of the economy for defined categories of qualified personnel.

264

Materials and services: Equipment provided for the university which does not include equipment under capital expenditure. Services provided by the university in order to facilitate all university activities.

Mechanism: A method or technique for planning.

Monograph: A publication in book form of a study concentrated in one area.

New media: Modern methods of communication—such as television, tape recordings or radio—used for instructional purposes.

Number of textbooks: The total number of 'textbooks', including multiple copies of the same textbook. See also 'library items', 'library titles', and 'textbook titles'.

Open admission system: A system of entrance to the university which allows all those who have successfully completed 'second-level education' to be admitted to the university.

Operating expenditure: Money spent for day-to-day operation of the university. It includes salaries, supplies, regular maintenance of buildings (but not remodelling). It does not include 'capital expenditures', which are long-term investments in buildings, equipment, etc.

Other books: Books which are not specifically 'textbooks' and include works of fiction or other works not closely related to the affairs of the university.

Overheads: Expenses not chargeable to a particular part of the university's activity.

Owner, manager: Persons who are not 'professionals' but who either own their own business or enterprise, or manage one (alone or as a member of a managerial group) for someone else.

Part-time day classes: Classes conducted during the day for part-time students. (The students may, for example, be on day-release from industry.)

Part-time graduate: (See also 'graduate student'.) As a general guide we mean a person who is working in normal graduate studies, but who for financial or other reasons also has other employment. He will presumably need longer than the full-time graduate to complete his degree.

Part-time student: (See also 'undergraduate student'.) As a general guide this means someone who is carrying *less* than the normal load or number of classes required to obtain the degree sought in the normal length of time. The definition is sometimes in terms of less than a certain number of hours per week spent in class, or number of courses, etc.

Physical planning: Planning for both *space* and *equipment*.

Professional: A category of people in occupations generally requiring some form of higher learning, e.g. doctors, lawyers, university professors, etc.

Programme: (See also 'course'.) A group of courses (or several related groups of courses in the same general subject area) which leads to a degree. Most of the courses in a group are integrated around a particular 'discipline' or general subject area, and most of these courses are obligatory. There is generally room within a programme, however, to take some optional courses either directly related to the field in which the degree is to be granted or in other fields.

Programme budgeting: A method of projecting and distributing resources according to requirements and cost estimates of individual planned programmes.

Programme planning: A method of organizing university activities on the basis of chosen objectives. These objectives are translated into sequential actions over time which form the programmes.

Refresher courses: Courses designed to bring a person who has been out of formal

265

education for a while up to date in subject matter once learned but since forgotten or subject matter that has changed since that person was in formal education.

Regular programme of classes: All classes counting toward and leading to a degree. Most of such classes are taught during the day, but others may in fact be taught at other times. The distinguishing feature is that they count toward a degree.

Research: (See also 'applied research', 'basic research' and 'development'.) The term 'research', when it appears alone and is not specified further, is used in the broad sense and includes both basic and applied research.

Research reports: Printed statements setting out the results of concluded research.

Research staff: Personnel at the university who are engaged, by the government, the university itself or some other agency, exclusively to carry out research. It does not include research support personnel—i.e. technicians, etc.

Requirements: Subjects which the student is obliged to study (as opposed to those he may select for himself) in his degree course.

Second-level education: For the purpose of this project we define second-level education as that which leads to higher education.

Second-level schools: Intermediate schools such as high schools, *colegios, lycées,* and preparatory schools for youth generally between 13 and 18 years of age.

Second degree: See 'second or higher degree'.

Second or higher degree: All degrees sought after receiving a first degree. For convenience, in some cases, we have asked for 'second' and 'higher-than-second degree' together. In other cases we have asked for 'second degree' and 'higher-than-second degree' separately. The second degree is equivalent to a master's degree under the American and British systems, but under other systems there is no equivalent. 'Higher-than-second degree' is equivalent to a doctorate in the American and British systems (for simplification we have combined all kinds of doctorates even though the requirements are varied) and to a candidate in the Soviet system.

Schools: Organizational structure within the 'faculty'—where the faculty structure exists. Schools may exist independently of faculty structure and group together a smaller number of 'departments' than a 'college'.

Selective admission system: A system of entry to the university in which some method of selection is applied by the government, by the university itself or by some other agency to qualified candidates seeking admission to the university.

Senior teaching and research staff: Staff members of the university engaged in teaching or research or both, who occupy academic positions above the middle rate in your scale of appointments.

Special degree or certificate: In some fields and in some universities, degrees are given that do not neatly fall into the category of 'first degree' (equivalent to a bachelor's), or 'second or higher degree' (equivalent to a master's or a doctorate or candidate degree). These are special degrees usually (but not always) requiring study beyond the first degree but not fulfilling the requirements of a second or higher degree. For example, such degrees or certificates can exist in education and in engineering.

Structural organization: For the purpose of the questionnaire, the administrative and decision-making structures in the university.

Student scholarships and support: Financial aid given directly to students to support them during their studies and money spent by the university on student activities which do not fall within the formal academic programme.

Student/teaching staff ratio: The number of students, divided by the number of teaching staff (excluding those members of staff engaged exclusively in research).

Student wastage: See 'drop-out'.

Summer classes: Classes which are given in the summer vacation when the regular students are on holiday.

Teaching and research staff: All staff members of the university engaged in either teaching or research or both of these activities. It does not include supporting or technical personnel.

Teaching staff: Teaching personnel at the university, who may also be engaged in research.

Team teaching: Method of teaching which involves the co-operative work of two or more members of staff and their presence together with the class.

Textbook: Written course of study, which is the principal recommended source of information for a subject.

Textbook titles: The total number of *unduplicated* textbooks. Multiple copies of the same textbook should not be included here. (See 'library titles', 'library items', and 'number of textbooks'.)

Theoretical research: See 'basic research'.

Total students: The total of all other columns in the question. If information is requested only for 'undergraduate students' and 'graduate students', then 'total students' is the sum of these two groups. However, if information is requested for 'undergraduate students', 'graduate students' and 'all other students', then 'total students' is the sum of all three groups.

Training: The term is used in several senses, depending on the question. In some questions it is used in its broadest sense, to include teaching courses for students working toward a degree, and teaching evening or correspondence courses for persons requiring special or updated knowledge but who are not in a programme leading to a degree. In other questions, training refers only to teaching of persons in programmes leading to degrees, while in still other questions it refers only to teaching students who are not in programmes leading to a degree. The exact meaning in each case is clear within the context of the particular question.

Updating of training: See 'refresher courses'.

Undergraduate students: Students in the university working towards their 'first degree' —that is, towards a degree corresponding to a bachelor's degree under the American and British systems.

Units: Any organizational academic structure. If this term is used, give a definition.

Unit cost: The total expenditure, divided by the total enrolment expressed in some form or another. This is a general formula, which should be modified by taking into account the characteristics of the system (e.g. in the case where there are 'part-time students' some weighting average is usually worked out so as to represent 'part-time students' as full-time equivalents).

Useable instructional space: All physical space directly involved in the instructional process. It includes classrooms, lecture halls, laboratories and libraries.

White-collar employee: An employee who is neither a member of a profession nor considered a labourer or worker (skilled or unskilled), for example, salesmen in stores, clerical workers (see 'blue collar, unskilled worker', and 'professional').

IIEP book list

The following books, published by Unesco/IIEP, are obtainable from the Institute or from Unesco and its national distributors throughout the world:

Educational cost analysis in action: case studies for planners (1972. Three volumes)

Educational development in Africa (1969. Three volumes, containing eleven African research monographs)

Educational planning: a bibliography (1964)

Educational planning: a directory of training and research institutions (1968)

Educational planning in the USSR (1968)

Financing educational systems (series of monographs: full list available on request)

Fundamentals of educational planning (series of monographs: full list available on request)

Manpower aspects of educational planning (1968)

Methodologies of educational planning for developing countries by J.D. Chesswas (1968)

Monographies africaines (five titles, in French only: list available on request)

New educational media in action: case studies for planners (1967. Three volumes)

The new media: memo to educational planners by W. Schramm, P.H. Coombs, F. Kahnert, J. Lyle (1967. A report including analytical conclusions based on the above three volumes of case studies)

Planning the development of universities (Vol. I, 1971; Vol. II, 1973. Further volumes to appear)

Planning the location of schools (series of monographs: full list available on request)

Population growth and costs of education in developing countries by Ta Ngoc Châu (1972)

Qualitative aspects of educational planning (1969)

Research for educational planning: notes on emergent needs by William J. Platt (1970)

Systems approach to teacher training and curriculum development: the case of developing countries by Taher A. Razik (1972)

The following books, produced in but not published by the Institute, are obtainable through normal bookselling channels:

Education in industrialized countries by R. Poignant
  Published by N.V. Martinus Nijhoff, The Hague, 1973

Managing educational costs by Philip H. Coombs and Jacques Hallak
  Published by Oxford University Press, New York, London and Toronto, 1972

Quantitative methods of educational planning by Héctor Correa
  Published by International Textbook Co., Scranton, Pa., 1969

The world educational crisis: a systems analysis by Philip H. Coombs
  Published by Oxford University Press, New York, London and Toronto, 1968

The International Institute for Education Planning

The International Institute for Educational Planning (IIEP) was established by Unesco in 1963 to serve as an international centre for advanced training and research in the field of educational planning. Its basic financing is provided by Unesco, and its physical facilities by the government of France. It also receives supplemental support from private and governmental sources.

The Institute's aim is to expand knowledge and the supply of competent experts in educational planning in order to assist all nations to accelerate their educational development. In this endeavour the Institute co-operates with interested training and research organizations throughout the world. The Governing Board of the Institute consists of eight elected members (including the Chairman) and four members designated by the United Nations Organization and certain of its specialized agencies and institutes.

Inquiries about the Institute and requests for copies of its latest progress report should be addressed to:
The Director, IIEP, 7-9, rue Eugène-Delacroix, 75016 Paris